ASSISTED REPRODL

Framing, Federalism, and Failure

The world has undergone a revolution in assisted reproduction, as processes such as in vitro fertilization, embryonic screening, and surrogacy have become commonplace. Yet when governments attempt to regulate this field, they have not always been successful. Canada is a case in point: six years after the federal government created comprehensive legislation, the Supreme Court of Canada struck it down for violating provincial authority over health. In *Assisted Reproduction Policy in Canada*, Dave Snow provides the first historical exploration of Canadian assisted reproduction policy, from the 1989 creation of the Royal Commission on New Reproductive Technologies to the present day. Snow argues the federal government's policy failure can be traced to its contradictory "policy framing," which sent mixed messages about the purposes of the legislation.

In light of the federal government's diminished role, Snow examines how other institutions have made policy in this emerging field. He finds provincial governments, medical organizations, and even courts have engaged in considerable policymaking, particularly with respect to surrogacy, parentage, and clinical intervention. The result – a complex field of overlapping and often conflicting policies – paints a fascinating portrait of different political actors and institutions working together. Accessibly written yet comprehensive in scope, *Assisted Reproduction Policy in Canada* highlights how paying attention to multiple policymakers can improve our knowledge of health-care regulation.

DAVE SNOW is an assistant professor in the Department of Political Science at the University of Guelph.

Assisted Reproduction Policy in Canada

Framing, Federalism, and Failure

DAVE SNOW

UNIVERSITY OF TORONTO PRESS
Toronto Buffalo London

© University of Toronto Press 2018
Toronto Buffalo London
utorontopress.com
Printed in the U.S.A.

ISBN 978-1-4875-0242-3 (cloth)   ISBN 978-1-4875-2319-0 (paper)

∞ Printed on acid-free, 100% post-consumer recycled paper with vegetable-based inks.

Library and Archives Canada Cataloguing in Publication

Snow, Dave, 1985–, author
Assisted reproduction policy in Canada : framing, federalism, and failure/
Dave Snow.

Includes bibliographical references and index.
ISBN 978-1-4875-0242-3 (cloth).   ISBN 978-1-4875-2319-0 (paper)

1. Reproductive technology – Government policy – Canada.   I. Title.

RG133.5.S66 2018   616.6'9206   C2018-902370-8

This book has been published with the help of a grant from the Federation
for the Humanities and Social Sciences, through the Awards to Scholarly
Publications Program, using funds provided by the Social Sciences and
Humanities Research Council of Canada.

University of Toronto Press acknowledges the financial assistance to its
publishing program of the Canada Council for the Arts and the Ontario Arts
Council, an agency of the Government of Ontario.

**Canada Council Conseil des Arts
for the Arts du Canada**

ONTARIO ARTS COUNCIL
CONSEIL DES ARTS DE L'ONTARIO
an Ontario government agency
un organisme du gouvernement de l'Ontario

Funded by the   Financé par le
Government   gouvernement
of Canada   du Canada

Canadä

For Alaina

Contents

Acknowledgments

The research for this manuscript was completed over eleven years, covering my time as a graduate student at the University of Calgary, a postdoctoral researcher at Dalhousie University, and an Assistant Professor at the University of Guelph. Accordingly, many have contributed to its development. First and foremost is my mentor, supervisor, and friend Rainer Knopff. This book, and my career, would never have come to fruition without Rainer's support, insight, and compassion.

I have been lucky to be guided along the way by many others. Tom Bateman fostered my love for political science as an undergraduate, Françoise Baylis facilitated my interest in interdisciplinary research and taught me to "work smart," and Dennis Baker has helped me navigate the academic world while achieving that elusive work/life balance. Over the last decade, Tim Anderson, Andrew Banfield, Alana Cattapan, Jocelyn Downie, Kelly Holloway, Emmett Macfarlane, Kate Puddister, and Mike Zekulin have helped this research in innumerable ways. Mark Harding deserves special mention, for contributing intellectually to virtually every project I have ever completed. I am also grateful to Leah Levac for organizing our "writing club" (often a club of just two!) that enabled me to write this manuscript, and to Dan Quinlan at the University of Toronto Press for making the publication process so seamless. This book would not have been possible without the generous financial support over the years from the Social Sciences and Humanities Research Council of Canada, the Killam Trusts, the Institute for Humane Studies, Dalhousie University, the University of Calgary, and the University of Guelph.

As someone whose research concerns family-building, I am constantly reminded of how blessed I am to have grown up in a loving family.

My parents Tim and Kathleen, grandmother Margaret Kerr, "Auntie" Jill Humphries, and late great-grandmother Jean Snow have provided me with unconditional love and support as I ventured further and further into this project. Of course, the most important person to acknowledge is my wife and soulmate Alaina. Her love, encouragement, and above all patience have taught me to cherish every minute of my life, including the many minutes I have spent writing this book.

Select parts of this book draw from previously published material. The six-part typology for assisted reproduction was originally published with Rainer Knopff for the University of Calgary School of Public Policy as "Assisted Reproduction Policy in Federal States: What Canada Should Learn from Australia" 5 (12): 1–28 (2012). The typology has since been revised and redefined. Chapters 2 and 3 draw from Dave Snow, "Explaining a Policy Failure: Policy Framing, Federalism, and Assisted Reproductive Technologies in Canada," *Canadian Public Policy* 41 (2): 124–36 (2015). Chapter 5 reproduces part of Dave Snow, "Measuring Parentage Policy in the Canadian Provinces: A Comparative Framework," *Canadian Public Administration* 59 (1): 5–25 (2016). In each case, the information has been updated and revised for incorporation into this book.

ASSISTED REPRODUCTION POLICY IN CANADA

Framing, Federalism, and Failure

Chapter 1

Understanding Assisted Reproduction Policy

This book provides an account of Canada's assisted reproduction policy landscape. It is an attempt to describe how Canada arrived at its current set of policies, and how a multitude of different institutions have contributed to the overall framework. To understand how this complex framework affects everyday decisions made by governments, stakeholders, and individuals using assisted reproduction, it is helpful to begin with a brief story.

In February 2012, the Royal Canadian Mounted Police (RCMP) raided Canadian Fertility Consulting's office in Brighton, Ontario, seizing computer equipment and company files. Canadian Fertility Consulting owner Leia Picard, whose business helped connect surrogates and egg donors to one or more intended parent(s), was initially given little information about the raid. Almost a year later, in February 2013 the RCMP announced that it was charging Picard with fifteen different criminal offences, including offering to purchase eggs, sperm, and the services of a surrogate, and receiving consideration for arranging these services. It subsequently emerged that Picard had referred some of her clients to a notorious American "baby-selling" ring dressed up as a similar consulting service, although, like the patients and clients defrauded by the ring, Picard knew nothing about the truth of the American scheme (Blackwell 2012, A1; 2013a, A1; 2013b, A2; 2013c, A1).

Why was a fertility consultant charged with arranging services for the payment of eggs, sperm, and surrogacy in the first place? Under sections 6 and 7 of Canada's federal 2004 *Assisted Human Reproduction Act* (*AHR Act*), it is a crime to offer "consideration" to a surrogate, and to purchase sperm or eggs from a donor. It is also a crime to act as an intermediary for a surrogacy arrangement, as Picard had done; all of these crimes are punishable by up to a $500,000 fine or ten years in prison. Unpaid surrogacy and egg/sperm donation remain legal, and the *AHR Act* permits reimbursement of surrogacy- and donor-related expenditures, but regulations to specify the limits of such expenditures, including those Picard had administered, have never been drafted. The *AHR Act* had been passed with the express goal of stopping "trade in the reproductive capabilities of women and men and the exploitation of children, women and men for commercial ends" (*Assisted Human Reproduction Act* 2004: 2(f)). However, the raid of Picard's offices marked the first – and to date only – charges laid under the *AHR Act*.

As the story developed, Picard, who was herself twice a surrogate, remained defiant. In one Facebook post, she announced that "I am … confident that in time, and through the judicial process, I will be cleared of all charges and, more importantly, laws will be changed" (quoted in Blackwell 2013b, A2). She suggested her case would involve a constitutional challenge that the *AHR Act* violated the *Canadian Charter of Rights and Freedoms*, claiming that the law was "abusive to those trying desperately to become parents … The Charter challenge my lawyers will launch will be a game changer." Canadian Fertility Consulting continued to operate, with one employee claiming "business has boomed" a month after the charges were laid (Blackwell 2013b, A2).

As the case neared trial, the wisdom of the *AHR Act* was itself litigated in the press. For critics of the law, the charges against Picard confirmed a long-standing belief in the wrong-headedness of the criminal prohibitions surrounding payment for surrogacy and human reproductive material. Picard's lawyer Frank Addario called the law "bewildering" and claimed enforcement was "uneven." For proponents of the law, Picard's case was the first piece of good news, signalling that the federal government was finally serious about enforcing the criminal prohibitions. Bioethicist Juliet Guichon hoped Picard's case would be the "tip of the iceberg" that would "send a strong signal to others" engaged in selling human reproductive material or surrogacy (quoted in Blackwell 2013a, A1). The case and the potential *Charter* challenge promised to serve as something of a litmus test for a law whose morality had been long debated.

The end result was anticlimactic. Picard and her company pleaded guilty to charges of buying eggs, paying surrogates, and receiving money for such surrogacy arrangements (Motluk 2014, E75). Collectively, she and her company were fined just $60,000 – what some described as an amount "so low that others involved in similar activities might just consider fines a 'cost of doing business'" (Baylis and Downie 2013b). Canadian Fertility Consulting continues to operate today with Picard at the helm; its website contains sections for intended parent(s), egg donors, and surrogates. The company's Twitter feed, from which Picard tweets regularly, boasts of providing services in London, Toronto, and Vancouver. While the *AHR Act* remains largely unchanged, liberalized laws designed to make surrogacy arrangements easier have come into force in Ontario and British Columbia since Picard's offices were raided, with Manitoba and Quebec contemplating change as well. Picard remains the only person ever charged (and found guilty) under the *AHR Act*, while stories of illegal payment and a "grey market" in eggs and surrogacy abound (Motluk 2010; CBC News 2014).

The story of Picard's charges, plea, and conviction serve as an example of the strange world of the law, policy, and practice of assisted reproduction in Canada. The federal *AHR Act*, passed in 2004, remains the law of the land, but has been emaciated through a constitutional challenge and minimal enforcement. The Agreed Statement of Facts in Picard's case references "Health Canada policy" that "permits reimbursement to donors and surrogates" – a policy that, because of a lack of regulations, does not actually exist apart from information listed on Health Canada's website. Only one regulation has been passed since the law was created in 2004, and Assisted Human Reproduction Canada, the federal agency that received the first complaint about Picard, was closed down before Picard's case went to trial. Jurisdiction over surrogacy is complicated by the division of powers; provinces draft permissive laws while federal prohibitions discouraging the practice remain in force. While the fertility business booms, patients, intended parents, and physicians all operate with uncertainty regarding whether they are breaking the law.

Overlapping authority, unclear responsibility, a lack of policy coherence, and exasperated stakeholders: How did Canada get to such a position? Why has the federal *AHR Act* resulted in such a mess, inviting scorn from critics and supporters alike? The answer has much to do with Canada's federal institutions, path dependence, and the unintended consequences of policy decisions several decades old.

The Canadian Case Study

Since its inception, assisted reproduction policy in Canada has been a work in progress. Beginning with the 1989 establishment of the Royal

Commission on New Reproductive Technologies, for fifteen years Canadian policymakers sought to achieve a comprehensive national framework to address assisted reproduction. In 2004, Parliament finally passed the *AHR Act*. The legislation included criminal prohibitions, a framework for forthcoming federal regulations, and a national agency to respond to emerging technologies. The federal government lauded the law as one of the most comprehensive pieces of assisted reproduction legislation in the world.

Over a decade later, such optimism seems wildly inappropriate. After the *AHR Act* passed, Quebec challenged much of it in court for violating provincial jurisdiction over health care, prompting the federal government to delay its regulatory framework. Transgressions of the law mounted, but the criminal prohibitions were not enforced. Assisted Human Reproduction Canada (AHRC), the federal agency created to monitor the development of assisted reproduction, was repeatedly subject to complaints about transparency and financial mismanagement, resulting in the sudden resignation of three board members in 2010. And then, in late 2010, after the federal government appealed a decision from the Quebec Court of Appeal, the Supreme Court of Canada narrowly declared unconstitutional nearly every regulatory authority contained in the *AHR Act* for violating provincial jurisdiction. Just six years after the federal government had triumphantly signalled its new role as a world leader for the regulation of assisted reproduction, its attempts to regulate the area had, according to one newspaper editorial, "collapsed in ruins" (*Victoria Times-Colonist* 2011).

This book surveys the ruins to explain how Canada arrived at a point that nearly every policymaker and stakeholder involved in the policy process would describe as suboptimal. It is the first scholarly exploration of the entire assisted reproduction policymaking process at the national and provincial levels, from the 1989 creation of the Royal Commission on New Reproductive Technologies to the present day. The story it tells is not one of success; the federal government gambled on the jurisdictional question, and it lost. Understanding this history of Canada's failed policymaking experiment can provide lessons for political scientists, public policy scholars, and policymakers alike.

This book has two primary goals: first, to identify the reason behind the federal government's policy failure, and second, to consider the state of Canada's assisted reproduction policy today. Drawing from a qualitative analysis of legislative debates, primary and secondary documents, and interviews[1] with policymakers, advocacy group leaders, and physicians, I argue that the federal government's policy failure can be traced to the 1993 report of the Royal Commission on New Reproductive Technologies. It is widely acknowledged that the Royal Commission heavily influenced the final product in the *AHR Act*. What this book adds is insight into the way the Royal Commission "framed" the policy field, in terms of both the *content* of assisted reproduction policy and which government had *jurisdictional competence* over such policy. By claiming that nearly every aspect of assisted reproduction policy should be decided by Parliament – regardless of whether the regulated activities were beneficial or harmful – the Commission set Parliament on a collision course with the provinces in the Supreme Court of Canada. The pursuit of a national assisted reproduction policy is thus a "tragedy" in the literary sense – wherein "failure to compromise" between competing ideals produces negative consequences (Ricci 1984, 22) – that can be traced back to its first act.

When the Supreme Court of Canada (and the Quebec Court of Appeal before it) ruled that much of the federal legislation violated provincial authority over health care, many experts and media outlets lamented "a return to the Wild West," an "unregulated nightmare" that would create a "patchwork" approach to governance across the country (Baylis 2011, 319; Guichon, Giroux, and Mitchell 2008 [cited in Snow and Knopff 2012]; Eggertson 2011). Now that more than seven years have passed since the Supreme Court reference, this book aims to assess its lasting impact. However, determining the current state of assisted reproduction policy in Canada requires that we first answer two questions: What is assisted reproduction policy in the first place? And who makes it?

Assisted Reproduction Policy: Undefined Terms, Unexplored Actors

Although the field of assisted reproduction policy is still relatively new, nearly every study acknowledges a few facts: that the world has

---

1 The author personally conducted fifty-five semi-structured interviews between May 2010 and July 2012 in Canada and Australia as part of a larger research project involving both countries. Eleven of those interviews, all from Canada, are cited in this book.

undergone a reproductive revolution since the 1978 birth of Louise Brown, the first child born through in vitro fertilization (IVF); that the implications of this revolution affect women far more than men; that there are potentially dangerous implications of a "brave new world" of genetic manipulation; and that, as a result, significant government intervention is warranted or, at the very least, likely.

Beyond that, there is a dearth of consistency in the policy field. Scholars cannot even agree on its name: assisted reproductive technology (ART), reproductive genetic technology (RGT), assisted human reproduction (AHR), "red" biotechnologies, and new reproductive technologies (NRTs) have all been used to describe the field (Bauer 2005; Engeli, Green-Pedersen, and Thorup Larsen 2012; Evans 2006; Jones and Salter 2010). Nor is there clarity on what the field includes. Does it include research that requires reproductive material but is not designed to create human beings, such as embryonic stem-cell research? What about surrogacy, technically a private social arrangement rather than a "technology"? What about rules regarding legal parenthood of children born through assisted reproduction?

These are not merely semantic questions. Definitional and typological consistency is imperative to enable precise measurement, one of the paramount goals of comparative political science and policy studies. For simplicity and consistency, I use the term "assisted reproduction policy" to describe the field, which I define as "the rules for the technologies, procedures, and activities related to the use of human reproductive material for the purposes of both non-coital reproduction and scientific research." This definition encompasses policies governing assisted reproduction at fertility clinics (such as surrogacy and IVF) as well as human embryonic research. The definition is deliberately broad because, as I will argue throughout, assisted reproduction policy is best conceptualized as consisting of six distinct subfields.

1. *Clinical intervention*: the use of technology to enhance the prospects of reproductive success. Policies in this subfield address rules for medical professionals, donors of human reproductive material, patients undergoing assisted reproduction, and patient insurance coverage, particularly for IVF and fertility drugs. This subfield is the one most commonly associated with assisted reproduction as a whole.

2. *Surrogacy*: a private social and often legal arrangement that occurs when a woman (the surrogate) gestates and bears a child with the

intention that the child will raised by someone else (the intended parent(s)). Surrogacy can be "traditional" (where the surrogate is genetically related to the child) or "gestational" (where she is not). Policy typically pertains to surrogacy arrangements, the surrogate's genetic relation to the child, and the permissibility of payment.

3. *Parentage*: the rules concerning the procedures and eligibility requirements used to determine legal parenthood for children born through assisted conception or surrogacy.

4. *Reproductive human cloning*: the artificial creation of two or more genetically identical individuals through the manipulation of human reproductive material.

5. *Screening and enhancement*: the application of technologies to determine and even manipulate the attributes of children before they are born, regardless of whether those children were conceived via assisted reproduction.

6. *Embryonic research*: the creation, preservation, and manipulation of human embryos for scientific research and medical treatment. Embryonic research is non-reproductive; it seeks to improve the lives of this and future generations rather than produce the next one.

Broadly speaking, these subfields are ordered from policy concerning fertility and childbirth to policy concerning scientific research. However, there is some conceptual overlap between the six subfields. Surrogacy obviously raises parentage issues and typically requires clinical intervention, while a total ban on embryonic research would make human cloning impracticable. Such overlap and debate are unavoidable with all typologies in the study of public policy, insofar as policy categories are themselves socially constructed (Schneider and Ingram 1997). While typologies have been criticized in the past for being inexhaustive or arbitrary (Smith 2002), when constructed with sufficient concept refinement and an eye to empirical reality, they can still provide a useful framework for comparison. The precise definitions contained in this assisted reproduction typology, coupled with elaboration in subsequent chapters, provide sufficient clarity to enable scholars to isolate differences between policy subfields and engage in meaningful cross-national comparison across and even within jurisdictions.

Having answered "What is assisted reproduction policy?," comparative scholars will be better equipped to answer "Who makes assisted reproduction policy?" Existing comparative studies of assisted reproduction have focused almost exclusively on policy created by national governments (Bleiklie, Goggin, and Rothmayr 2004; Engeli, Green-Pedersen, and Thorup Larsen 2012; Montpetit, Rothmayr, and Varone 2007). However, a quick glance at jurisdictional federations such as the United States, Canada, and Australia shows that other policymakers – particularly subnational governments, medical organizations, and courts – have engaged in considerable policymaking. Yet the policy contribution of these institutions has yet to be systematically integrated into the comparative literature on assisted reproduction. We have been told only partial stories.

To understand Canada's history of assisted reproduction policymaking, this book applies the above typology to examine the work of policymakers beyond the federal government. The Canadian case study demonstrates the benefit of these strategies. The typology offers a better way to understand the "division of labour" in which policymakers engage; the inclusion of subnational governments, medical organizations, and courts adds other labourers to the discussion. In terms of Canadian assisted reproduction policy, this analysis contributes to our knowledge of how and when these institutions make policy. Applied comparatively, this typology can offer opportunity for cross-national comparison and eventually contribute empirical evidence of the effectiveness of public policy.

Outline and Argument of the Book

While this typology marks the beginning of a more expansive comparative research project, the book focuses on Canada, where the federal government played the dominant role throughout the early stages of policy development. In this vein, chapters 2 to 4 explore three historical events that produced and eventually rendered unconstitutional the majority of legislation at the federal level: the 1993 Royal Commission, the 2004 *AHR Act*, and the 2010 Supreme Court of Canada *Reference re Assisted Human Reproduction Act*.

Chapter 2 sets out to explain how and why two decades of national policymaking collapsed in ruins in 2010. I draw from the scholarly literature on historical institutionalism and policy framing to demonstrate that the Royal Commission on New Reproductive Technologies adopted important framing strategies concerning both the content of, and the jurisdictional competence over, assisted reproduction policy. As to content, the Commission distinguished between aspects of assisted reproduction that were medically beneficial and ought to be regulated (the medical-scientific frame) and other aspects of assisted reproduction that were harmful and ought to be criminally prohibited (the moral frame). At the same time, the Commission's jurisdictional framing claimed that all of assisted reproduction policy except for parentage, regardless of whether it was medically beneficial or morally harmful, should be administered by the federal Parliament. Applying this "national" jurisdictional frame to both criminal prohibitions and a regulatory health framework was a constitutionally risky strategy given provincial jurisdiction over health policy. The Royal Commission downplayed the potential risk, however, arguing that nearly all aspects of the new assisted reproduction policy realm (with the exception of parentage policy) were too important to leave to the provinces, and that national legislation could be justified in relation to the "national concern" doctrine under the "Peace, Order, and Good Government" clause in the Canadian Constitution.

Chapter 3 moves beyond the Royal Commission to examine the federal policymaking process from 1993 to 2004, which led to the eventual creation of the *AHR Act*. Drawing from Hansard debates, policy documents, proposed legislation, committee hearings, and interviews, I demonstrate how the Royal Commission's framing strategies and policy recommendations were systematically adopted by the federal government, and that the work of the Commission therefore constitutes a "critical juncture" in the development of assisted reproduction policy in Canada. One might have expected the federal government's approach to change during this intervening decade, as assisted reproduction became more frequently used and public opinion liberalized. However, the proposed legislative content and policy frames remained the same. In the end, Parliament's historic legislation covered every subfield of assisted reproduction policy except parentage. The *AHR Act*'s combination of prohibitions, regulatory authority for "controlled activities," and provisions to establish a national agency almost exactly mirrored the Commission's overarching recommendations.

This legislation resulted in a constitutionally unstable framework, particularly with respect to medically beneficial "controlled activities" and regulatory authority. Just as it had threatened, the Quebec government challenged the *AHR Act*'s regulatory authority in court for violating provincial jurisdiction over health care. Chapter 4 details the judicial process, explaining precisely why a majority of justices in both the Quebec Court of Appeal and the Supreme Court of Canada held that the regulatory components of the legislation violated provincial jurisdiction. These justices explicitly referred to the Royal Commission and adopted its distinction between beneficial and harmful activities. However, in their constitutional analyses, majorities on both courts found that the medically beneficial technologies fell under provincial jurisdiction. Drawing from the Supreme Court's federalism jurisprudence throughout the 1990s and 2000s, I explain why this outcome was even more likely in 2010 than it was in 1993, as the Peace, Order, and Good Government (POGG) clause – the major piece of constitutional ammunition put forward by the Commission – had become watered down. Chapter 4 concludes with an analysis of the aftermath of the reference, and shows how the academic and journalistic commentary collectively articulated the belief that Canadian assisted reproduction policy would become an unregulated "Wild West" that would produce a "patchwork" going forward.

Chapter 5 considers whether, seven years after the Supreme Court reference, assisted reproduction policy in Canada reflects these commentators' initial concerns. I begin by describing how the federal government, through various mechanisms, still effectively regulates much of three subfields (reproductive human cloning, embryonic research, and screening/enhancement) and also maintains some regulations and prohibitions concerning surrogacy and clinical intervention. However, other policymakers now make the vast majority of policy pertaining to surrogacy, parentage, and clinical intervention.

The chapter then moves on to define and assess surrogacy and parentage policy in Canada. I show how surrogacy itself contains three dimensions: payment (subject in Canada to a federal ban), the distinction between traditional and gestational surrogacy (a distinction that is not governed by legislation), and surrogacy arrangements. Because surrogacy arrangements involve the transfer of parental rights and responsibilities, I argue that these aspects of surrogacy arrangements are best conceptualized as falling within the subfield of parentage policy. I then apply a framework to measure parentage policy – including parentage in the case of surrogacy – to the Canadian provinces. I find that considerable policymaking has occurred in the last several years, and that policy is slowly leaning towards permissiveness. In the absence of clear provincial rules, the courts have played an important role in moving parentage policy in a permissive direction and placing an onus on provincial legislatures to act. Ontario's recent comprehensive legislative change also shows that provinces have engaged in policy learning and transfer, drawing lessons from other provinces (Alberta and British Columbia) to influence new legislation. With respect to parentage in particular, it is incorrect to refer to Canada as "unregulated," although it is certainly correct that these regulations are subject to considerable provincial variation.

Chapter 6 focuses on clinical intervention policy, the subfield most commonly associated with assisted reproduction policy as a whole, and most subject to critical commentary in Canada. I define this policy subfield as constituting three categories: rules targeting clinical professionals, rules targeting patients and donors, and rules for patient coverage. I then examine who regulates this area and how they regulate it. In addition to a few federal regulations and prohibitions, Quebec introduced comprehensive policy in 2009, and Ontario introduced more minimalist policy in 2015. Although Quebec and Ontario are the only provinces to legislate in this subfield, their initiatives demonstrate that provinces certainly have the capacity for effective regulation of clinical practice, both with and without the carrot of state funding for fertility treatment.

What this legislation cannot explain, however, is why the other eight provinces have been largely absent from the field. For greater understanding, I turn to medical organizations, which include federal and provincial professional associations such as the Canadian Medical Association and the Ontario Medical Association, national specialist associations such as the Canadian Fertility and Andrology Society, and regulatory colleges such as the College of Physicians and Surgeons of Ontario. While provincial medical colleges themselves have not engaged in policymaking, they have delegated their authority to national specialist associations, who have over time created a number of clinical guidelines. Moreover, there is some evidence that medical practitioners are following the guidelines, as demonstrated by Canada's declining multiple birth rate. I argue that the existence of medical self-regulation provides an institutional explanation for why most provinces have not yet regulated clinical intervention, insofar as the organizations are doing enough to prevent a true policy vacuum, obviating the incentive for provinces to become engaged in this morally contentious subfield. I also suggest that the Royal Commission's "medical-scientific" policy frame, which influenced the Supreme Court majority, has further entrenched the position that clinical policy in health care should remain the purview of professionals, not governments. Finally, I explore the possibility of judicial influence on this subfield, detailing the *Pratten* cases (*Pratten v. British Columbia (Attorney General)* [2011]; *Pratten v.*

British Columbia (Attorney General) [2012]) concerning donor anonymity. As with other subfields of assisted reproduction, it is not surprising to see judicial policymaking over morally contentious policy, particularly in the absence of provincial legislation.

Chapter 7 draws together these various threads to explain why Canadian assisted reproduction policy developed as it did, and to assess Canada's current assisted reproduction policy. Using a combination of policy framing and the identification of critical junctures, I argue that the development of assisted reproduction policy was initially path dependent, reflecting the Royal Commission's framing of this emerging and unregulated policy field. However, a series of tensions embedded in this initial stage led to increasingly less predictable patterns of policy development in the mid-term. These tensions were of two orders: First, at the ideational level, there was an inability to adopt a universal framing strategy for the diverse elements captured under the assisted reproduction policy umbrella; instead, some elements were deemed beneficial and others harmful. Second, at an institutional level, there was an assertion that the federal government should have responsibility for all of these various, distinct policy components. The Royal Commission's strict adherence to a national framing strategy meant that the competing ideational justifications for government action in this diverse policy field were obscured by the desire for one level of government to speak with one voice. The initial legislative vacuum that characterized the new field, coupled with the moral framing strategy used to justify criminal prohibitions, diminished federal incentives to collaborate and coordinate with the provinces.

The collision of the initial path-dependent framing of the policy arena with the realities of federalism and judicial action has led Canada to the current state of assisted reproduction policy, which is often subject to rules and regulations from various policymakers that differ by province. Overall, the existence of provincial, judicial, and even medical policymaking demonstrates that assisted reproduction policy in Canada is far from unregulated. The permissiveness of Canadian assisted reproduction policy ranges from subfield to subfield (and even among provinces). On the continuum from permissive to restrictive, assisted reproduction policy in Canada represents an "intermediate" policy compared with other countries, but it is not until we delve deeper that we develop a more complete understanding of which elements are more restrictive (such as human cloning) and which are, in several provinces, more permissive (clinical intervention and parentage).

While the constitutionally unstable framing strategy ultimately ended in failure from the federal government's perspective, Canada's assisted reproduction history provides lessons for scholars and policymakers alike. Federal policymakers' failure to produce comprehensive assisted reproduction policy should provide a valuable lesson to future over-zealous policymakers desirous of national uniformity at all costs, who ignore the constitutional division of powers and developing Supreme Court jurisprudence at their peril. The emphasis on jurisdictional framing also demonstrates how the language policymakers use when justifying legislation matters, and can even shape judicial outcomes. I also stress that, in Canada and comparatively, there is a greater need to recognize the role of the judiciary and medical professionals as policymakers in their own right. Moreover, in jurisdictional federations with competencies divided between national and subnational jurisdictions, the interaction of federalism with health-care policymaking can lead to unforeseen consequences and limit government policymaking, as it has with Canadian clinical intervention policy in particular.

Finally, for comparative scholars of assisted reproduction, the policy framing lens and the six-part typology should set the stage for increased understanding of the reasons behind policy variation in this growing field of public policy. By looking closely at the diverse array of policymakers and policy subfields involved in the creation and maintenance of assisted reproduction policy in Canada, this book provides evidence about the important way in which qualitative case studies can contribute to theory building and a better understanding of policy outcomes in new fields of public policy. As with much else, the Canadian story has significant implications for countries across the world.

The Royal Commission
on New Reproductive Technologies
and the Legacy of Past Frames

In Canada, assisted reproduction policy has long been conceptualized by policymakers and scholars as a singular and unified field. Throughout the federal government's long and tortured history of policymaking in this field, a common thread was that assisted reproduction should be legislated holistically, as part of a uniform approach. The origins of this thread, and its subsequent influence on policy, can be traced directly to the 1993 Royal Commission on New Reproductive Technologies.

This chapter details the history and continued relevance of the 1993 Royal Commission on New Reproductive Technologies. Drawing from the historical institutional literature on critical junctures and path dependence, it shows how various institutional factors provided the Commission with a disproportionately high ability to influence subsequent policy. This chapter begins with a brief description of historical institutionalism, the theoretical lens through which the history of assisted reproduction policy is examined throughout the book. I argue that historical institutionalism is an especially appropriate lens through which to view assisted reproduction policy for a number of reasons, including the novelty of the policy field and the importance of ideational factors in shaping outcomes. The chapter then describes the Royal Commission's comprehensive recommendations, and shows how they covered five of the six subfields of assisted reproduction policy described in chapter 1.

The latter part of the chapter details the Royal Commission's framing strategies, both substantive and jurisdictional. Substantively, the Commission adopted a "medical-scientific" frame for much of assisted reproduction, which it viewed as largely beneficial. However, the commissioners were deeply ambivalent about the field as a whole, and adopted a "moral" frame to recommend strong criminal prohibitions for other aspects of assisted reproduction. Jurisdictionally, there was no such ambivalence: in spite of weak constitutional justifications, the Commission recommended that virtually the entire field of assisted reproduction should be governed by an overarching national framework in which the federal Parliament would take the policymaking lead. The combination of these substantive and jurisdictional policy-framing strategies set Canadian policy down a constitutionally risky path: by framing much of assisted reproduction as medically beneficial but nevertheless requiring federal intervention, the Commission created a framing discourse that did not fit with Canada's constitutional division of powers and the Supreme Court of Canada's jurisprudence. This frame incongruity, which would remain throughout the legislative process in the years to come, can explain much of the subsequent development of Canadian policy over the last two decades.

Historical Institutionalism and the Study of Unintended Consequences

Fundamentally, much of political science is concerned with answering one question: What drives politics? To answer this question, new institutional scholars emphasize how political institutions constrain, proscribe, and prescribe certain forms of behaviour; they share the belief that institutions "matter more than anything else that could be used to explain political decisions" (Peters 2005, 164). One branch of new institutional thought, known as historical institutionalism, emphasizes the importance of time and history in understanding policymaking. Historical institutionalism's "deceptively simple" idea, according to B. Guy Peters (2005, 71), "is that policy choices made when an institution is being formed, or when a policy is initiated, will have a continuing and largely determinative influence over the policy far into the future." In this sense, historical institutionalists do not accept the ontological view of the political world as "governed by causal relationships that take the form of lawlike regularities operative across space and time," and instead argue that similar developments may have different impacts across cases, depending on when they are initiated (Hall 2003, 373, 385). Because policy choices can become embedded and lead to unintended consequences, historical institutionalists reject functionalist accounts by which "institutions take the form they do because powerful actors engaged in rational, strategic behavior are seeking to produce the outcomes observed" (Pierson 2004, 14).[2] In this vein, historical institutionalists stress the importance of ideas – particularly those ideas that are prevalent early in policy development – in shaping political dynamics and institutional development. Such ideas exist independent of institutional setting, but require the "support of powerful actors that have an interest in promoting them" (Béland 2005, 10; see also Béland and Cox 2011; Broschek 2010).

According to Capoccia and Kelemen (2007), many historical institutional accounts posit a dualist model of institutional development with two characteristics: long periods of path dependence and stability, and short periods that produce significant institutional change. These latter situations occur when structural influences are "significantly relaxed for a relatively short period," providing greater latitude for political actors. These periods are known as "critical junctures," which are "relatively short periods of time during which there is a substantially heightened probability that agents' choices will affect the outcome of interest" (341, 343, 348). The potential for agency is higher during critical junctures than in periods of stability.

Much of the political science scholarship on Canadian federalism implicitly or explicitly adopts a historical institutional approach to explain how the allocation of the division of powers in the 1867 *British North America Act* (later renamed the *Constitution Act, 1867*) affects policymaking. As Broschek (2012, 672–4) notes, Canada's "dualistic allocation of authority" was shaped by critical junctures preceding the *British North America Act*, including "deadlock and stalemate in the United Province of Canada" and the horror of the American Civil War (see also Stevenson 1993). However, the ambiguities built into this dualistic allocation meant that many matters could plausibly be construed as either provincial or federal jurisdiction. This ambiguity gave the Judicial Committee of the Privy Council considerable authority to influence Canada's federal trajectory in path-dependent ways, enabling provinces to develop state capacities within a dynamic federal system that continues to oscillate between "centrifugal and centripetal forces" (Broschek 2012, 678).

---

2 This study adopts Peter Hall's (1986, 19) definition of institutions as the "formal rules, compliance procedures, and standard operating practices that structure the relationship between individuals in various units of the polity and economy." This broad definition lends itself, in the words of Paul Pierson (2004, 78, 165), to the analysis of "microphenomena," allowing us to view specific public policies as institutions in their own right.

With its emphasis on critical junctures and path dependence, historical institutionalism is a particularly valuable approach for understanding the evolution of assisted reproduction policy in Canada for
four related reasons. First, historical institutional accounts, given their
focus on policy legacies, are most useful when the beginning of the
policy process can be readily identified. With assisted reproduction,
the medical technology only gained prominence in the late 1970s, and
most states (including Canada) did not begin their legislative processes
until the 1990s. As assisted reproduction is a relatively new policy field,
it is easier to identify the initiation of policy development and the impact of institutions – in short, to identify critical junctures. Second, because historical institutionalists reject functional explanations of public
policy, they are best suited to describe policy outcomes whose consequences were unintended. Again, assisted reproduction in Canada fits
the bill: even those satisfied with Canada's policy status quo would
not deny that it represents a wildly divergent outcome from what was
intended by policymakers throughout the 1990s and 2000s. Third, historical institutionalists have long stressed that ideas – and crucially, the
way that political elites frame those ideas to the public – can have lasting effects on institutional arrangements. This focus on ideas is especially relevant given the importance of policy framing in new policy
fields such as assisted reproduction. Finally, in previous historical institutional work on critical junctures, the "unit of analysis" has often
been an "institutional setting in which actors' decisions are constrained
during phases of equilibrium and are freer during phases of change"
(Capoccia and Kelemen 2007, 349). The Royal Commission on New
Reproductive Technologies provides such a setting.

Proceed with Care: The Royal Commission on New Reproductive Technologies

The Royal Commission's origins can be traced to the 1980s, a time of
widespread concern about the implications of what were then called
"new reproductive technologies." After several smaller studies of the
legal and medical implications of assisted reproduction,[3] a collection of

---

3 These included the *Ninth Report of the British Columbia Royal Commission on Families
and Children's Law* and the Ontario *Report of Human Artificial Reproduction and
Related Matters*, as well as an inquiry from the Medical Research Council of Canada.
As Scala (2002) notes, these inquiries were smaller in scale and "did not challenge

Canadian feminist academics and women's health organizations created the Canadian Coalition for a Royal Commission on New Reproductive Technologies in 1987. As its name attests, this organization lobbied the federal government to create a Royal Commission that would initiate a large-scale policy discussion on this developing field. In 1989, Prime Minister Brian Mulroney announced the creation of the Royal Commission on New Reproductive Technologies, which was given a mandate to "inquire into and report on current and potential medical and scientific developments related to new reproductive technologies, considering in particular their social, ethical, health, research, legal and economic implications and the public interest" (Royal Commission on New Reproductive Technologies 1993, 2).

There are many reasons that Mulroney chose to appoint a Royal Commission rather than legislate immediately. Most obviously, as its name suggests, the Canadian Coalition for a Royal Commission on New Reproductive Technologies was convinced that a large, independent study was needed to gauge how best to legislate in this field. Royal commissions can serve as a way to provide an information source for public policy, particularly in a novel field like assisted reproduction. For decades, they have also enabled governments "to postpone action on a politically embarrassing question" (Doern 1967, 421). By referring the subject to a panel of non-partisan experts and giving the Commission a sweeping mandate, Mulroney was able to delay public policy on such a divisive issue and avoid confrontation with women's groups, religious groups, legal organizations, medical organizations, and disability organizations concerned or excited about the prospect of these new technologies.

It took four years before the Commission finally reported. After consultation with over 15,000 Canadians, the Commission published its final report, *Proceed with Care*, on 15 November 1993. The report comprised 1,275 pages, two volumes, and 293 recommendations. These recommendations largely fit into three overarching categories: prohibiting certain activities and technologies using the federal *Criminal Code*; creating a regulatory framework for permissible activities; and establishing a federal regulatory and licensing agency. Stressing the principle

---

the medical-scientific discourse on reproductive technologies"; the focus on rights
effectively amounted to the "legal appropriation and validation of medical
definitions of reproductive technologies" (97).

of "non-commercialization of reproduction," the report recommended criminalizing the purchase and sale of eggs,[4] sperm, zygotes, fetal tissue, and embryos, as well as payment for surrogacy. It also recommended criminal prohibitions for non-medical sex selection, germ-line alteration, cloning human embryos, creating animal-human hybrids, retrieving gametes from fetuses or cadavers, and other forms of research on human reproductive materials (Royal Commission on New Reproductive Technologies 1993, 915–17, 942, 1022, 1049; see also Harvison Young 2005, 131). The report recommended that various other technologies, such as prenatal diagnosis and assisted insemination, be subject to oversight and licensing by a new national agency, the National Reproductive Technologies Commission (NRTC).

In terms of the six subfields of assisted reproduction, the Commission recommended that most should be subject to a combination of regulation and prohibition. With respect to *clinical intervention*, it recommended that payment for sperm and eggs be criminalized, but also that other aspects – sperm collection and storage, assisted insemination, assisted conception, and egg retrieval, to name a few – be subject to compulsory licensing by the national agency. It called for an "integrated, uniform approach" to donor insemination, and for standardized "sperm collection, service provision, and record-keeping practices." Although it recognized that "much of the responsibility" for adapting practices for issues such as donor insemination would lie with provincial health authorities, the Royal Commission (1993, 472–5) ultimately decided that the proposed NRTC should bear responsibility for creating and licensing the overall system. For *surrogacy*, the Commission recommended criminal prohibitions for paid surrogacy. Although it suggested that unpaid surrogacy should not be "undertaken, sanctioned, or encouraged," it stopped short of recommending a criminal ban if no payment was involved. It also recommended that provinces and territories amend their family law legislation to make all surrogacy arrangements unenforceable (689–90).

The final report recommended a ban on *human cloning* and various components of *screening/enhancement*, including ectogenesis (creating an artificial womb) and creating animal-human hybrids; however,

---

4 Unless quoting, I use the word "egg" rather than "ova" throughout this book. Although medical studies tend to use the word ova, the terms are used interchangeably.

it also recommended national policy for screening and enhancement, claiming that there should be a regulatory licensing regime for prenatal diagnosis (xxxiii). For *embryonic research*, the Commission sought to ban research directed towards the sale of fetal tissues, and the use of human zygotes/embryos after fourteen days. It recommended that the proposed NRTC create compulsory regulations for research on zygotes, and that informed consent be a principle in such research (108, 636–45).

Clearly, the Royal Commission envisioned that the federal Parliament would be the key driver of assisted reproduction policy. Between the criminal prohibitions and the proposed national agency's regulations, each subfield of assisted reproduction would be subject to federal involvement, with the exception of parentage (see Table 2.1). The Commission recognized that provincial consultation and cooperation was necessary, but generally limited such cooperation to public health educational campaigns concerning "infertility prevention, occupational health and safety, and adoption policy" (1041). The only subfields where it recommended provincial legislation were for all of *parentage* (to clarify parental responsibility for children born through assisted conception) and for certain aspects of *surrogacy* (nullifying surrogacy arrangements, which would have precluded parentage transfer) – each with the goal of unified national standards in mind. It claimed that "matters so important to women and children, in terms not only of their health but of their legal status and how they are viewed, cannot differ from province to province" (xxvi). Yet it stopped short of recommending federal law, instead advocating uniform provincial legislation regarding legal parenthood for children born through assisted conception (468). The Commission doubtless recognized that, whatever the wisdom of having federal policy for parentage, parental responsibility was unquestionably provincial jurisdiction, falling under the umbrella of family law.[5]

The Commission was highly critical of the regulatory role of medical professionals, claiming that "levels of self-regulation and accountability vary enormously from one area of practice to another," and "many health care professionals are not well informed" about infertility and prenatal

---

5   As Boyd and Baldassi (2009, 112) note, jurisdiction in Canada's family law system is divided. The federal government defines marriage and divorce and administers certain benefits for couples. However, most family law matters, including those pertaining to parentage, are provincial jurisdiction.

Table 2.1
Royal Commission Recommendations

	Federal Prohibitions	Federal Policy (Non-Criminal)	Provincial Policy	Medical Regulations
Clinical Intervention	*	*		
Surrogacy	*		*	
Parentage			*	
Human Cloning	*			
Screening/Enhancement	*	*		*
Embryonic Research	*	*		

diagnosis (Royal Commission on New Reproductive Technologies 1993, 111, 1044). It made various recommendations for "education, training, and practices of health care professionals," and for professional guidelines (1044–6), but considered it "unrealistic to expect self-regulating professional bodies, or the provinces, individually or together, to provide the necessary level of regulation and control" for these issues (12). As a result, its recommendations for professional medical organizations were minimal, and mostly related to continued medical education, proposed standards for training, informed consent, and increased collaboration. The only recommendation that amounted to a regulatory role for medical professionals was that accreditation by the Canadian College of Medical Geneticists should be a precondition for licensing genetic centres (1043–6).

Framing Assisted Reproduction: Medical-Scientific with a Moral Asterisk

Equally important to the Commission's recommendations of future policy content was the way in which it engaged in policy framing. Policy framing involves structuring and manipulating how social or political debate over a policy issue is contested by influencing the perception of available choices; frames are "normative concepts that elites use to legitimize these programs to the public" (Campbell 1998, 385). The goal when framing policy is not to come to an overarching truth about a given issue but rather to construct, simplify, and emphasize a particular aspect of that issue to constrain the perceived range of choices (Daviter 2011). As assisted reproduction was a new and relatively unknown field in the 1990s, there was considerable opportunity for interest groups and policymakers to frame the debate during proceedings of the Royal Commission on New Reproductive Technologies.

The policy framing literature has traditionally focused on how actors frame the *substance* of a policy, or what I call "substantive frames." In her analyses of the Royal Commission, Francesca Scala (2002, 2007, 2008) identifies different substantive frames present during the Canadian debate on assisted reproduction. The most prominent, which she refers to as the "medical-scientific" frame, "regards reproductive technologies as neutral and necessary, and transforms the patient into a client" (2002, 87). Those who subscribed to the medical-scientific frame were generally pro-technology; while they saw a role for the state in setting boundaries, they argued that the potential harms associated with assisted reproduction could be "easily contained by suitable modes of regulation" (2002, 240). In large part, this frame was created and sustained during the Royal Commission's proceedings by representatives from the medical and scientific community, who engaged in "boundary work," using their privileged societal position and expertise to "protect their autonomy and authority" by opposing criminal sanctions and the creation of a regulatory body (Scala 2007, 220).

As Daniel Béland (2005, 11) notes, frames are "dialogical in nature: they anticipate what potential opponents could say to undermine the support for specific policy alternatives." Scala (2002, 8) notes that the medical-scientific frame was highly contested during the Royal Commission's work by what I will refer to as the "moral" frame, whose adherents applied a "broader critique of science and medicine" to assisted reproduction. Such opponents of assisted reproduction included religious organizations, social conservatives, and some – though not all – feminists concerned with commodification of women's bodies. These groups called for outright prohibitions and moratoria on the use of many technologies, and were generally pessimistic about the prospects of these technologies for society. They frequently made reference to the language of commodification, exploitation, and commercialization. Because the debates about assisted reproduction involved first principles about life and sex, adherents of the medical-scientific and moral frames held largely incommensurable positions with little room for compromise (Scala 2002, 210).

Of these two perspectives, Scala and others (Ariss 1996; Eichler 1993; Weir and Habib 1997) detail how the medical-scientific frame triumphed over the moral frame during the Royal Commission's proceedings, as the structure and content of the final report consolidated medical-scientific authority and marginalized critics of assisted reproduction. Scala identifies three interrelated reasons for this: the organizational structure of Commission, the privileged position commissioners ascribed to the scientific community and scientific knowledge, and the Commission's "individual rights" discourse, stemming from Canada's then-recent legacy of abortion politics. Organizationally, the Commission was centralized and hierarchical; the buck stopped with the chair, Patricia Baird, whose background in genetics left her open to the criticism that she was overly sympathetic to the medical-scientific frame. Although other commissioners (particularly Louise Vandelac and Maureen McTeer) were more inclined towards the moral frame, they were frequently marginalized. After four commissioners, including Vandelac and McTeer, openly complained about Baird's management style, in December 1991 the Prime Minister's Office fired all four and replaced them with commissioners more sympathetic to the medical-scientific frame (Scala 2002, 46, 163–5; 2008, 97, 104).

Scientific expertise was also privileged over social scientific and philosophical expertise throughout the Royal Commission process. Medical and legal organizations were positioned as neutral "experts" while other advocates were viewed as more "traditional" interest groups lobbying on behalf of a particular policy preference. The principle of "evidence-based research" guided the Commission's work, as Baird and her staff frequently asked for quantitative data to substantiate claims counter to the medical-scientific frame. However, because arguments opposing assisted reproduction are often based on difficult-to-quantify concerns such as dehumanization, exploitation, and commodification – particularly when those arguments are future-oriented – evidence-based research tends to marginalize moral claims in favour of medical-scientific ones. The legacy of abortion rights also contributed to a liberalized discourse that complemented the organizational dominance of the medical-scientific frame, as feminist concerns about patriarchy and the exclusion of women from medicine were systematically ignored (Scala 2008, 109–14).

Overall, the scholarly consensus (Ariss 1996, 46; Baylis and Herder 2009b, 353; Roberts 1999, 20; Scala 2002, 7, 79, 147; Scala 2008, 107–9) is that those opposing assisted reproduction were marginalized, and the medical-scientific frame dominated the Commission's proceedings. The Royal Commission rejected moratoria, promoted medicalization, cited the benefits of embryonic research, and gave legitimacy to new procedures such as IVF and assisted insemination (Royal Commission on New Reproductive Technologies 1993, 14, 34, 140, 1004). In this vein, Scala (2007, 215) notes that the Commission was another example of what Anne L. Schneider and Helen M. Ingram (1997, 167) describe as professional and scientific groups successfully "commandeer[ing] an issue with important social value implications and transform[ing] it into a matter of elite scientific and professional concern."

Yet this consensus regarding the Royal Commission's medical-scientific dominance requires an important qualification, as the Commission significantly deviated from the medical-scientific frame in one crucial respect: it declared that several technologies and activities were unacceptable, and that Parliament's criminal law power was the only instrument capable of policing transgressions. When it came to practices that "conflict so sharply with the values espoused by Canadians" (Royal Commission on New Reproductive Technologies 1993, 1022), the Commission used the moral frame. These practices included commercial for-profit activities related to human reproductive materials and surrogacy arrangements; human cloning; various types of embryonic research; genetic engineering; and unjustified medical interventions that threaten the autonomy of pregnant women (108–9). The Commission's proposed prohibitions were so extensive that they encompassed five of the six subfields of assisted reproduction (see Table 2.1).

In contrast to the Commission's structure and its regulatory recommendations, the criminal recommendations did not stem from medical-scientific framing. The entire twenty-fourth chapter of the report, "Commercial Interests and New Reproductive Technologies," frequently criticized commercial interests and the "profit motive." A by no means exhaustive list of such statements includes:

- "No profit should be made from the selling of any reproductive material ... because of its ultimately dehumanizing effects" (447).
- "The impact of market forces in the area of human reproduction could, if not properly regulated, undermine important social values and ethical principles and harm people by leading to inappropriate, unethical, or unsafe use of technology" (699).
- "The presence of a profit motive means that commercially funded research is particularly in need of independent research ethics board approval" (713).
- "The Commission strongly opposes the development of a two-tier health care system" (716).

- "To allow commercial exchanges of this type would undermine respect for human life and dignity and lead to the commodification of women and children" (718).
- "Adoption of these recommendations would ensure that the commercial impetus is contained and regulated so that the vulnerable interests of individuals and society are protected" (725).

By speaking of dehumanization, human dignity, commodification, two-tier health care, and by condemning commercial exchange, the Commission employed the moral frame. Criminalizing payment for surrogacy and reproductive material, opposing private health insurance, and banning various types of genetic and embryonic research are antithetical to the medical-scientific frame, which views science as "neutral, necessary, and client-centred" and privileges "technological values and the positivist notion of 'scientific progress'" (Scala 2002, 9, 79). Medical professionals themselves strongly opposed the proposed prohibitions; the Canadian Medical Association at one point complained that the proposed criminal prohibitions were "an unjustified intrusion of the government's criminal law power into the patient-physician relationship" and would "create a chill on much needed research on reproductive and genetic technologies." Likewise, the Canadian Fertility and Andrology Society (CFAS) and the Society of Obstetricians and Gynaecologists of Canada (SOGC) felt prohibitions would amount to "total control by the government" (Scala 2007, 223; see also Healy 1995).

In sum, while there is considerable evidence that the Commission privileged the medical-scientific over the moral frame, when it came to certain activities and technologies, both the method (criminal prohibition) and the language were hostile to medical-scientific assumptions and reflective of the moral frame. What explains this ambivalence? One reason is that the Royal Commission was not *uniformly* in favour of assisted reproduction, particularly the commercial aspect. However, another reason lies in a different type of frame the Commission adopted throughout its report: that assisted reproduction was an issue of inherent national, rather than provincial, concern.

Jurisdictional Framing: Assisted Reproduction and the National Interest

Although the Royal Commission was ambivalent about the substance of assisted reproduction policy, there was no such ambivalence concerning jurisdictional capacity. Throughout its entire report, the

Commission was resolute in its determination that the federal Parliament had to be the dominant policymaker for assisted reproduction. This too was a type of policy framing, but one that differed in kind. Whereas substantive framing emphasizes aspects of a policy to make a certain outcome more feasible, the Commission was engaging in what I call "jurisdictional framing": defining a policy field as properly belonging to one level of government rather than another. Jurisdictional framing can be "positive," when governments assert authority over policy, or it can be "negative," when governments place responsibility, and often blame, with a different level of government. Regardless of whether such frames are positive or negative, they often include both normative and procedural components: a *normative* component explains why a government should or should not create policy, whereas a *procedural* component asserts that a government has or lacks the legal authority to do so. This conceptualization is crucial to understanding how the Royal Commission's positive jurisdictional framing of assisted reproduction – as a policy field that only the federal Parliament could properly regulate – continues to affect Canadian policy today.

Canada is a "jurisdictional federation," with legislative competencies distributed between its federal and provincial governments (Montpetit, Rothmayr, and Varone 2005, 129; Braun 2000). Both the federal Parliament and the provincial legislatures have primary responsibility for policy formulation and implementation in specific policy fields, enumerated through sections 91 and 92 of the *Constitution Act, 1867*. In many fields, jurisdiction is clear; few would dispute federal authority over military and national defence (section 91.7) or provincial authority over municipalities (section 92.8). Yet the Constitution is less clear about relatively new policy fields, because existing constitutional provisions are often described in broad, general terms. This jurisdictional uncertainty manifests itself in ideational uncertainty about the Canadian federation: there have always been competing visions of how Canada ought to operate, and how authority ought to be divided (see Rocher and Smith 2003; Schertzer 2016, 48–58). Because no dominant idea of the federation has ever achieved hegemonic "lock in" (Broschek 2010), one should expect jurisdictional framing to occur regularly in Canada.

With respect to assisted reproduction, the Canadian Constitution does not contain a clear grant of jurisdiction; in fact, it does not even grant clear jurisdiction over health care to either level of government. Over time, however, Canadian courts have specified that three provincial grants of jurisdiction (sections 92(7), 92(13), and 92(16)) give the provinces primary though not exclusive jurisdiction over health care. Provinces thus retain primary responsibility for health-care spending and the administration of hospitals and health insurance plans.[6] However, health-care jurisdiction is complicated by two federal grants in the *Constitution Act, 1867*. First, section 91 gives Parliament a residual power to make laws for the "Peace, Order, and Good Government of Canada." Second, section 91(27) grants Parliament jurisdiction over criminal law.

Given the predominance of provincial governments in the creation of health policy, the Royal Commission ought to have recognized considerable ambiguity over whether policymaking authority for assisted reproduction fell under federal or provincial jurisdiction. Parliament has a broad scope to legislate under the criminal law power; under section 91(27) of the *Constitution Act, 1867*, it is granted exclusive authority over "the Criminal Law, except the Constitution of Courts of Criminal Jurisdiction, but including the Procedure in Criminal Matters." Provided a law includes a prohibition backed by a penalty with a criminal law purpose – and provided the purpose is defined by a criminal-law "substance" such as public order and safety – courts have generally considered it valid criminal law (Baker 2014, 277–8; see also *Reference re Firearms Act* 2000, para. 27). Thus the Royal Commission could be reasonably certain that its recommended criminal prohibitions would have constituted valid federal law under section 91(27). However, the constitutionality of policies related in principle to those laws, such as clinic licensing, physician permits, and rules for embryo donation and research, was less certain.

Yet with few exceptions, the Commission called for the federal Parliament to play the dominant role in assisted reproduction. Its efforts to frame assisted reproduction as a field necessitating federal intervention – the normative component of its jurisdictional frame – were ubiquitous.

---

6 These sections are the "Establishment, Maintenance, and management of Hospitals, Asylums, Charities, and Eleemosynary Institutions"; "Property and Civil Rights in the Province," and "Generally all Matters of a merely local or private Nature in the Province." Parliament distributes billions of dollars annually to the provinces for health care, ensures compliance and enforcement through Health Canada, and establishes standards for funding in the *Canada Health Act*. However, its main contribution is financial, by offering block grants to the provinces through the Canadian Health Transfer and threatening to withhold funds from the provinces for violating the principles in the *Canada Health Act* (Maioni 2012, 162–9).

It claimed that assisted reproduction was "unique in Canada's health care system" because this policy field raised "issues that require national attention" (Royal Commission on New Reproductive Technologies 1993, 16). It stressed that "the field is developing too rapidly, [and] the consequences of inaction are too great" for fragmented policy (16, xxxv). It rejected the idea that this field could be "subdivided into component parts and left to provincial legislatures, or delegated to self-governing professional bodies" (18). It even claimed that a national response was the preferred strategy of the general public, as it found "consistent and widespread demand for national leadership and action in relation to new reproductive technologies" (11). Overall, assisted reproduction was "too important ... to be left to be resolved by a fragmented and disjointed sector-by-sector or province-by-province approach" (17). The title of the first chapter, "A Comprehensive Response to Issues of National Importance," sums up the commissioners' views on the jurisdictional question.

Several factors explain this commitment to centralization. The first is the Commission's terms of reference, which, under Order-in-Council 1989–2150, were to "inquire into and report on current and potential medical and scientific developments related to new reproductive technologies, considering in particular their social, ethical, health, research, legal and economic implications and the public interest, recommending what policies and safeguards should be applied." The terms of reference were framed broadly, so as to examine "in particular" the implications of assisted reproduction for "women's reproductive health and well-being," "the status and rights of people using or contributing to reproductive services," and "the impact of these services on all concerned parties, particularly the children" (Royal Commission on New Reproductive Technologies 1993, 3). This broad scope lent itself to recommendations for federal action. Women's reproductive health, the rights of donors and patients, and the impact on children are issues that do not fit neatly into provincial boundaries. The overall tone of the terms of reference was conducive to national recommendations.

Another obvious factor is that the Commission was appointed by the federal government. Yet this does not in and of itself explain the Commission's jurisdictional framing strategy. While royal commissions rarely recommend a robust provincial response to issues of perceived national importance, not every federal commission makes as strong a case for national uniformity as the Royal Commission on New Reproductive Technologies did. For example, the 2002 Royal Commission

on the Future of Health Care (the Romanow Commission) made recommendations for sustained federal intervention in health, but it did
not suggest that provincial governments abandon the field. Instead,
Romanow recommended intergovernmental collaboration and national standards, and emphasized a continued provincial role. Unlike
the Royal Commission on New Reproductive Technologies, the Romanow Commission had to navigate an existing decades-long policy
framework for health care that privileged provincial authority. It was
restricted by a well-developed policy field where constitutional jurisdiction over health care was fairly clearly defined. By contrast, in the
late 1980s and early 1990s, there was a policy vacuum in the six subfields of assisted reproduction policy; the Royal Commission on New
Reproductive Technologies did not need to work around existing provincial policies, which meant that creating an almost entirely national
plan was much more feasible. It is not particularly surprising that the
nationally appointed Commission was inclined towards national action in this new and developing field.

Justifying National Action: A Weak Procedural Component

While the Commission was committed to a national strategy, it did recognize, albeit without sufficient attention, that there were concerns
over whether Parliament had the constitutional authority to create a
national body with permanent regulatory power over certain areas of
health care policy. The Royal Commission's recommendations were
justified not just as a matter of desirable policy but also of constitutional
law; it was convinced that the Canadian Constitution supported a centralized scheme.

To make the case for national action, the Commission needed to adopt
a *procedural* component for its jurisdictional frame. To do so, the Commission cited both the criminal law power and Parliament's authority
to make laws for "Peace, Order, and Good Government" (POGG). It
relied on the POGG clause most heavily. By 1993, the Supreme Court
of Canada (and the Judicial Committee of the Privy Council before it)
had determined that POGG enables Parliament to enact legislation
that might otherwise come within provincial jurisdiction in one of two
instances. First, it can do so temporarily (and very extensively) in order to respond to emergency situations (see *Re Board of Commerce Act*
1922; *Fort Frances Pulp & Power Co. v. Manitoba Free Press* 1923; *Toronto
Electric Commissioners v. Snider* 1925). However, while some of the Royal

Commission's rhetoric reflected an "emergency" tone – such as its pronouncement that "the field is developing too rapidly, the consequences of inaction are too great" – it did not intend the federal legislation to be a temporary response to an emergency. Indeed, its recommendation that "permanent mechanisms should be put in place" was antithetical to temporary action (Royal Commission on New Reproductive Technologies 1993, xxxv, 1049).

Absent an emergency, Parliament has the authority to invoke POGG to justify permanent legislation in matters that implicate provincial jurisdiction if those matters have attained a sufficient "national dimension" or "national concern." The Commission referenced this branch of POGG early and often in its first chapter, suggesting it gave the federal Parliament a "clear basis for seeking national action" over assisted reproduction. It claimed, without reference to any cases, that the Supreme Court permitted invoking POGG when Parliament was legislating in areas of "genuine national concern" that possess "a degree of singleness, distinctiveness, and indivisibility." The Commission also claimed that the Court had permitted Parliament to invoke POGG in the case of a "province's failure to regulate the intraprovincial aspects" of a matter through interprovincial cooperation, particularly if the policy area had "extraprovincial dimensions." While acknowledging that assisted reproduction touched on "health issues," the Commission insisted that the convergence of "other individual and societal issues" necessitated a national response. Overall, assisted reproduction had attained such "profound importance" and exhibited such "inter-relatedness" that federal restriction of traditional provincial jurisdiction was justified (Royal Commission on New Reproductive Technologies 1993, 18–19).

From a constitutional law perspective, the Commission's evidence was not particularly convincing. While "indivisibility," "distinctiveness," and "provincial inability" were all doctrinal tests that Supreme Court justices had accepted as constitutional justification for federal action in the past (*Munro v. National Capital Commission* 1966; *R. v. Crown Zellerbach* 1988; see also Baier 2006, 128–42), the Commission made insufficient comparison between the content of some of those cases – such as the creation of a national capital region and combating environmental pollution – and assisted reproduction. Overall, its procedural reliance on POGG's "national concern" doctrine was fairly weak (see Healy 1995).

The second constitutional lever the Royal Commission used as a procedural component of its jurisdictional frame was Parliament's power to create criminal law. The Commission justified the criminal law as an instrument for those activities that "conflict so sharply with the values espoused by Canadians and by this Commission" (1022). Its recommendations for outright prohibitions relied on this power; however, the Commission limited this power to activities that would be criminally proscribed and not, as would become important in the future, regulatory authority attached in principle to those prohibitions. The Commission also briefly mentioned other areas of federal jurisdiction – including jurisdiction over environmental regulation, health care on Indian reserves, federal penitentiaries, and the federal spending power – that could theoretically justify federal intervention (79). However, it dedicated virtually no time to these supplementary arguments, and minimal time to criminal law justifications relative to POGG.

In sum, while the Royal Commission did engage in procedural jurisdictional framing, its jurisprudential basis was weak, and the Commission emphasized the procedural component far less than the normative jurisdictional frame. In other words, it did not draw a close enough connection between justifications based on effectiveness and arguments based on constitutionality. The Commission instead relied on broad normative arguments, such as the fact that assisted reproduction was "so important to women and children," was "unique in Canada's health care system," raised "fundamental social, moral, legal, and ethical implications," and had "social implications" that could not be contained "within the boundaries of a single province." The Commission's only reference to a "clear precedent" in terms of jurisprudence was that "radio and television broadcasting is regulated and monitored through a licensing agency for the Canadian public interest" (Royal Commission on New Reproductive Technologies 1993, xxxvi, 16, 21). While the recommended criminal prohibitions would almost certainly pass constitutional scrutiny, the reliance on POGG's "national concern" doctrine rested on a shaky constitutional foundation, which the Commission dangerously underplayed.

Conclusion: The Commission's Unintended Consequences

Like other royal commissions, the Royal Commission on New Reproductive Technologies was ad hoc, public, and investigatory. It made recommendations but it did not legislate, and the mere publication of a final report did not necessarily mean that policy would be forthcoming. However, the Royal Commission's recommendations would have a formative, lasting effect beyond the scope of other federal commissions. Its chief recommendations – federal prohibitions, federal regulatory authority, and a national agency – would come to fruition in the *Assisted Human Reproduction Act*. Just as importantly, the wide latitude granted to the Commission meant that the way it framed the emerging debate would become especially crucial. This latitude meant that the Royal Commission was a "critical juncture" in the development of assisted reproduction policy in Canada – both in terms of content and framing strategies.

Its framing strategy was especially important. The Commission selected, emphasized, and manipulated particular aspects of the policy issue to influence and limit the perception of choices available to future policymakers. To understand the Commission's influence, it is important to separate its substantive framing strategy from its jurisdictional framing strategy. Substantively, others have argued that the Commission's organizational structure, the scientific community's privileged position, and the individual rights discourse meant that the "medical-scientific" frame dominated (Ariss 1996; Eichler 1993; Scala 2002, 2007, 2008). However, the Commission's substantive framing strategy reflected more ambivalence than this. While the medical-scientific frame was prominent, the Commission effectively created a discursive "division of labour" between positive (medical-scientific) practices that should be regulated and negative (immoral) practices that should be proscribed.

The Commission also engaged in jurisdictional framing by arguing that five of the six subfields of assisted reproduction should be subject to a national regulatory framework. Much of this frame was reliant on normative concerns about importance, uniqueness, and national leadership. However, the procedural component of its jurisdictional frame was lacking. Because the Commission relied primarily on broad normative arguments, federal authority was from the outset built on a shaky constitutional foundation; a constitutional power (POGG's "national concern" doctrine) was used to justify federal intervention in a field of provincial authority in spite of limited jurisprudential support. The implications of these framing strategies would be far-reaching, both in the justifications used to frame the federal *AHR Act* and, eventually, in the Supreme Court of Canada.

Chapter 3

The *Assisted Human Reproduction Act* Comes to Fruition

While the Royal Commission made recommendations for immediate and comprehensive national intervention, there was no inherent reason why the federal government needed to adopt them. The commissioners themselves held no political power; a royal commission is "dismantled once it has carried out its investigatory function on a specific policy topic" (Doern 1967, 418). Moreover, by the time the Commission reported in November 1993, the Canadian power structure had changed. Jean Chretien's Liberal Party had swept to power with a majority government, while the governing Progressive Conservatives were decimated, returning just two seats in the 1993 federal election. Although the Commission was non-partisan, the new government was not obliged to listen to its recommendations.

And yet the federal government did act in concert with the Royal Commission's recommendations, albeit not with any great immediacy. Through an analysis of legislative proposals, legislative debates, committee hearings, and journalistic and academic commentary from 1993 to 2004, this chapter will show how, with minor exceptions, the Royal Commission's framing strategy and its recommendations regarding content were reproduced in the 2004 *Assisted Human Reproduction Act* (*AHR Act*). The combination of prohibitions, regulatory authority for "controlled activities," and a national agency contained in the *AHR Act* almost exactly mirrored the Commission's overarching recommendations.

However, the Commission's most lasting legacy would come in the form of its framing strategies. The Commission's ambivalence in substantive framing was also reflected during parliamentary debates: the medical-scientific frame was used to justify certain activities and technologies, while the moral frame was used to justify criminal prohibitions.

Jurisdictionally, the national frame dominated the entire process, and was rarely questioned by policymakers. The Royal Commission's determination that Ottawa had the authority to lead clearly gave the federal government the constitutional confidence to "go it alone" on the entire field of assisted reproduction except parentage. The relative legislative vacuum and the unwillingness of provinces to legislate reinforced this strategy, as the federal government perceived a greater ability to set policy for assisted reproduction than it would have in policy fields where the jurisdictional question was more definitively settled. In effect, the frames produced by one temporary institution (the Royal Commission) created a new policy (*AHR Act*), albeit one whose institutionalization would be long in the making and never fully completed.

For these reasons, this chapter concludes that the Royal Commission constitutes *the* critical juncture for assisted reproduction policy in Canada, although not in a way that the commissioners would have intended. Indeed, the incompatibility between the Commission's substantive and jurisdictional frames would ultimately contain the seeds of the legislation's demise.

A Long Gestation: Parliament Debates Assisted Reproduction

Although the Royal Commission on New Reproductive Technologies had been appointed by Brian Mulroney's Progressive Conservatives, the incoming Liberal government indicated that it would take seriously its recommendation for a national framework for assisted reproduction. Beginning in 1994, the year after the Commission reported, there were a series of federal initiatives that would continue for a decade until the *AHR Act* was passed in 2004. Table 3.1 lists these initiatives, which fall into three stages of parliamentary development: the process leading to the failed Bill C-47 and companion discussion paper; the Standing Committee on Health's report on draft legislation in 2001 (the "Brown Committee"); and the three subsequent legislative attempts that ultimately culminated in the 2004 *AHR Act*.

Bill C-47: Criminalizing Issues of Grave Concern

In 1994, Health Canada began consultations with stakeholders regarding the Commission's final report. A year later, Minister of Health Diane Marleau announced a voluntary moratorium on nine of the practices for which the Royal Commission had recommended criminal

Table 3.1
Federal Responses to Assisted Reproduction

	Date Created*	Initiated By	Content	Outcome
Royal Commission	October 1989	Federal Government	Prohibitions Regulations Agency (recommended)	Reported 15 November 1993
Voluntary Moratorium	July 1995	Federal Government	Moratorium	Announced
Bill C-47	June 1996	Federal Government	Prohibitions	Died on Order Paper (Election) 27 April 1997
Setting Boundaries	June 1996	Minister of Health	Regulations (recommended)	Sent to public
Bill C-247	October 1997	Bloc Québécois MP	Prohibitions	Died on Order Paper (Prorogation) First Reading 18 September 1999
Bill C-336	April 2001	Bloc Québécois MP	Prohibitions	Died on Order Paper (Prorogation) First Reading 16 September 2002
Draft Legislation	May 2001	Minister of Health	Prohibitions Regulations	Referred to Standing Committee on Health
Brown Committee	December 2001	All-Party Committee	Prohibitions Regulations Agency	Presented to Government
Bill C-56	May 2002	Federal Government	Prohibitions Regulations Agency	Died on Order Paper (Prorogation) Referral to Committee 16 September 2002
Bill C-13	October 2002	Federal Government	Prohibitions Regulations Agency	Died on Order Paper (Election) Second Reading in Senate 12 November 2003
Bill C-6	February 2004	Federal Government	Prohibitions Regulations Agency	Royal Assent 29 March 2004

* For legislation, this is the date of first reading.

prohibitions. The activities included in the moratorium covered five of the six areas of assisted reproduction policy (with the exception of parentage), including

- clinical intervention (purchasing or selling eggs, sperm, and embryos; egg donation in exchange for IVF);
- surrogacy (commercial surrogacy arrangements);
- human cloning (reproductive human cloning);
- screening/enhancement (germ-line engineering, non-medical sex selection, retrieval of reproductive material from cadavers and fetuses, ectogenesis, creating animal-hybrids); and
- embryonic research (non-reproductive human cloning).

Evidence soon surfaced that certain clinicians and physicians were not abiding by the moratorium,[7] and in 1996 the federal government introduced Bill C-47, the *Human Reproductive and Genetic Technologies Act*. In addition to the activities contained in the moratorium, Bill C-47 would have criminalized the use of sperm/ova without consent, the transfer of embryos between human and other species, research on embryos after fourteen days, the creation of embryos solely for research, and offers to pay for any prohibited practices. The government intended to subsequently create a second bill that would introduce a regulatory framework consistent with the Royal Commission's recommendations (Baylis and Herder 2009a, 113–14; Health Canada 1996; Norris and Tiedemann 2015).

By focusing on the most unacceptable practices, Bill C-47 did not at all fit with the Royal Commission's "medical-scientific" frame; indeed, it began with the preamble that Parliament was "gravely concerned" about threats to human dignity, health, and safety. One commentator claimed that the bill's tone was "quite simply hostile to reproductive technology," as it made no mention of individual rights and "essentially ignored" the *Canadian Charter of Rights and Freedoms* (Harvison Young 2005, 128). It was poorly received by medical and professional organizations, and

---

7 According to Health Canada's 1996 report, many physicians were openly ignoring the moratorium: "Two sex selection clinics operate in Canada; payment to sperm donors continues to occur in most facilities; seven advertisements have appeared to date in student newspapers seeking women to sell their eggs; and one physician has reported that he has been approached by women to have sperm removed from the corpses of their dead husbands so that they may attempt pregnancy" (Health Canada 1996, 25; see also Jones and Salter 2010, 428).

physicians perceived it as "almost a slap on the wrist" for not abiding by the terms of the moratorium (Jones and Salter 2010, 427).

At the same time, Health Canada released a discussion paper entitled *New Reproductive Technologies: Setting Boundaries, Enhancing Health*. This paper was the first to put forward the federal government's proposed regulatory framework, and it was far more consistent with the medical-scientific frame than the moral frame – although it did endorse the criminal prohibitions in Bill C-47. Like Bill C-47, *Setting Boundaries* also saw Parliament as the key actor to implement all the proposals, albeit with one small gesture to the provinces: it was the first federal proposal to include a provision for the creation of "equivalency agreements," whereby federal regulatory controls could be suspended if a province or territory enacted a policy that was "substantially the same as, but not necessarily identical to, the federal legislation in substance and enforcement" (Health Canada 1996, 33). Nevertheless, by mandating that such agreements would be the same as existing federal policy, provinces would be clearly subservient to Parliament under the equivalency provision.

In terms of actually creating a national agency to oversee assisted reproduction, *Setting Boundaries* proposed that the federal regulatory structure "could" include an agency separate from Health Canada, which would report to the Minister of Health, but was not as definitive about the need for a specialized agency as the Royal Commission was. Regardless of whether it would take place within a separate agency or simply within Health Canada, the federal government would have responsibility for issuing licenses, monitoring compliance through enforcement, creating and maintaining information registries, and developing national standards for the use of reproductive materials. These standards would be subject to ministerial approval. The department's goal was to pass Bill C-47 and then introduce these regulatory aspects as an amendment to that legislation, in order to produce a "single piece of legislation containing both prohibitions and regulatory controls" (Health Canada 1996, 27; see Table 3.2). However, after an election was called in 1997, Bill C-47 died on the order paper.[8]

---

8 During the same session of Parliament, Bloc Québécois MP Pauline Picard also introduced private member's legislation in the form of Bill C-247. The legislation sought to prohibit human cloning through the *Criminal Code*. Picard sponsored a similar bill in 2001 (Bill C-336, see Table 3.1). Like most private members' legislation, both bills died on the order paper before they made it to second reading.

Table 3.2
Autonomy of the National Regulatory Agency

	Less Autonomy < – – – > More Autonomy			
	No agency; Minister of Health creates regulations	Agency exists, but regulations made by Minister of Health	Agency creates regulations; Minister of Health must approve	Agency creates regulations, fully arms-length
1993 Royal Commission				X
1996 Setting Boundaries			X	
2001 Draft Legislation	X			
2001 Brown Committee		X		
2004 Assisted Human Reproduction Act		X		

Overall, these documents continued to demonstrate the Royal Commission's influence in terms of content and, especially, framing: substantively, there was "grave concern" in Bill C-47 but a recognition in *Setting Boundaries* that "some [reproductive technologies] can enhance health and well-being" (Health Canada 1996, 5). Jurisdictionally, the national frame dominated, with Parliament taking the lead role for assisted reproduction policymaking. The discussion paper recognized that "some important issues related to [reproductive technologies] fall within provincial/territorial jurisdiction," including family law, but that those issues were "not addressed in this document" (10). Insofar as everything covered by Bill C-47 and *Setting Boundaries* was assumed to fall within federal jurisdiction, Health Canada clearly did not perceive intergovernmental collaboration on these issues to be a requirement.

The Brown Committee: Continuing Centralization

Following the 1997 election, the pace of legislative development was slow. Health Canada consulted with stakeholders and issued a feedback report in 2000. As provincial governments showed no strong desire to legislate, the federal government was ready to try again. Rather than tabling the draft legislation as a bill in the House of Commons, federal Minister of Health Allan Rock asked the House of Commons Standing Committee on Health to first examine and provide recommendations on the document entitled *Proposals for Legislation Governing Assisted Human Reproduction*. The primary difference between the draft legislation and Bill C-47 was the distinction between "prohibited activities," which were banned by the legislation itself, and "controlled activities," which could only be carried out with a license in accordance with regulations. Under this framework, both prohibitions and controlled activities would be brought in at the same time by Parliament, and regulations would be drafted after the legislation was passed. This draft legislation was given to the Brown Committee (chaired by Liberal MP Bonnie Brown) in May 2001. After extensive hearings, the committee released its recommendations in December 2001 in a report entitled *Assisted Human Reproduction: Building Families*.

The Brown Committee's majority report made thirty-three recommendations based on the draft legislation. It recommended only minor adjustments to the proposed criminal prohibitions, approving of bans for reproductive and non-reproductive human cloning, germline engineering, ectogenesis, creating embryos solely for research, the removal of gametes from embryos in order to create another embryo, animal-human reproductive experimentation, non-medical sex selection, paid surrogacy, the purchase of gametes and embryos, and the use of reproductive materials without consent. Like those in the moratorium, these bans encompassed five of the six subfields of assisted reproduction policy, with the exception of parentage. Like the Royal Commission, the committee argued that Parliament should play the dominant role: the only mention of interprovincial collaboration concerned the legal status of donors and offspring and the creation of a sexual and reproductive health database concerning infertility (Canada 2001a, 22, 32). Both issues were clearly provincial jurisdiction, and neither was part of the legislation.

The draft legislation had left open the possibility for an arm's-length body to deal with monitoring, licensing, and regulations. As Health Minister Allan Rock told the committee, "we need your advice on how this body could be structured – whether it should be part of Health Canada or an external organization" (Canada 2001a). In Canadian law, comprehensive legislation can delegate authority to create regulations

to a body (most often part of the executive branch), and the draft legislation contemplated the possibility of future regulations. Such regulations typically add specificity to legislation; while they must undergo
legal examination, registration, and formal publication in the *Canada
Gazette*, they are not subject to the same level of scrutiny as the enabling legislation (Privy Council Office 2001). During committee hearings, there was considerable debate over which body would be charged
with creating such regulations, as well as the timing and content of
those regulations. The Brown Committee, like the Royal Commission,
found "most witnesses felt that an arm's length agency would be more
appropriate" (Canada 2001p, 25).

Unlike the Royal Commission, however, the committee did not recommend giving the agency as much autonomy. Under the committee's
recommendations, regulatory authority would rest with the Minister
and Health Canada, who "would be responsible for establishing general policies and standards" as well as enforcement and inspection.
The committee defended its approach by claiming that "requiring the
agency to report to the Minister is more in keeping with the principle
of ministerial accountability," and would also facilitate intergovernmental cooperation (Canada 2001p, 25). The committee further recommended that all regulations coming from the Minister would be
subject to approval or modification by the House of Commons within
thirty sitting days. The new national agency, given a statutory base
with a board of governors, would be tasked with maintaining a personal health information registry, keeping abreast of national and
international trends, issuing licenses, ensuring compliance, and public
reporting. However, the overall direction of the agency, as well as the
authority to create regulations pursuant to the legislation, would rest
with the Minister of Health.

The committee also made recommendations regarding regulations.
While it did not suggest that regulations be created contemporaneously with the passage of legislation, it did recommend the subsequent development of regulations for areas such as counselling, eligibility requirements for donors, and the maximum number of eggs that
could be harvested (Canada 2001p, 17). The committee made a host
of recommendations relating to the legislation's proposed Personal
Health Information Registry, which would collect information about
donors and donor offspring. Along these lines, it recommended that
the federal Minister of Justice collaborate with the provinces and territories in order to create uniform parentage legislation, as the Royal

Commission had recommended (22). Additional recommendations included a three-year parliamentary review clause (the draft legislation had set it at five years), and the replacement of a legislative preamble with a statutory declaration, which would have greater legal force. The Royal Commission's framing strategies continued to loom large, as substantive ambivalence over the medical/moral benefits was reflected in different aspects of the legislation, with all the work to be done by the federal Parliament.

Bills C-56, C-13, and C-6: The AHR Act *Is Born*

Following the committee's recommendations, Bill C-56, *An Act Respecting Assisted Human Reproduction*, was introduced in May 2002. The *Act* was far more comprehensive than Bill C-47, containing prohibitions, provisions outlining a regulatory framework, and a semiautonomous national agency. Bill C-56 was referred to committee, but died on the order paper when Parliament was prorogued in September. Bill C-13, an exact replication of Bill C-56, was introduced on 9 October 2002. Although the bill passed all three readings in the House of Commons, Parliament was once again prorogued before it passed third reading in the Senate, and the bill died on the order paper in November 2003. In February 2004, Bill C-13 was reintroduced as Bill C-6, *An Act Respecting Human Reproduction and Related Research*. The House deemed it adopted at all stages and passed it quickly. It then passed through the Senate, and received Royal Assent on 29 March 2004, with most sections of the *Act* coming into force on 22 April 2004. Almost fifteen years after the Royal Commission was established, Canada finally had legislation with respect to new reproductive technologies: the *Assisted Human Reproduction Act* (*AHR Act*).

The *AHR Act* prohibited several activities, including the creation of animal-human hybrids, human cloning, embryonic sex selection, and commercial surrogacy. Those who violated the terms of these activities would be subject to criminal sanctions of up to a $500,000 fine or ten years in prison. The legislation created a federal regulatory structure for controlled activities, which would be prohibited unless carried out in accordance with future regulations and a license. As the Brown Committee recommended, Health Canada was given authority for creating subsequent regulations defining the parameters of such activities. The *Act* also created Assisted Human Reproduction Canada (AHRC), a federal agency charged with monitoring compliance and enforcement, creating and administering a licensing framework for the controlled activities, and maintaining a health data registry. The legislation included equivalency agreements, which stated that federal law would be withheld if the federal government agreed that provincial regulations were "equivalent to those sections and the corresponding provisions of the regulations" (*Assisted Human Reproduction Act*, s. 68).

In terms of the six subfields of assisted reproduction policy, the *AHR Act* did the following:

- *Clinical intervention:* The legislation prohibited compensation for gametes, although it permitted reimbursement for certain receipted expenditures in accordance with future regulations and a license. In addition, Health Canada's broad regulatory power could have, if implemented, applied to nearly all aspects of clinical intervention by setting rules for artificial insemination, IVF, and licensing fertility clinics.[9]
- *Surrogacy:* In keeping with the anti-commercialization spirit evident with respect to gametes, the *AHR Act* prohibited paid surrogacy but permitted unpaid surrogacy. It did not legislate with respect to the distinction between traditional and gestational surrogacy.
- *Parentage:* The *AHR Act* did not legislate with respect to parentage, whether for children born through assisted conception or through surrogacy.
- *Reproductive Human Cloning:* The *AHR Act* enacted an absolute prohibition on reproductive human cloning, and on transplanting a human clone into a human being.
- *Screening/enhancement:* The *AHR Act* banned germ-line engineering and non-medical sex selection. It also prohibited putting human reproductive material into a non-human life form for the purpose of creating a human being, creating chimeras, and creating human-animal hybrids.
- *Embryonic research:* The *AHR Act* prohibited creating animal-human chimeras or hybrids, paying for embryos, creating an embryo from part of another embryo or fetus, maintaining an embryo outside a woman's body for more than fourteen days, and "therapeutic"

---

9   While the Brown Committee recommended ending the practice of donor anonymity, the government did not implement this recommendation in the subsequent legislation in part because it felt that donor identification was provincial jurisdiction (Canada 2001p; see chapter 6).

(non-reproductive) human cloning. It also limited embryonic research to surplus embryos from assisted conception, thus prohibiting the creation of embryos solely for research.

While the legislation did not please everyone, it was viewed by many as a compromise. Bioethicists, academics, and infertility support organizations frequently used the term "compromise" to describe the legislation (Jones and Salter 2010, 428–9). Even religious organizations defended the legislation as an important compromise: one interview respondent from the Evangelical Fellowship of Canada, which was "supportive" of the prohibitions, said that while "we had hoped that for something like embryonic research there would have been clear parameters … on the whole we were pleased with the outcome" of the *AHR Act* (Interview 2011e). Insofar as the legislative content drew heavily from a Royal Commission that itself framed the policy field in ambivalent medical/moral terms, the language of compromise is not surprising.

In 2007, Health Canada passed the *Assisted Human Reproduction (Section 8 Consent) Regulations*, which expanded on the qualified prohibitions in section 8 of the *AHR Act*, which ban the use of reproductive material without consent (*Assisted Human Reproduction (Section 8 Consent) Regulations*, SOR/2007–137). These regulations specify the rules for patient consent when donating human gametes and embryos, and stipulate the purposes for which those reproductive materials can be used. To date, this is the only regulation Health Canada has passed pursuant to the *AHR Act*, although in July 2017 it released a set of policy proposals to create a number of new regulations pursuant to reimbursement, safety of reproductive materials, and administration and enforcement (Health Canada 2017).

**The Royal Commission's Influence:
Continued Medical-Moral Ambivalence**

By any reading, the Royal Commission had an enormous influence on every stage of the policymaking process. It was frequently referenced by parliamentarians and ministers: Early in the process, Liberal cabinet minister Stan Keyes noted that the bill was "based on extensive research and consultations with the Royal Commission on New Reproductive Technologies"; six years later, Canadian Alliance MP and Brown Committee member Rob Merrifield referred to the legislation as "a child of the Royal Commission on New Reproductive Technologies" (Canada 1996, 1750; Canada 2002a, 1030). Both the form and content of the legislation were in line with the Commission's recommendations. Indeed, all three of the Royal Commission's overarching recommendations – prohibitions, the creation of a permanent agency to respond to developing technologies, and regulatory capacity (if not outright regulations) – were realized in the legislation.

Why was the Royal Commission so influential? One reason, as Scala (2002, 68) suggests, is that an institution's ability to create change is often dependent on the "unique characteristics of the policy field and the policy issue in question." In his study of Canadian Royal Commissions, Doern (1967, 420) suggests that most fall into one of two categories: "non-recurring issues" related to novel circumstances, and "recurring issues" of generalized social, economic, and/or cultural interest. The Royal Commission on New Reproductive Technologies seems to straddle both categories. On the one hand, it was created in response to a particular set of circumstances – the recent development of new reproductive technologies and the desire from interest groups to see some legislation. Yet it would be a mistake to call assisted reproduction a "non-recurring issue"; indeed, one of the Commission's overarching recommendations was to put in place "permanent mechanisms" that could "provide a flexible and continuing response" to assisted reproduction as the field evolved and that would adapt to changing and unforeseen technologies (Royal Commission on New Reproductive Technologies 1993, 1049). Thus, the Commission dealt with a novel issue, albeit one that would have a continuing impact into the future.

In this sense, the Royal Commission's opportunity for influence was quite wide. Unlike the Royal Commission on Aboriginal Peoples and the Royal Commission on the Future of Health Care, it was not working within an existing legislative framework. It is true that the technologies had been around for over a decade and, as such, the Commission's need to accommodate existing practices from the medical communities meant it was not working with a completely blank slate. However, to use the Commission's own language, the field in 1993 was characterized by "chaos" (Royal Commission on New Reproductive Technologies 1993, 16). There was no federal or provincial legislation in any of the six subfields, and the level of self-regulation varied depending on the subfield.

The Royal Commission was equally influential in terms of policy framing. The Commission's ambivalence between the "medical-scientific" framing of beneficial technologies and the "moral" framing of negative ones persisted throughout the legislative debates and committee hearings. Sometimes parliamentarians and witnesses treated the issue as health-related. Health Minister Allan Rock noted that "there is enormous potential and great hope here that Canadians can benefit from research in such areas as infertility but also inherited disorders" (Canada 2001a, 1120). Subsequent Health Minister Anne McLellan said the legislation "speaks to one of the most fundamental human desires, having a family" and that "there is great merit in other types of research in the field" (Canada 2002a, 1015–20). With some exceptions, most witnesses were supportive of assisted reproduction.

On the other hand, when it came to prohibited activities, the government's language clearly reflected the moral frame. Health ministers Allan Rock and Anne McLellan claimed that "there must be a higher notion than science alone ... that can guide scientific research," and that the prohibitions concerned "activities that Canadians simply will not countenance because they offend our shared values" (Canada 2001a, 1110; Canada 2002a, 1015–20). Deputy Minister of Health Ian Shugart claimed the bill reflected the principle that "science is not free from civil society's oversight" (Canada 2001b, 1215). As with the Royal Commission, this language was strongest when it came, in the words of Health Committee chairperson Bonnie Brown, to "eliminat[ing] commodification and commercialization" (Canada 2001l, 1310).

Many witnesses – including fertility doctors, law professors, and members of the British Columbia Civil Liberties Association, the Canadian Medical Association, and the Canadian Bar Association – spoke out against the prohibitions. Among these witnesses, there was frequent reference to the criminal law, in the words of Dr Eugene Bereza, as a "blunt instrument" that was incapable of flexibility (Canada 2002f, 1600). However, these witnesses were often criticized by MPs. In one particularly poignant exchange, a nurse from sperm bank Xytex Canada described the processes for compensating sperm donors. Canadian Alliance MP James Lunney then thanked her for "painting such a clear picture of where the committee was quite determined we did not want to see this process go" (Canada 2002d, 1720). The criminal law remained the preferred legislative instrument for eliminating certain behaviours; in words that echoed the Royal Commission, the Brown Committee's majority report argued that "an outright statutory ban signals more clearly that certain activities are either unsafe or socially unacceptable" (Canada 2001p, 9).

The *AHR Act* did not follow the path laid down by the Royal Commission in every respect, however. In particular, it moved away from the Royal Commission's model of independent expertise for Assisted Human Reproduction Canada (AHRC), the national regulatory agency. Table 3.2 displays the degree of autonomy given to the agency under the major legislative initiatives. As it shows, the 2004 *AHR Act* followed the Brown Committee rather than the Royal Commission in subjecting AHRC to government control. Whereas the Commission recommended an arm's-length body outside of Health Canada and accountable to Parliament, the *AHR Act* kept AHRC largely under the control of the Minister of Health and Health Canada. The content of regulations would be set by the Minister of Health, who was permitted to "issue policy directions to the Agency concerning the exercise of any of its powers" (*Assisted Human Reproduction Act*, s. 25(1)). Maintaining ministerial responsibility represents the one major area where the institutional outcome offered by the *AHR Act* differed from that prescribed by the Royal Commission.

The Persistence of the National Frame

While the government was ambivalent regarding medical-scientific and moral frames, there was no ambivalence with respect to jurisdiction. Allan Rock described the legislation as "surely an area where federal leadership is needed, where the Government of Canada is uniquely positioned to lead, where a consistent approach is needed to deal with national issues that reflect national values" (Canada 2001a, 1115). As with the Royal Commission, Rock frequently made reference to the uniqueness of assisted reproduction. He noted, "This legislation is like no other. These issues are like no others" (Canada 2001a, 1110).

Echoing the Royal Commission, MPs and government officials cited "provincial inability" as another common theme. Canadian Alliance MP Preston Manning noted that there "appears to be a lack of desire on the part of the provinces to do it, mainly for political reasons" (Canada 2001m, 1135). Chairperson Brown commented, "No province has rushed in to fill this void ... I think they're probably going to be quite happy that someone else is carrying this particular responsibility" (Canada 2002c, 1215). A former senior civil servant at Health Canada recalled that "no [provincial] jurisdiction was acting in a significant fashion to deal with the fundamental issues," and it was "very evidently a policy and regulatory vacuum" (Interview 2011a). Another

MP who sat on the Brown Committee said, "If the provinces had legislation and you were stepping over their turf, that's one thing, but it's a harder argument to say when they don't have legislation" (Interview 2011h).

This dominant national frame was not limited to MPs and government officials. Witnesses were uniformly in favour of a national approach, with not a single witness suggesting that provincial governments could more effectively or efficiently regulate assisted reproduction. Law professor Martha Jackman represented most witnesses' views when she stated, "It is clear that by the total inaction of the provinces in effectively regulating these activities ... the provinces, individually and collectively, are unable to effectively regulate this area" (Canada 2001m, 1145). The Royal Commission's normative jurisdictional frame – that the federal government *must* be the main actor in order to create good public policy – remained ubiquitous.

Like the Royal Commission, those involved in the creation of the *AHR Act* recognized that constitutional issues could arise in principle. Equivalency agreements were included to assuage some of these concerns: one civil servant noted that they were "very deliberately put in place to mitigate concerns of provinces that we were taking up space that was theirs" (Interview 2011a). However, apprehension over the legislation's constitutionality varied depending on partisan affiliation. The Brown Committee's majority Liberal report made no mention of constitutional concerns, and in fact worried that "a patchwork might develop" from equivalency agreements (Canada 2001p, 23). The committee's dissenting reports, by contrast, were more concerned about federal/provincial conflict. The sovereigntist Bloc Québécois urged coordination with the provinces, asserting that "large sectors of the field of medically assisted reproduction are matters of provincial responsibility" (Canada 2001p, 85). Bloc MP Réal Ménard frequently commented that the legislation violated provincial jurisdiction. At one point Ménard said, "If the regulatory agency were established, there would be serious incompatibility between ... Quebec statutes and the [federal] bill" (Canada 2002e, 1010). The Progressive Conservatives asserted that "the provinces and territories should *have* to be involved" (Canada 2001p, 93; emphasis in original). And the Canadian Alliance expressed concern that "attempted federal regulation of assisted human reproduction facilities may raise constitutional challenges" (80). Preston Manning, the highest-ranking Alliance member of the Brown Committee, repeatedly pressed witnesses on questions of constitutionality, at one point stating, "If this [bill] is passed in the current form, we're going to end up having all kinds of litigation on the regulation of assisted human reproduction, on whether it's a federal or provincial responsibility" (Canada 2001m, 1135).

While Manning was prescient in this respect, he was virtually alone among non-Bloc MPs in fearing Parliament lacked constitutional authority. As one parliamentary researcher involved with the *AHR Act* recalled in an interview, there was satisfaction that the criminal prohibitions created a constitutional "anchor" that would allow Parliament to enact its national regulatory scheme (Interview 2011c). One standing committee member recounted that "we didn't hear an awful lot of testimony saying, 'you guys shouldn't be playing in this field' … Most of the provinces were saying, 'we dodged a bullet on this one, let them do it'" (Interview 2011h). In fact, every single witness except one claimed that Parliament had the authority to launch its regulatory scheme. Constitutional lawyers were among the most adamant. Brent Windwick, on behalf of the Canadian Bar Association, stated that the legislation "will meet the appropriate legal test for the federal government to assume jurisdiction over the activities it seeks to regulate" (Canada 2001n, 1145). Law professor Timothy Caulfield, drawing explicitly from Supreme Court jurisprudence in *R. v. Hydro-Québec* (1997), claimed that the federal government "should retain jurisdiction so long as the regulatory scheme has criminal prohibitions and is aimed at a legitimate public health concern … If the model went forward as proposed, I don't think there's any doubt that the feds would keep jurisdiction" (Canada 2001g, 1140–5). And law professor Patrick Healy stated, "The legislation as a whole can properly be characterized as criminal law … because the criminal law power available to Parliament has a rather wide scope" (Canada 2001h, 1150).

The lone holdout was Gerald Chipeur, an independent lawyer. He maintained that the mere existence of equivalency agreements logically took away "the very basis for the argument a Parliament could make that they needed to incidentally affect health care in order to achieve their objective." Chipeur asserted that, while the prohibitions were valid, the creation of a regulatory agency – even with subsequent regulations to be created by the Minister of Health – could be justified neither by POGG nor by the criminal law power. But Chipeur did not persuade the government. Glenn Rivard from the Department of Justice responded to him directly, stating, "We're quite satisfied as to the constitutionality of the legislation" (Canada 2002c, 1210–15). Health

Minister Allan Rock was likewise "satisfied … as a minister, as a person, as a lawyer, that the draft legislation we put before you would be upheld by the courts if it were challenged on the basis of constitutional competence." And Deputy Minister of Health Ian Shugart claimed that "the basis upon which the government is proposing to legislate and regulate in this area is the criminal power," and that "there ought not to be any issue" with regulations related to criminal prohibitions (Canada 2001a, 1135; Canada 2001g, 1140). This constitutional confidence displayed by most legal experts and federal officials, combined with the theme of "provincial inability" and the lack of provincial legislation for assisted reproduction, likely explains why the federal government felt little need to engage in meaningful intergovernmental collaboration before passing its legislation.

What is most notable about this is not that the federal government adopted a national jurisdictional frame. It is common for a federal government to assert constitutional authority when introducing a new national policy that could potentially intrude on provincial authority. This occurs even with less centralizing federal governments, as when the Harper Conservatives began their (ultimately failed) attempt at national securities regulation (Ivison 2009; *Reference re Securities Act* 2011). Rather, what is most notable from the above discussion is that the federal government had completely shifted away from POGG's national concern doctrine to the criminal law power as its sole constitutional defence for its national assisted reproduction policy. Somewhere between the Royal Commission and the legislative debates, the procedural component of the national jurisdictional frame shifted – a shift that reflected less constitutional certainty over POGG than the Royal Commission had envisioned. This was true for MPs, bureaucrats, and independent witnesses. While law professors Jocelyn Downie and Martha Jackman both briefly cited Parliament's POGG power and its "national concern" doctrine at committee (Canada 2001k, 1605; Canada 2001f, 1110), all other defences of federal jurisdiction invoked the federal authority over criminal law – even when discussing the *AHR Act*'s regulatory framework.

Because the Royal Commission had relied on POGG as its primary constitutional justification for federal regulatory authority, the importance of this shift cannot be understated. The development of the Supreme Court of Canada's federalism doctrine also played an important role, as during the 1990s the Court shied away from POGG to justify federal intervention while the criminal law power became something of a "proxy for national concern" (Baier 2006, 141; see chapter 4). One former civil servant at Health Canada recalled that he did not believe "at the end of the day the Department of Justice was actually persuaded by the argument that it could be done under Peace, Order, and Good Government" (Interview 2011a). Most witnesses and government lawyers were convinced that the criminal law power would act as a suitable "anchor" for federal authority. Crucially, however, the language used to justify the use of the criminal power often reflected the national concern branch of POGG more than targeting criminal law "evils." MPs and government officials cited "federal leadership," "a lack of desire on the part of the provinces," and fears of a "patchwork" – arguments typically used to justify federal intervention in an area of national concern, not the criminal law (Canada 2001a, 1115; Canada 2001f, 1135; Canada 2001p, 23). In terms of how the government framed the legislation, the language of national concern was far more prominent than the elimination of harmful behaviour.

Frame Stability and Critical Junctures

Like the Royal Commission, parliamentarians and government officials adopted both substantive and jurisdictional framing strategies. Substantively, they were ambivalent about the benefits of technologies and activities related to assisted reproduction. The regulatory and licensing functions of Health Canada and AHRC were framed using a "medical-scientific" discourse, as the goal of these agencies would be to facilitate the development of research and permit the creation of new families within certain regulatory boundaries. The criminal prohibitions, by contrast, were routinely justified using the "moral" frame, with frequent reference to avoiding the commodification of human life, the exploitation of women and children, and the commercialization of reproduction. However, there was no such ambivalence to the ever-present jurisdictional frame: to have uniform standards for Canadians across the country. As Minister of Health Allan Rock stated, the goal was to create a "comprehensive pan-Canadian approach that would not follow the patchwork situation that exists in the United States" (Canada 2001a, 115).

What is remarkable when analysing the policymaking process from 1993 to 2004 – from the Royal Commission to the *AHR Act* – is the extent to which the content and the frames remained almost entirely the same. This period was characterized in part by the proliferation of assisted reproduction, as well as advances in research that created Dolly the Sheep, the first animal to be cloned using somatic cell nuclear trans-fer. While there is little public opinion research on Canadian attitudes towards assisted reproduction during this period, there was significant normalization of assisted reproduction in the Western world over this period, including in Canada. Yet the content and the framing strategies were almost entirely identical for the Royal Commission and for the federal government, with the notable exception of Health Canada being given greater regulatory authority. The Royal Commission's recommendations were pervasive throughout the entire legislative period.

For these reasons, the Royal Commission on New Reproductive Technologies constitutes a "critical juncture" in the development of assisted reproduction policy in Canada. Critical junctures are "relatively short periods of time during which there is a substantially heightened probability that agents' choices will affect the outcome of interest"; they are more likely to occur when structural influences on political actors are "significantly relaxed for a relatively short period," resulting in an expanded "range of plausible choices" for which the outcome is "potentially much more momentous" (Capoccia and Kelemen 2007, 348, 343). Such junctures are especially likely to produce "path-dependent" outcomes, whereby "once a country or region has started down a track … entrenchments of certain institutional arrangements obstruct an easy reversal of the initial choice" (Levi 1997, 28).

This almost perfectly describes the creation and subsequent influence of the Royal Commission. The Commission functioned for a "relatively short" time period under "significantly relaxed" structural constraints. The legislative vacuum, the novelty of the technologies, and the wide scope of inquiry gave the Royal Commission the capability to institute "momentous" change. Its effect on the policy outcome was undeniable; its recommendations for prohibitions, a national agency, and regulatory authority all made their way into the legislation, even after four bills, countless consultations with stakeholders, hundreds of witnesses, an all-party legislative report, and eleven years. While the legislative process did not necessary produce full-fledged institutionalization, the dominant frames and recommendations were nevertheless reproduced, with the expectation that the institutions would soon follow. In many ways, the Commission was the "first mover" for assisted reproduction policy in Canada.

This path-dependent period was also likely stabilized by the state of national party politics at the time. From 1993 to 2004, the Liberal Party had a majority of seats in the House of Commons. As a centre-left party

with pro-business leanings, the Liberals did not have a particular policy agenda concerning assisted reproduction; as Éric Montpetit (2004,
79) notes, their own internal documents offered "no indication of preferred policy directions" for assisted reproduction. However, while the
Liberals' "big tent" has included conservative and progressive members with respect to social policies such as abortion and same-sex marriage, its members uniformly support a strong federal government. As
future leader Michael Ignatieff (2005) said to a national convention in
2005, the Liberal Party's "first task as a party is to preserve the national
unity of Canada ... Federal Liberals say yes to strong provinces, but no
to a balkanized Canada ... We stand for one country, not ten." While
it has been accused at times of lacking a coherent ideology, the Liberal
Party has for decades supported national programs and a strong federal government. It is thus no surprise that, in the face of ambivalence
concerning the medical-scientific and moral frames on assisted reproduction, the governing Liberals uniformly adopted the national jurisdictional frame during the legislative process.

Conclusion

During Canada's assisted reproduction policymaking process, both
the Royal Commission and the federal government sought comprehensive legislation to produce two goals: promoting beneficial aspects
of assisted reproduction and prohibiting its more harmful possibilities.
These two goals were reflected in language that, not surprisingly, relied
on two contradictory substantive frames: assisted reproduction as a
medically beneficial way to build families (the medical-scientific frame),
and as a set of harmful technologies that required criminal prohibition
(the moral frame). It is thus helpful to conceive of the *AHR Act* as containing a "division of labour" between regulated activities (justified by
the medical-scientific frame) and prohibited activities (justified by the
moral frame). To tie the two goals together, federal policymakers, start-
ing with the Royal Commission, employed a jurisdictional frame to
square the circle: assisted reproduction was a policy field requiring national rather than provincial attention. While assisted reproduction
policymaking constituted a division of labour, the work required the
same labourer.

This was a constitutionally risky proposition, and one that did not
ultimately produce what policymakers sought. It would be a mistake,
however, to suggest that such decisions were made with bad intentions,

or with complete foresight of what would transpire. As Paul Pierson (2004, 47) notes, when studying the institutional development of public policies, "rather than assuming relative efficiency as an explanation, we have to go back and look." Having looked at the Royal Commission, legislative debates, and committee hearings leading up to the 2004 *AHR Act*, it is clear that the Commission believed that federal control of the entire field of assisted reproduction (with the exception of parentage) was preferable, feasible, and constitutional. The Liberal federal government, itself partial to national initiatives, built on the positive feedback owing to the lack of provincial legislation and endorsed the Commission's centralized preferences. Over the years, the dominant frame justifying a national policy was recreated as the only solution.

That the Royal Commission influenced the *AHR Act* is not a controversial proposition, nor is it controversial to suggest that it was unwise, in retrospect, for the federal government to adopt this centralized model. However, the federal government's framework was not a foregone conclusion. As Pierson (2004, 47) notes, "many alternatives to the outcome in question might have been possible, and a dynamic of positive feedback may have institutionalized a particular option even though it originated by accident." Given jurisdictional uncertainly, the Commission could have opted for a provincial jurisdictional frame – as it did for parentage policy. However, it chose to go forward with a national frame for which there was limited jurisprudential support in 1993 and, although the Commission could not have known this, even less support by the 2000s. This jurisprudence would become manifest as the *AHR Act* quickly made its way into the courts, culminating in the Supreme Court of Canada's 2010 *Reference re Assisted Human Reproduction Act*.

Chapter 4

The *Assisted Human Reproduction Act* Goes to Court

From 1989 to 2004, nearly every stakeholder accepted that Canadian assisted reproduction policy would be created, administered, and monitored by the federal government. Provincial governments and medical organizations were largely left out of policy recommendations. As many federal MPs, civil servants, and witnesses involved during the legislative process made clear, few provinces showed any desire to act.

While most MPs were aware that assisted reproduction touched on health concerns, the inclusion of equivalency agreements in the *AHR Act* were designed explicitly to assuage the concerns of the provinces. Nevertheless, some provincial and federal politicians from Quebec repeatedly claimed that the legislation violated provincial jurisdiction over health care. Bloc Québécois MPs were particularly vocal at committee, and at one point Quebec Minister of Health François Legault (then of the governing Parti Québécois) wrote a letter to the federal Minister of Health that, in the words of Bloc Québécois MP Réal Ménard, asked "that this bill not be passed" because it was incompatible with "a dozen acts" including the Quebec Civil Code (Canada 2003b, 1210). The federal government did not simply hand-wave such threats away, nor did it intentionally intend to call Quebec's bluff. As one former civil servant from Health Canada noted at committee, "We knew all along that there was the potential for jurisdictions, the provinces, to say, this is really our responsibility." But at the end of the day, "whether it was the health and safety or the broader societal implications, we were confident that a very strong case could be made that the federal government's criminal law head of power was relevant in both situations" (Interview 2011a). At committee, government lawyer Glenn Rivard flatly said to Bloc MP Réal Ménard, "There is no incompatibility between

Quebec legislation that touches on these issues and federal legislation" (Canada 2002e, 1010). All but one constitutional expert who testified at committee agreed. The federal government was confident that it had the legislative authority to act, and that if challenged in court, it would win.

In 2006, the government of Quebec – now led by the federalist Liberal Party – launched an official legal challenge by initiating a reference case in the Quebec Court of Appeal. The reference asked the Court of Appeal whether most of the non-criminal components of the *AHR Act* violated provincial jurisdiction over health care. Quebec won the case, first unanimously in the Quebec Court of Appeal and then narrowly on appeal by a 5–4 margin in the Supreme Court of Canada. The result, which rendered most federal regulatory authority contained in the *AHR Act* unconstitutional, surprised the legal community, infuriated stakeholders across the country, and put the onus on the provinces to create much of assisted reproduction policy. This chapter explains how this happened and asks a simple question: Why did a majority of Supreme Court justices strike down legislation when its creators were so confident it would withstand constitutional scrutiny?

There are two main reasons. First, from 1993 to 2004 the Supreme Court of Canada's federalism jurisprudence shifted in such a way that made the Royal Commission's constitutional justifications even more tenuous. Over several cases the Court rejected the "national concern" branch of the Peace, Order, and Good Government (POGG) power under section 91 of the *Constitution Act, 1867*, which had been the Royal Commission's primary constitutional justification for federal action. This meant the federal government ended up relying on one constitutional instrument (the criminal law power) to justify large parts of legislation that had originally been justified through an altogether different instrument (POGG). In the absence of the "national concern" branch of POGG as a constitutional justification, the federal government's legal argument was even more strained than it would have been in 1993.

Second, the framing strategies employed by federal policymakers from the Royal Commission to the *AHR Act* also influenced the way a majority of justices came to understand assisted reproduction. Like the Royal Commission, the federal government adopted ambivalent substantive frames for the legislation: beneficial aspects were framed using the medical-scientific frame, and negative aspects with the moral frame. In the Supreme Court *Reference*, a majority of the Court referred precisely to this linguistic ambivalence, drawing from the Royal Commission's report and the legislative debates to draw a clear distinction between morally harmful (prohibited) practices and medically beneficial activities that would be subject to regulation and licensing. The Supreme Court's growing reluctance to use POGG as a justification for national action meant that, by framing many aspects of the legislation as medical but nevertheless requiring national intervention, the federal government had set itself on a collision course with the provinces in court. In retrospect, the crash looks all too predictable.

Federalism in the Supreme Court, 1993–2004: A Shift in Emphasis

Sections 91 and 92 of the *Constitution Act, 1867* describe the heads of power through which federal and provincial governments may legislate, but these constitutional provisions are described in broad, general terms; as Gerald Baier (2006, 126) notes, the structure of the Canadian Constitution "effectively put the enumerated powers in competition with one another ... with some exceptions, for every federal grant of power, there is a provincial grant that might be characterized in such a way as to justify provincial control over a roughly similar power" (see also Lederman 1976). In Canada, judicial review has become the most definitive mechanism for resolving disputes between governments. The British-administered Judicial Committee of the Privy Council (JCPC) had the final authority to determine such issues for much of Canada's early history, but following the abolition of appeals to the JCPC in 1949, the Supreme Court of Canada became the final stop for judicial review of federalism disputes. Some argue that, in the twenty-first century, the judicial role in adjudicating federalism disputes has diminished due to greater intergovernmental collaboration (Baier 2012). However, there can be little doubt that the courts continue to play a crucial role in resolving disputes between levels of government. The Supreme Court of Canada rendered thirty decisions concerning the division of powers between 2000 and 2010 (Schertzer 2016, 105–6), and it has subsequently ruled on momentous federalism disputes such as Senate reform, the federal gun registry, and appointments to the Supreme Court itself (*Quebec v. Canada* 2015; *Reference re Senate Reform* 2014; *Reference re Supreme Court Act* 2014).

The history of federalism adjudication in Canada is long and complicated; it has been the subject of much debate, analysis, and criticism. While there is considerable dispute about the extent to which decentralization was caused by the JCPC or by other political and sociological factors (see Baier 2006; Cairns 1971; Saywell 2002; Vaughan 2010), there is a consensus that during the JCPC's tenure as court of last resort from 1867 to 1949, provincial authority grew while federal authority diminished. Most early federalism disputes concerned several broadly worded clauses in the *Constitution Act, 1867*: the "Peace, Order, and Good Government" (POGG) clause; Parliament's authority over trade and commerce (section 91.2); provincial authority over property and civil rights (92.13); and matters of a merely local or private nature (92.16). In these disputes, the provinces fared better. As Baier (2006, 56) summarizes, "The JCPC largely interpreted the POGG and trade and commerce clauses narrowly and the civil rights power expansively" and "clearly favoured the provinces in doing so." By several accounts, Canada became one of the most decentralized federations in the world.

Many hoped the federally appointed Supreme Court would reverse the trend by systematically favouring Ottawa, particularly following the appointment of legal scholar (and JCPC critic) Bora Laskin as chief justice in 1973. However, the extent to which the Court has favoured the federal government remains contested. Some argue that the Supreme Court's federalism jurisprudence has been largely "balanced" between the provinces and the federal government (Baier 2006; Hogg 1979; Russell 1985). Others dispute such balance, arguing that the Supreme Court's view of federalism has been centralizing by promoting "efficiency over diversity," and that the JCPC's jurisprudence has been "gradually eroded by a centralizing interpretation of powers" (Brouillet 2011, 602; Leclair 2003). Still others have avoided the centralization/decentralization dichotomy, instead focusing on how Supreme Court jurisprudence has managed conflict over national identity (Gaudreault-DesBiens 1999; Schertzer 2008). In his comprehensive study of the Supreme Court of Canada's federalism decisions (including references) from 1980 to 2010, Robert Schertzer (2016) distinguishes between those decisions in which the Court *imposes* one model of the federation versus those when it *recognizes* the legitimacy of multiple models. For Schertzer, the Court's "imposition" cases are problematic, not least because those cases are far more likely increase federal government power "in important areas and with far-reaching implications" (211–12). However, Schertzer also finds that the Court has been far more likely to "recognize" multiple models since the 1998 *Reference re Secession of Quebec*, and that these recent cases are more likely to "depict the federation in an inclusive manner" (279).

Whether the Supreme Court's jurisprudence has been balanced, centralizing, or inclusive, few would argue that it has systematically favoured the provinces. Yet this did not necessarily give the federal government *carte blanche* to legislate for assisted reproduction. The Royal Commission initially relied on POGG as its primary justification for federal action, which the Commission claimed gave Parliament a "clear basis for seeking national action" due to the "profound importance" of assisted reproduction (Royal Commission on New Reproductive Technologies 1993, 18–19). The Commission's reliance on POGG was already questionable in 1993, as the Supreme Court had generally allowed Parliament to rely on POGG in only two situations: when federal legislation responds to a "national emergency," or when it addresses an area of "national concern." The *AHR Act*, whatever the tone of some of its proponents, was not primarily meant to address a national emergency. However, the Court had in the past allowed "national concern" to justify federal legislation implicating provincial jurisdiction in matters sufficiently "distinct" and limited in scope that the overall federal balance remains undisturbed – for example, the creation of the National Capital Region (*Munro v. National Capital Commission* 1966). Along with distinctiveness, the Supreme Court also endorsed the "provincial inability" test, whereby Parliament can act if the provinces are unable to achieve the same purpose working together (*R. v. Crown Zellerbach* 1988).

However attractive "national concern" may have been to supporters of the *AHR Act*, there was no guarantee that the federal legislation would actually be upheld on that basis. From the *Reference re Anti-Inflation Act* (1976) up to 1993, the Court's "national concern" jurisprudence had been ambiguous and conflicted. The test had been used as often to deny federal jurisdiction as to sustain it, and decisions in either direction typically involved narrow majorities prevailing over substantial dissents. A single, comprehensive, national policy on assisted reproduction was thus constitutionally risky. Nevertheless, the Commission clearly considered the risk worth taking, and it bet heavily on the national concern branch of POGG. The combination of a "medical-scientific" substantive frame for some aspects of assisted reproduction with a "national" jurisdictional frame was constitutionally unstable, at least insofar as it included regulatory authority for the kind of medically beneficial health care that fell within provincial jurisdiction.

What the Commission could not know was that after 1993 the Supreme Court would begin avoiding POGG (including the "national concern" branch) as a potential support for disputed federal legislation. Even when constrained by criteria such as "provincial inability," the national concern test came to be seen as too much of a threat to the

Court's approach to federalism, leading the justices to rely more heavily on other grants of federal power. In particular, the federal criminal law power (91.27) became the Court's favoured alternative to POGG as a justification for federal legislation. Ever since the Court upheld federal employee–government relations legislation on the basis of POGG in *Ontario Hydro v. Ontario* (1993), "when the court has been faced with the opportunity to choose between criminal law and the POGG power, it has increasingly opted for the former" (Baier 2006, 142).

This shift occurred primarily in a string of cases throughout the 1990s – coincidentally, the time during which different iterations of the *AHR Act* were being debated and justified in Parliament. In *RJR-MacDonald Inc. v. Canada* (1995), a majority of justices upheld (on federalism grounds) legislation prohibiting tobacco advertising under the criminal law power and "dispensed with a POGG analysis almost entirely" (Baier 2006, 139). Two years later, in *R v. Hydro-Québec* (1997), a majority of justices opted to justify federal environmental legislation under the criminal law power rather than POGG. When the Court upheld federal gun control legislation for having only "incidental" effects on provincial jurisdiction in *Reference re Firearms Act* (2000), it found it was "unnecessary" to consider whether the legislation could have been upheld using POGG (para. 59). Finally, in *R v. Malmo-Levine* (2003), a case that upheld Parliament's marijuana ban via the criminal law power, a majority of justices again held that it was "unnecessary" to deal with POGG, opting to "leave this question open for another day (para. 72)."[10]

Thus, just as Parliament was debating federal legislation governing assisted reproduction, the Supreme Court was adapting the rules that would permit the government to do so. On its face, this jurisprudence made it unclear whether the federal *AHR Act* would withstand constitutional scrutiny. Although Supreme Court justices had moved from POGG to the criminal law, majorities still upheld federal legislation in each case. Baier himself asserted in 2006 that it was "too early" to determine whether the criminal law power had simply become a "proxy" for the national concern component of POGG (141). Yet Baier (2006, 142) was prescient in predicting that Parliament's winning streak

---

10 In both *RJR-MacDonald* and *Malmo-Levine*, the Court subsequently considered whether the federal legislation, having been declared constitutional on federalism grounds, nevertheless violated the *Canadian Charter of Rights and Freedoms*. The Supreme Court struck down parts of Parliament's legislation in *RJR-Macdonald* as a *Charter* violation, but upheld the marijuana ban from *Charter* scrutiny in *Malmo-Levine*.

could not continue forever, claiming that the criminal law power likely had a "more restricted scope" than POGG's national concern doctrine. In spite of a string of victories at the Supreme Court of Canada, the federal government ought to have noticed – and, as its strategy in court demonstrates, certainly did notice – that it had lost the constitutional instrument most amenable to defence of the *AHR Act*.

Whether because of the Commission's weak constitutional justifications or the shift in Supreme Court jurisprudence, the federal government seemed aware that POGG was no longer the best instrument to justify the *AHR Act*. At committee in Parliament, almost every legal witness, including government lawyers, relied on the criminal law power rather than POGG as the specific constitutional power through which the legislation would be justified. By the time the case was heard by the Quebec Court of Appeal, the federal government did not even bother to invoke POGG, and instead relied entirely on its criminal law power.

The Quebec Court of Appeal Rules

Although there was some uncertainty about the *AHR Act*'s constitutionality throughout the legislative process, most provincial governments did not express any desire to legislate in this field. Quebec was the lone exception: provincial government officials wrote several letters to the federal Minister of Health insisting that the *Act*'s regulatory aspects were unconstitutional, and several federal Bloc Québécois MPs claimed the legislation violated provincial authority. The strongest Bloc voice was Health Committee member Réal Ménard, who said the legislation "clearly interferes in an extremely important area of provincial jurisdiction, that being health" (Canada 2003a, 1350). As it turns out, this was no bluff. On 14 February 2006, the Government of Quebec launched a reference in the Quebec Court of Appeal to clarify the constitutionality of the federal legislation. In 2007, Quebec Health Minister Philippe Couillard tabled Bill 23, *An Act Respecting Clinical and Research Activities Relating to Assisted Procreation*, in the National Assembly. Although this bill played no part in either reference, it was reintroduced and eventually passed as Bill 26 in 2009.[11]

---

11   The legislation contains many provisions similar to the regulatory components of the *AHR Act*, including licensing, reporting, and ministerial authority to create regulations. It also provided for public funding of IVF under provincial health insurance, although that funding was largely eliminated in 2015 (see chapter 6).

While Quebec did not challenge the majority of the criminal prohibitions in the federal scheme, it asserted that virtually every regulatory provision was provincial jurisdiction under sections 92(7), 92(13),
92(16), and 93 of the *Constitution Act, 1867*. The reference question asked
whether sections 8 to 19, 40 to 53, 60, 61, and 68 of the *AHR Act* were
ultra vires (beyond the authority of) Parliament. These sections included

- certain prohibited activities, including the consent to use
  reproductive materials and the use of gametes obtained from
  a minor (sections 8–9);
- all the "controlled" activities, which were only permitted if done in
  accordance with federal regulations and a license. These activities
  included the use of human reproductive material; storage of gametes
  and embryos; the combination of genes from different species;
  and reimbursement of expenditures for gamete donation, surrogacy,
  and the "maintenance or transport" of embryos (sections 10–13);
- privacy and information management provisions (sections 14–19);
- certain administrative matters pertaining to licensing controlled
  activities (sections 40–44) and inspection and enforcement
  (sections 45–53); and
- penal sanctions (offences and punishment) and equivalency agreements to the extent they related to the impugned provisions
  (sections 60–61 and 68).

Most of the *Act*'s outright criminal prohibitions, contained in sections
5–7, were not challenged (*Reference re Assisted Human Reproduction Act*
2010, paras. 141–55; see also Ogbogu 2011, 155–7).

In June 2008, the Quebec Court of Appeal issued its opinion in *Reference
re Assisted Human Reproduction Act* (2008). All three justices unanimously sided with the Government of Quebec, ruling that all the impugned
provisions were unconstitutional. In practice, this would have removed
from Parliament its entire regulatory and licensing power, which is to
say virtually every power that did not relate to an outright criminal
prohibition. It also found unconstitutional the outright prohibitions
concerning consent and using reproductive material from minors.

A few things of note stand out in the Court of Appeal's reference
opinion. First, the federal government justified the legislation entirely
on the basis of its criminal law power, dispensing with POGG entirely.
In doing so, it relied on the "double aspect" doctrine, whereby "both
levels of government may legislate on different aspects of the same

matter, such as health" (*Reference re Assisted Human Reproduction Act* 2008, para. 25). According to the federal government, the impugned provisions – which mostly involved regulatory authority rather than outright prohibitions – were intended to protect vulnerable persons, public morality, and health and safety. Or, as the Court of Appeal summarized, "unsafe or ethically reprehensible access to assisted reproduction constitutes an 'evil' that requires the legislative intervention of Parliament" (para. 38). This was the moral frame par excellence; without the ability to use POGG's "national concern" doctrine, the federal government had to downplay the extent to which its legislation had relied on the medical-scientific frame at all.

Second, although the federal government did not justify the legislation on the basis of Parliament's ability to legislate for matters of "national concern" under POGG, the Quebec Court of Appeal rejected the argument anyway. The Court denied that the growth of assisted reproduction constituted a "national emergency," stating that "if there was [an emergency] at the time of the Royal Commission, it is no longer present, since fifteen years have passed between the first intervention at the House of Commons on medically assisted reproduction and the enactment of the Act" (para. 79). Likewise, it claimed that the national concern doctrine could not apply, as the *AHR Act* sought to protect only individual users of and children born through assisted reproduction, not the "national interest." The justices warned that courts must resist "the temptation to legitimize the Act out of a desire for uniformity across the country" (para. 80). By rejecting POGG, the Court of Appeal rejected the normative component of the federal government's jurisdictional frame entirely.

With the federal government omitting its POGG argument and the Court of Appeal rejecting it anyhow, the case focused on whether the impugned provisions were in "pith and substance" health care (provincial) or criminal law (federal). The justices relied on a close reading of the legislative history of the legislation to inform their opinion, including lengthy excerpts from the Royal Commission and ministers of health (paras. 3–17, 115–39). Drawing from this evidence, the justices were convinced that the *AHR Act* contained "two main parts," which were, on the one hand, "a formal and complete prohibition of certain practices" and, on the other, support for "desirable" practices that "promote fertility and, consequently, the creation of new families" (paras. 118–19). For the justices, the *AHR Act* envisioned a division of labour, whereby the prohibited and non-prohibited activities were designed to address qualitatively different issues, and would be addressed by different institutions.

The Court of Appeal allowed that Parliament could criminally prohibit the "evils" associated with assisted reproduction. It accepted that certain components of the legislation – namely, the unchallenged federal prohibitions in sections 5–7, which covered aspects such as paid surrogacy, human cloning, non-medical sex selection, and germ-line engineering – were designed to do precisely that. However, the impugned provisions themselves (controlled activities and the licensing, inspection, and enforcement related to those activities) were designed "not to prohibit wrongful acts but to ensure that ... desired and encouraged activity is carried out properly" (para. 128). For the Court of Appeal, the criminal law was not the proper instrument for adopting national standards for beneficial practices: "The appropriateness of a single piece of legislation applying to Canada as a whole and regulating a permitted and recognized activity is not a purpose that confers criminal law jurisdiction." For the purposes of constitutional analysis, it did not matter "whether the Act is good or bad, or whether it achieves its objectives or not"; all that mattered was "whether its purpose is criminal in nature," which it decidedly was not (para. 137). According to the Court of Appeal, the criminal law could not act as a proxy for POGG's national concern doctrine.

A Divided Supreme Court Rules

While the Quebec Court of Appeal's reference opinion was a blow to the federal government, most knew the case would go to the Supreme Court of Canada, which soon granted leave to appeal. The governments of Alberta, Saskatchewan, and New Brunswick intervened on behalf of the government of Quebec. Although these provinces did not have any forthcoming legislation tabled, their intervention against the *AHR Act* demonstrates that provinces do not need to legislate in order to forcefully defend their provincial autonomy in a policy field.[12] The

---

12 Dr Michael Awad, a Red Deer physician trained in assisted reproduction and licensed to practise with the College of Physicians and Surgeons of Alberta, intervened on behalf of Quebec. Dr Awad claimed that he could not practise in his field, because the *AHR Act* required that he obtain a license, but the federal government had not made the proper regulations for licensure (Mitchell 2011, 646, 650). The Canadian Conference of Catholic Bishops and the Evangelical Fellowship of Canada, two conservative religious organizations, intervened on behalf of the federal government.

questions were the same as those posed at the Quebec Court of Appeal; Quebec claimed that the impugned provisions were of pith and substance related to health care under sections 92(7), 92(13), 92(16), and 93[13] of the *Constitution Act, 1867*; the federal government countered that these provisions were necessary to proper functioning of the criminal prohibitions, and thus a valid use of Parliament's criminal law power (91(27)). Once again, the federal government did not attempt to justify the legislation under the Peace, Order, and Good Government (POGG) power, which had been the Royal Commission's main constitutional plank.

There were early indications that the case was especially difficult for the court. As with everything pertaining to assisted reproduction policy in Canada, proceedings developed slowly; the Court originally heard the case in April 2009 and did not rule for twenty months.[14] In December 2010, a divided (4–1–4) Supreme Court of Canada finally issued its opinion in *Reference re Assisted Human Reproduction Act* (2010). In a rare federalism case divided by a single vote, the Court's majority largely accepted Quebec's argument, and found most of the *AHR Act*'s controlled activities and regulatory authority to be *ultra vires* the Parliament of Canada. While the reference contained many legal and doctrinal disagreements, the fundamental debate among the justices concerned the overall purpose, or "pith and substance," of the legislation. Here, substantive framing strategies throughout the legislative process were crucial to the justices' legal reasoning. The Court was primarily divided over whether the controlled activities and regulatory authority were designed to provide a "good" or to limit an "evil"; whether, in effect, Parliament's legislative authority stemmed from the medical-scientific or the moral frame of assisted reproduction.

Chief Justice McLachlin (writing for herself and Justices Binnie, Fish, and Charron) agreed with the federal government's submission, and held that the legislation was primarily designed to create a number of prohibitions supported by the authority to create a few ancillary regulations. Interestingly, and unlike the other five justices, she examined the impugned provisions in the context of the legislation as a whole. For

---

13   All nine justices rejected Quebec's assertion that the *AHR Act* violated section 93 (education) with respect to health professionals (para. 261).

14   In 2010 the average time between hearing and judgment was 7.7 months; between 2005 and 2015, the Court averaged 6.0 months (Supreme Court of Canada 2015).

the Chief Justice, the *AHR Act* was primarily designed to "prohibit practices that would undercut moral values, produce public health evils, and threaten the security of donors, donees, and persons conceived by assisted reproduction" (*Reference re Assisted Human Reproduction Act* 2010, para. 255). The "dominant thrust" of the legislation was prohibitory, as it was "essentially a series of prohibitions, followed by a set of subsidiary provisions for their administration" (paras. 24–5). Chief Justice McLachlin effectively adopted the moral frame to describe the entire legislation.

Chief Justice McLachlin's method – reading the legislation as a whole, then subsequently determining the constitutionality of individual provisions – led her to accept that the *AHR Act* "incidentally permits beneficial practices through regulations"; however, this incidental permission did not render the legislation unconstitutional (para. 30). She went through the impugned provisions individually, and found that they were all tied to the overall scheme of prohibiting an "evil": privacy and information management provisions were "closely tied" to valid criminal prohibitions; licensing was "directly related … to prohibiting harmful and immoral conduct, while excepting beneficial activity"; inspection and enforcement provisions were "part and parcel" of the overall prohibitory scheme; and the offences and rules for punishment "simply provide the penal sanctions that are necessary for criminal law provisions" (paras. 146, 149, 150, 155). Chief Justice McLachlin also held that the equivalency agreements were indicative of a "flexible approach to federal-provincial cooperation, which is appropriate to modern federalism" (para. 1152). The group of four justices led by the Chief Justice would have upheld the *AHR Act* in its entirety as a valid exercise of the criminal law power.

Justices LeBel and Deschamps (writing for themselves and Justices Abella and Rothstein), by contrast, supported the medical-scientific frame as a rationale for the controlled activities, information gathering, and federal licensing authority. Unlike Chief Justice McLachlin, they examined the impugned provisions individually, rather than as part of the *AHR Act* as a whole. They found that the fundamental purpose of these impugned provisions was to set national standards for "a specific type of health services provided in health-care institutions by health-care professionals" (para. 227). Just like the Court of Appeal, Justices LeBel and Deschamps frequently referenced the Royal Commission on New Reproductive Technologies. In doing so, they found the *Act*'s non-criminal components did not concern "an evil needing to be suppressed," but instead "a burgeoning field of medical practices and research that … brings benefits to many Canadians" (para. 251).

Also like the Court of Appeal, LeBel and Deschamps effectively saw a division of labour between prohibited (harmful) and non-prohibited (medically beneficial) components of the legislation. The criminal prohibitions did "not depend on the existence of the regulatory scheme" but were able to "stand alone … regardless of whether a scheme regulating other activities existed," just as "the regulation of activities associated with assisted human reproduction [does] not depend on other activities being prohibited completely" (paras. 276–7). Moreover, Justices LeBel and Deschamps claimed that the provision for equivalency agreements did not remedy the legislation's "constitutional defects," insofar as provincial policymaking would be "tolerated only if the provinces in question adhere to the federal scheme" (para. 272). While the unchallenged criminal prohibitions were certainly a valid exercise of the federal criminal law power, this second group of four justices would have upheld the Quebec Court of Appeal reference in its entirety by rendering *ultra vires* the prohibitions contained in sections 8–9, all the controlled activities, and the licensing, inspection, and enforcement pertaining to those activities. They would have left intact only sections 60 and 61, insofar as those punitive measures applied to unchallenged criminal prohibitions in sections 5–7 (para. 281).

Justice Cromwell, at that time the most junior justice on the Court, cast the decisive vote in a brief thirteen-paragraph set of reasons. He stated that the purpose of the legislation was the "regulation of virtually every aspect of research and clinical practice in relation to assisted human reproduction" (para. 285). He generally agreed with Justices LeBel and Deschamps that most of the impugned provisions fell under provincial jurisdiction over health, as these provisions "permit[ted] minute regulation of every aspect of research and clinical practice" and were not created to "simply prohibit 'negative practices'" (para. 286). However, he found that three impugned provisions – concerning donor consent, age of consent, and reimbursement for donor- and surrogacy-related expenditures – were sufficiently criminal in nature to qualify as criminal law (para. 289). Thus, he upheld sections 8, 9, 12, 19, and 60, as well as several other provisions only insofar as they related to the constitutionally valid provisions.[15]

---

15 These included sections 40(1), (6) and (7), 41 to 43, 44(1) and (4), 45 to 53, 61, and 68 (para. 294).

Some commentators criticized Cromwell for his "sparse reasons," the brevity of which arguably came across as "Delphic" (von Tigerstrom 2011, 43; Mitchell 2011, 654). However, Justice Cromwell was clear that on the subject matter of the impugned provisions, he agreed "substantially" with "the reasons given by Justices LeBel and Deschamps at paras. 259–66" (*Reference re Assisted Human Reproduction Act* 2010, para. 287). Thus, although Justice Cromwell sided with aspects of both groups of justices, his opinion generally adopted Justices LeBel and Deschamps's analysis. As a result, Justices LeBel and Deschamps's opinion "represents the majority view on matters of doctrine," while Cromwell's opinion "is dispositive and governs the result" (Mitchell 2011, 640). Justice Cromwell's vote effectively found most of the *AHR Act*'s controlled activities and regulatory provisions to be unconstitutional, leaving a void yet to be filled by most provinces concerning many facets of assisted reproduction policy.

Policy Framing, Legislative History, and the Division of Labour

The most fundamental disagreement between the two sets of justices, which coloured all other analysis, concerned the pith and substance of the impugned provisions – effectively, which substantive frame they accepted. Chief Justice McLachlin agreed with the federal government that the purpose and effect of the legislation was to ban certain practices associated with assisted reproduction that constituted a public health "evil," and that any beneficial activities were incidental to those prohibitions. Justices LeBel and Deschamps, by contrast, read the impugned provisions individually, and found that they were primarily designed to set national standards for health care in order to promote fertility and help build families. In effect, Chief Justice McLachlin thought the legislation *as a whole* was designed to eliminate evils, while Justices LeBel and Deschamps recognized that the legislation had two different goals: eliminating harmful practices through prohibitions, and promoting beneficial health outcomes through regulation, data gathering, and licensure. Justice Cromwell's vote largely concurred with the LeBel and Deschamps opinion, although it moved a few activities from the "beneficial" to the "harmful" category.

There are several reasons why the Justices LeBel and Deschamps/ Cromwell combination produced the proper legal outcome. The first has to do with constitutional doctrine. The primary doctrine over which the justices disagreed was the "ancillary powers" doctrine which, first articulated by Chief Justice Dickson in *General Motors of Canada Ltd. v. City National Leasing* (1989), prescribes that impugned provisions must be read *by themselves*, rather than as part of the overall scheme: "The issue is not whether the Act as a whole is rendered *ultra vires* because it reaches too far, but whether a particular provision is sufficiently integrated into the Act to sustain its constitutionality" (*General Motors* 1989). This logic produces a three-part test: first, whether the impugned provisions "intrude" on provincial powers; second, whether the Act as a whole is valid; and third, if the answer to the first two questions is yes, "whether the impugned provision is sufficiently integrated" with the overall legislative scheme (ibid.). According to this doctrine, impugned provisions should be analysed first, the legislative scheme second. However, as Ubaka Ogbogu (2011) notes, by "assessing whether the entire statutory scheme [was] … a valid exercise of federal power and not whether the impugned provisions intrude on provincial legislative powers," Chief Justice McLachlin's analysis reversed this order, departing from the ancillary powers doctrine (169–70, 173).

Second, Chief Justice McLachlin's decision to lump all of the legislation into having one purpose, beyond its lack of basis in legislative history, lacks clarity. As Ogbogu (2011) notes, Chief Justice McLachlin's statement that Quebec was challenging the "bulk" of the *AHR Act* is what led her to reverse the order of analysis for the ancillary doctrine. However, she provides no guidance as to "what constitutes the 'bulk' of a statute"; indeed, Quebec challenged fewer than half of the *AHR Act*'s provisions and left the vast majority of the criminal prohibitions unchallenged (172). Further, Ian B. Lee (2012, 480) observes that it is not "immediately obvious that the licensed sphere will be much smaller than the prohibited sphere, or that the obligations of licensees are not substantial." One might add that if the criminal prohibitions constitute the "dominant thrust" of the legislation, as the Chief Justice found, then an opinion that leaves most of those prohibitions intact would not affect the bulk of the legislation.

Third, there must be limits to the extent to which the criminal law can simply be used as a "proxy" for national concern. In the words of John D. Whyte (2011, 52), it is problematic when the criminalization of activities "takes the form of regulating through a public agency and adopts the regulatory instruments of investigation, standard setting through regulations, granting licences and administrative approvals."

Criminal law, as an instrument, usually includes an absolute prohibition. However, if criminal conduct can only be determined "after an administrative determination," it is not at all clear that this activity falls within the criminal law power, even if such regulation could be construed as an area of national concern. This is especially true with respect to the licensing requirements contained in the *AHR Act*, which clearly intrude on medical licensing, an area of provincial jurisdiction. As Lee (2012, 492) writes, it is one thing to declare an aspect of assisted reproduction to be a criminal offence; it is another "to assume control over all assisted reproduction activities by requiring them to be carried out under a federal licence."

Constitutional doctrine aside, the Chief Justice's analysis also failed to give proper weight to the legislative history of the *Act*, particularly in her portrayal of the Royal Commission's influence. Chief Justice McLachlin gave the Commission minimal weight, dismissing its proceedings as mere "policy analysis" that did little to inform the efforts behind the *AHR Act*: "The fact that the Royal Commission may have referred to positive aspects of assisted reproduction technology ... does not establish that these benefits were the focus of Parliament's efforts" (*Reference re Assisted Human Reproduction Act* 2010, para. 29). In principle, this could be true. However, as chapter 3 demonstrates, the Royal Commission was central to every stage of legislative development. Chief Justice McLachlin and her colleagues did not need to undertake a detailed qualitative survey to determine the extent to which the Royal Commission influenced the legislation; even a cursory analysis shows that Parliament produced legislation that was remarkably similar to the Commission's recommendations, and referenced the Commission at every single stage of legislative development. Commissioners including Suzanne Scorsone (Canada 2001k, 1540–1600) and Patricia Baird (Canada 2001d, 1145–1230) appeared as witnesses before committee to laud the legislation, and one opposition MP even referred to the legislation as a "child of the Royal Commission" (Canada 2002a, 1030). Justices LeBel and Deschamps correctly criticized Chief Justice McLachlin's account for containing "no factual basis whatsoever" (para. 177).

Even discounting the Royal Commission's influence, government statements demonstrate that the goal of the legislation was not simply to eliminate evil practices – after all, the influential 2001 Brown Committee report on draft legislation was called *Building Families*. Contrary to what its lawyers argued in court, the federal government showed ambivalence between the medical-scientific and moral frames throughout the process. In addition to criminalizing certain harmful behaviours, the goal of the legislation was to implement national standards in the area of assisted reproduction, even when those standards intruded on provincial jurisdiction over health. A desire to establish national standards given provincial inaction may be a laudable goal, but in the words of Justices LeBel and Deschamps, "neither a desire for uniformity nor the very novelty of a medical technology can serve as the basis for an exercise of the federal criminal law power" (2010, para. 255). In other words, when governments justify legislation, the procedural component of the jurisdictional frame – not the normative component – must align with the substantive frame.

While the LeBel/Deschamps opinion gives a more precise reading of the legislative history of the Royal Commission, Justice Cromwell's slight alteration is also more in keeping with the content of the legislation. Although Justice Cromwell has been criticized for not adequately articulating his reasoning in his brief opinion (Mitchell 2011, 654–6), his decision to uphold the outright prohibitions in sections 8 and 9 (the use of reproductive material without donor consent and the use of reproductive material from a minor) was correct, as those prohibitions clearly contained penal sanctions directed towards a public purpose. Moreover, the provision in section 12 of the *AHR Act* that enabled Health Canada to create regulations permitting reimbursement of expenditures, which Cromwell also upheld, is directly connected to the prohibition on payment contained in section 6; as government lawyer Glenn Rivard noted during parliamentary hearings, this provision is consistent with the intent of the criminal prohibition, the objective of which was "to prevent any financial gain" from being a surrogate (Canada 2004a).

From a doctrinal and legislative-historical perspective, a bare majority of the Court seems to have got the case just about right. Indeed, the legal commentary on the case has been largely positive about the majority opinion (Mitchell 2011; Ogbogu 2011; Posyniak 2011; Whyte 2011), although a few commentators have quibbled with certain details (Carter 2011, 8; Hogg 2012; Lee 2012, 472; von Tigerstrom 2011, 37, 43). However, when it comes to commentary about the implications of the reference – about how assisted reproduction policymaking must now occur – the immediate reaction from outside the legal academy has been almost uniformly negative.

Fallout from the *Reference*: Federal Policy Diminished, but Not Extinguished

The *Reference re Assisted Human Reproduction Act* was clearly consequential. Rarely has the Supreme Court declared unconstitutional so much of a piece of legislation so comprehensive or so long in the making. In practical terms, a majority of justices held that the provinces have sole authority to regulate non-criminal research combining human and non-human material, the transfer and storage of human reproductive material, the oversight and licensing of fertility clinics, and the creation and maintenance of patient databases. AHRC was gutted, with virtually all of its regulatory functions rendered unconstitutional; having "lost much of its *raison d'être*" (Baylis and Downie 2013a, 197), it was wound down in 2012 and subsumed into the broader Health Canada structure. Over twenty years after the Royal Commission began its work on creating a national framework, the Supreme Court had, in the eyes of many, set much of assisted reproduction policy in Canada back to square one and, in the eyes of some, even left Canada in a worse situation than it was in 1989 (see Baylis 2011).

When the reference was released, academics, health law experts, and media commentators quickly condemned it, with one newspaper claiming that Canada's attempts to regulate the fertility industry had "collapsed in ruins" (*Victoria Times-Colonist* 2011). There was a concern, articulated by law professor Vanessa Gruben, that provinces would be unable to protect women and children. Patricia Baird, the chair of the 1993 Royal Commission, said that the reference would "lead to a patchwork of clinical standards." Others feared the outbreak of "fertility tourism," with an op-ed in the *Canadian Medical Association Journal* concerned that women "may opt to travel to a province that permits multiple implantations" for IVF (all quoted in Eggertson 2011). Some feared that, apart from Parliament's criminal prohibitions, assisted reproduction policy was now largely unregulated. Other than legislation pertaining to surrogacy and parentage transfer, Quebec was the only province with legislation governing clinical intervention at the time.[16]

---

16 Quebec has several Civil Code provisions (articles 11–25 and 541) and other pieces of legislation that concern assisted reproduction, including *An Act Respecting Clinical and Research Activities Relating to Assisted Procreation and Regulation Respecting Clinical Activities Related to Assisted Procreation*. See chapters 5 and 6.

By 2012, the other nine Canadian provinces had yet to produce a legislative response, and as a result many scholars were concerned that "in some provinces there will be no legislation, and therefore no regulatory oversight of practices that may be unsafe for the mother or the eventual offspring" (Hogg 2012, sections 18–34). In short, many feared a return to the "Wild West culture of the past" that characterized the early days of assisted reproduction (Baylis 2011, 319; see also Kirkey and Tibbetts 2010; *Toronto Star* 2010).

These responses to the Supreme Court reference share three assumptions: first, provinces are unable and/or unwilling, individually or collectively, to effectively regulate assisted reproduction; second, provincial variation in assisted reproduction policy is suboptimal; and finally, outside of Quebec, the non-prohibited aspects of assisted reproduction policy were effectively unregulated. The first two are normative assumptions that can be traced back to the Royal Commission, while the third is an empirical claim. Subsequent chapters will explore the first two assumptions, and demonstrate that they require some adjustment in light of existing provincial and medical policymaking. However, it is important to clarify the extent to which the third assumption – that assisted reproduction is unregulated – downplays existing federal policy. The *AHR Act* still contains prohibitions that cover five assisted reproduction subfields: clinical intervention (payment for gametes); surrogacy (payment); reproductive human cloning (a total ban); screening/enhancement (germ-line manipulation, ectogenesis, and non-medical sex selection); and embryonic research (the creation of embryos for non-research purposes as well as certain types of embryonic research). Parliament has also retained important regulatory authority pertaining to certain sections of the *AHR Act*, which it exercised when creating the section 8 consent regulations in 2007 (*Assisted Human Reproduction (Section 8 Consent) Regulations*, SOR/2007–137). While some commentators (Downie and Baylis 2013) have criticized the federal government for not properly enforcing the prohibitions in the face of blatant violations, and even I have criticized the federal government for delaying regulations (Snow, Baylis, and Downie 2015), it has certainly retained some of its legal authority.

Additional federal policies, outside of the *AHR Act*, also exist. Health Canada inspects fertility clinics every three years; there is a federal directive to process and distribute semen for assisted conception, created in 1996 and updated in 2006 (*Processing and Distribution of Semen for*

Assisted Conception Regulations ["Semen Regulations"]);[17] and a federal *Tri-Council Policy Statement on Ethical Conduct for Research Involving Humans*, created in 1998 and updated in 2014. The latter governs federal funding for research involving humans and embryos, including embryonic stem cell research. Together, these federal guidelines and prohibitions set additional rules beyond the *AHR Act* for ethical acceptability concerning several practices in the subfields of clinical intervention, reproductive human cloning, screening/enhancement, and embryonic research.

To understand how and why policy has developed in the years since the Supreme Court reference, it is necessary to recognize that the federal government still does retain an important role. Indeed, two responses from the federal government detail the extent to which the Supreme Court reference leaves room for federal policymaking. In 2012, as part of its 425-page omnibus budget implementation bill, Parliament (then under a Conservative majority government led by Prime Minister Stephen Harper) amended the *AHR Act* to comply with the Supreme Court ruling. The amendments repealed the provisions the Court had found *ultra vires*, closed down AHRC, removed the distinction between "controlled" and prohibited activities, and eliminated all licensing requirements. The amendment also replaced section 10 of the *AHR Act* – which had made using, altering, and manipulating human reproductive material a "controlled activity" – with a new qualified prohibition. The amendments will not come into force until regulations pursuant to those sections are created by Health Canada. Once in force, the new section 10 will prohibit the distribution, use, and importation of human gametes, unless quality assurance and tests have been conducted in accordance with regulations (Downie and Baylis 2013, 228–9).

The most interesting aspect of the amendment is the wording in section 10(1), which states: "The purpose of this section is to reduce the risks to human health and safety arising from the use of sperm or ova for the purpose of assisted human reproduction, including the risk of the transmission of disease" (Bill C-38). While legislative purposes are frequently articulated at the beginning of a law through a statement of principles or a statutory declaration, it is unusual for a particular

---

17 In its 2017 policy proposals for regulations pursuant to the *AHR Act*, Health Canada noted that the *Semen Regulations* would "be repealed once section 10 of the AHR Act is brought into force" (6).

subsection to include such an interpretive statement. After the *Reference re Assisted Human Reproduction Act*, Parliament clearly recognized that its framing strategy needed to change. While Parliament could not go back in time and infuse the language used to justify regulatory authority with the moral frame, it could amend the legislation in such a way that made the moral frame as clear as possible. The new subsection explicitly identifies a criminal law purpose – reducing risks to health and safety including disease transmission – that is directly connected to the new prohibition. It is, as a result, far more likely to withstand judicial scrutiny. It is also a recognition on Parliament's part that the connection between substantive and jurisdictional frames is important in federalism disputes, particularly when the Supreme Court looks closely at legislative history. If courts are digging deeper into government justifications, then the way those justifications are framed will matter more. The government seems to have recognized that the Court has created a greater incentive to explicitly emphasize the public health "evil" it is trying to eliminate.

Apart from this amendment, however, the Harper government was slow to respond to the assisted reproduction file. In 2009, it ignored a legislative requirement to review the *AHR Act*, and simply removed that requirement in its 2012 amendment. By the time the Conservatives lost the 2015 federal election, Health Canada had yet to create the regulations to give the 2012 amendments legal force (Snow, Baylis, and Downie 2015). In October 2016, the *Toronto Star* reported that the Canadian Standards Association subcommittee on assisted reproduction had, at the request of Health Canada, drafted rules that would require sperm and egg banks to conduct additional genetic testing and review donors' medical records (Boyle 2016). Also in October 2016, Justin Trudeau's Liberal government announced that Health Canada planned to "proceed with bringing into force sections 10, 12 and 45 to 58 of the *Assisted Human Reproduction Act* (AHRA) and to draft supporting regulations, as required." The announcement added that there was a "clear need to update regulations" due to "scientific and technological advances" and because "the attitudes of Canadians towards assisted human reproduction may have shifted" (Canada 2016). In July 2017, Health Canada released its policy proposals for regulations to the public. Proposals included processing and record-keeping requirements for human reproductive material (section 10); a list of permitted expenditures for reimbursement for sperm, eggs, and surrogacy (section 12); and administration and enforcement (sections 45–58). This set of proposals suggests that the Liberal government is more likely than its predecessor to use federal authority to give force to assisted reproduction policy for the first time since 2007.

Conclusion

After fifteen years of hand-wringing in the Royal Commission on New Reproduction Technologies and in Parliament, federal policymakers could have been forgiven for thinking their hard work was done with the passage of the 2004 *Assisted Human Reproduction Act*. However, the tragedy that became Canada's assisted reproduction policy had one final act. Quebec quickly challenged the legislation for violating provincial authority over health, and in 2010 a majority of the Supreme Court justices agreed with Quebec's claim. Most non-criminal aspects of the legislation were declared unconstitutional, Assisted Human Reproduction Canada closed up shop, and analysts lamented that Canadian assisted reproduction policy had returned to "the Wild West."

By the standards of the Royal Commission and the Liberal government that passed the *AHR Act*, this was clearly a policy failure. To be sure, the Royal Commission did not deliberately introduce a constitutionally unstable framework, nor did subsequent federal actors simply ignore the legal advice they received. The commissioners and their staff acted in good faith, making policy recommendations that they felt best suited the rapidly emerging field of assisted reproduction in Canada. Yet, especially at the early stage of policy development, policy frames and policy choices can lead to unintended consequences. As Paul Pierson (2004, 15) notes, "Even where actors may be greatly concerned about the future in their efforts to design institutions, they operate in settings of great complexity and high uncertainty. As a consequence, they will often make mistakes." With hindsight, the Royal Commission made a mistake. Its decision to frame certain aspects of assisted reproduction as a medical issue requiring national policy led it down a risky road, and its own constitutional analysis severely overstated Parliament's authority to regulate in this area.

Yet this was not a foregone conclusion, particularly given the Supreme Court's closely divided reference, The Supreme Court's developing jurisprudence in the 1990s and early 2000s – precisely the time during which the *AHR Act* was being created – was also a factor. Throughout this period, the Supreme Court moved away from accepting the "national concern" test derived from the federal authority to make legislation for the

"Peace, Order, and Good Government" (POGG) of Canada, and increasingly relied on the more limited criminal law power instead. By the time of the Commission, "national concern" had faded into the background of constitutional jurisprudence; nevertheless, the federal government accepted and implemented the Commission's advice. This is yet another example of a public policy producing unintended consequences because "the factors that gave it an original advantage have long since passed away" (Pierson 2004, 47). The constitutional advantage of a centralized framework was always a tricky proposition, and changing jurisprudence further contributed to the Supreme Court reference.

In the context of this changing jurisprudence, the most important factor explaining the outcome is the federal framing strategy, which loomed large throughout proceedings at both the Quebec Court of Appeal and the Supreme Court of Canada. From the Royal Commission to the *AHR Act*, federal policymakers had articulated the need for national legislation by relying on an ambivalent framing strategy that included two contradictory substantive frames: the medical-scientific frame, by which the legislation sought to promote beneficial activities; and the moral frame, by which the legislation sought to eliminate harmful behaviour by preventing commodification, exploitation, and threats to human dignity. They were wedded together under a "national" jurisdictional frame, which contained a normative component (that the federal government was the policy actor best suited to address these dual goals) and a procedural component (that it had the constitutional authority to do so under POGG's "national concern" doctrine and the criminal law power). As the Supreme Court's jurisprudence changed from 1993 to 2004, the procedural component was whittled down to the criminal law power, but the normative component remained the same.

These framing strategies reappeared in the courts, which were primarily concerned with determining the main purposes of the non-criminal aspects of the *AHR Act*. In both the Quebec Court of Appeal and the Supreme Court of Canada, a majority of justices relied on legislative history and held that, consistent with the federal government's ambivalent substantive framing, the legislation had a dual purpose – to prohibit harmful practices and promote beneficial ones – and that the impugned provisions dealt solely with the latter. The federal government tried in vain to defend the *AHR Act* as legislation entirely designed to eliminate harmful practices; Chief Justice McLachlin and three other justices accepted this argument largely by downplaying the importance of legislative history. But a majority of Supreme Court justices rejected this moral framing, holding that the impugned provisions were created with the intention of promoting research and building families, pointing to the government's medical-scientific framing throughout the 2000s. These justices held that the federal government's procedural component of its jurisdictional frame, the criminal law power, was not sufficient. The majority opinion effectively found that the dual purposes of the *AHR Act* mandated a division of labour by provincial legislatures and the federal Parliament, whereby Parliament would be solely responsible for policing harmful practices associated with assisted reproduction, and the provinces would be responsible for promoting the benefits.

However, the Supreme Court reference is not the end of Canada's assisted reproduction policy story. While many have lamented that Canadian assisted reproduction policy now constitutes the "Wild West" – an odd claim given the continued existence of criminal prohibitions – this view understates the role played by provincial governments, medical associations, and even courts. It is therefore necessary to move beyond the federal government, exploring what action other policymakers have taken with respect to assisted reproduction policy before and after the Supreme Court ruled.

Chapter 5

Surrogacy and Parentage Policy in the Provinces

Since the Supreme Court's 2010 *Reference re Assisted Human Reproduction Act*, many have characterized Canadian assisted reproduction policy as unregulated. Assisted Human Reproduction Canada has closed down; as of January 2018, Health Canada has yet to create new regulations in its absence, and enforcement of criminal prohibitions has been nearly non-existent. While some federal authority over assisted reproduction remains, there exists no comprehensive national policy of the sort the Royal Commission and Parliament intended. It is thus important to examine which provinces have created assisted reproduction policy, both before and after the Supreme Court reference. In particular, by reforming their family law frameworks in response to the growth of surrogacy and gamete donation, provinces have made significant changes to parentage policy to address new ways of building families.

In three subfields of assisted reproduction – human cloning, screening/enhancement, and embryonic research – there is effectively no provincial legislation, largely because Parliament has introduced a number of absolute bans in the *Assisted Human Reproduction Act* (*AHR Act*). The *AHR Act* also contains an absolute prohibition on *reproductive human cloning*, and it prohibits transplanting a human clone into a human being. With respect to *screening/enhancement*, the *AHR Act* bans germ-line engineering, non-medical sex selection, ectogenesis, and using human reproductive material in a non-human life form to create chimeras or hybrids. Finally, with respect to *embryonic research*, the *AHR Act* prohibits the creation of animal-human chimeras or hybrids, the creation of an embryo from part of another embryo or fetus, non-reproductive or "therapeutic" human cloning, and the creation of embryos solely for research. The federal *Assisted Human Reproduction (Section 8 Consent)*

Regulations, passed in 2007, add further specificity to these prohibitions. With the federal government largely covering these three subfields, it is not surprising that provinces have yet to act. While there is not an absolute ban on all aspects of screening/enhancement or embryonic research (as there is with reproductive human cloning), the breadth of the federal bans makes it unlikely that provinces would seek to regulate the small areas, such as preimplantation diagnosis, for which the *AHR Act* leaves room.

By contrast, provincial authority over health care and family law does permit the provinces a wide range of legislative and regulatory capability concerning other subfields of assisted reproduction. Consider the example of a child conceived via donor gametes in a fertility clinic, gestated by a surrogate, and transferred to the custody of the intended parent(s). First, many matters surrounding conception itself – the origin of donor gametes, the number of embryos that can be legally transferred into the surrogate, the rules regarding licensing of fertility clinics, the number of times a man can donate sperm, the age at which a woman can legally receive IVF, and the extent to which the costs of fertility treatment are covered by the government – all fall within the subfield of clinical intervention. Next, the extent to which the surrogate can be paid, the legal distinction between traditional and gestational surrogacy, and the legality of surrogacy itself fall within surrogacy policy. Finally, before and after birth, both the rules for who can become a parent and the processes used to add or transfer parentage, even in the context of a surrogacy arrangement, depend on parentage policy.

After the Supreme Court reference, certain aspects of surrogacy, and nearly all of clinical intervention and parentage policy, are in the hands of the provinces. Some of this authority was recognized well before the reference. While the Royal Commission's recommendations were dominated by its national jurisdictional frame, it did call for "family law reform to clarify and standardize in all provinces the parentage of children born as a result of donor insemination," including provisions that egg and sperm donors be denied parental rights. It also recommended that provinces and territories amend family laws to make surrogacy arrangements "unenforceable against the gestational woman" regardless of whether payment occurred (Royal Commission on New Reproductive Technologies 1993, 489, 595, 600). The Commission argued (ultimately unsuccessfully) that clinical intervention should be regulated by the federal government, but accepted that provinces had primary jurisdiction over parentage, including parentage in the case of surrogacy. While the pace of change has often been slower than many activists would like, over the past twenty years parentage has seen the most active policymaking of any subfield from provincial governments and, at times, provincial courts. Whether those rules were created by legislation or through judicial decisions, every province has rules for parentage – most of which also address the acceptability of surrogacy arrangements. The combination of jurisdictional certainty, successful litigation, and policy diffusion across some provinces has contributed to far more provincial policymaking in parentage than any other subfield.

This chapter begins by defining surrogacy and parentage policy; after a brief description of the different components of surrogacy policy, I then adopt a framework to enable measurement and comparison of parentage policy and apply it to Canada. In keeping with the comparative literature on assisted reproduction (Bleiklie, Goggin, and Rothmayr 2004; Engeli, Green-Pedersen, and Larsen 2012), I create a scale ranging from "restrictive" to "permissive" parentage policy. This framework shows that parentage policy certainly varies by province, but also that the provinces are far from unregulated. Moreover, this analysis demonstrates the importance of the courts as policymakers in their own right. When legal rules surrounding surrogacy and parentage are absent or unclear, judicial policymaking increases – almost always in a permissive direction. Finally, it demonstrates that parentage policy reform is by no means complete. Ontario's *All Families Are Equal Act*, passed in 2016, represents the most significant changes to parentage policy in Canada yet, changes that could very well be emulated by other provinces.

Surrogacy Policy in Canada

Perhaps more than any two subfields of assisted reproduction policy, surrogacy and parentage are conceptually related. However, it is possible to distinguish between laws concerning surrogacy and those concerning parentage when we consider that parentage policy occurs last temporally. Once governments have determined the rules governing the validity/enforceability of surrogacy arrangements, they then deal with how parentage can be transferred or added. This chapter follows this temporal sequence, addressing surrogacy first and parentage second.

Surrogacy is a method of achieving assisted reproduction through a private social and legal arrangement in which a woman gestates and bears a child to be raised by someone else. When governments make policy concerning surrogacy, they effectively deal with three separate issues: whether the surrogate is genetically related to the child (traditional vs. gestational surrogacy); whether the surrogate is paid or unpaid; and whether surrogacy arrangements are enforceable. Because surrogacy arrangements involve rules for transferring legal parental responsibility, they are best conceptualized as part of parentage policy.

In Canada, surrogacy policy involves both criminal law and family law, and is therefore regulated by a combination of federal and provincial legislation (Nelson 2013, 328). Of the three components of surrogacy, the federal government has only addressed payment: section 6 of the *AHR Act* bans paying, offering to pay, or advertising "consideration" to a surrogate. It also bans acting as an intermediary for paid surrogacy, paying an intermediary for paid surrogacy, or counselling someone under twenty-one years of age to be a surrogate. Section 12 of the *AHR Act* includes a provision that allows reimbursement of surrogacy-related expenditures, as long as that reimbursement is in accordance with federal regulations (*Assisted Human Reproduction Act*, ss. 6, 12). In 2017, Health Canada released policy proposals for reimbursement for surrogacy expenditures that would bring section 12 of the legislation into force. Under the proposal, eligible expenditures would include items such as travel, maternity clothes, medication, counselling and legal services, and the loss of work-related income (Health Canada 2017).

Although those regulations have not yet been created and section 12 is not yet in force, Health Canada (2013) has stated on its website that surrogates "may be repaid for out-of-pocket costs directly related to her pregnancy (i.e., maternity clothing, medications)," although they cannot be compensated for the act of surrogacy itself. One Ontario surrogacy lawyer noted in 2011 that with surrogacy arrangements at her firm, "in the absence of that regulation ... generally the surrogate will be paid expenses that will be capped at something like $15,000, and it's staged over the course of the pregnancy." These monthly payments are meant to cover aspects such as "childcare if they need assistance, loss of work-related income in accordance with the legislation ... transportation, communication costs ... maternity wear, specialty foods, that sort of thing," for which receipts are kept (Interview 2011d). Because the *AHR Act* deals comprehensively with payment, provinces have not introduced regulations on that issue. For reimbursement for surrogacy, there is Canadian uniformity in principle, but legal opacity in practice.

Federal law addresses neither the distinction between traditional and gestational surrogacy nor the enforceability of surrogacy arrangements. In fact, no level of government has legislated directly concerning traditional and gestational surrogacy. There is some evidence that traditional surrogacy – in which the surrogate is genetically related to the resulting offspring – is uncommon in Canada. In 2001, fertility lawyer Sherry Levitan claimed that traditional surrogacy was "not done" in Canadian fertility clinics, as physicians were unwilling to perform insemination and lawyers were unwilling to draft a surrogacy agreement (Canada 2001e, 1125). In 2011, another Canadian fertility lawyer confirmed in an interview that "traditional surrogacy is quite rare," and that her firm did not create traditional surrogacy arrangements (Interview 2011d). In 2016 committee hearings for Ontario's *All Families Are Equal Act*, fertility lawyer Sara Cohen stated that "although the empirical evidence is incomplete, it is clear that the vast majority of surrogacy in Ontario is gestational," and estimated that only 5 per cent was traditional (Ontario 2016d, SP-35). Traditional surrogacy can be achieved in the privacy of one's home, as in the famous case of Cathleen Hachey, a New Brunswick surrogate who conceived using a syringe and donor sperm, and whose intended parents subsequently backed out of the agreement (CBC News 2011).[18] While traditional surrogacy is uncommon in Canada, it is not illegal. As such, both traditional and gestational surrogacy are permitted across Canada, with the exception of Quebec, where all surrogacy arrangements are null and void. Like payment, on the issue of the traditional versus gestational surrogacy, there is uniformity, with one exception: the extent to which a traditional surrogacy arrangement can be used to influence parentage transfer, which depends on the rules regarding genetic association in each province's parentage legislation (see below).

In terms of surrogacy policy, the major point of province-to-province variation in Canada concerns the enforceability of surrogacy

---

18   Hachey, from Bathurst, New Brunswick, was interested in being a surrogate and found a British couple online who were looking for a surrogate. The couple visited her and signed an agreement, and Hachey performed home insemination using the intended father's sperm. She became pregnant with twins. However, Hachey was later notified via text message that the couple had split up, and no longer wished to raise the children. She was subsequently able to find a Nova Scotia couple willing to adopt the children.

arrangements – a pre-birth agreement between a surrogate and one or more of the intended parent(s) that they will raise the child. The purpose of a surrogacy arrangement is to enable successful transfer of parentage from the birth mother to the intended parent(s) with as few legal roadblocks as possible. It is a recognition of new family forms prominent in the age of assisted reproduction; as Australian legal scholar Jenni Millbank (2011, 78) notes, transferring legal parentage to the intended parent(s) "is justified by and consistent with a functional family approach to relationship law" that legitimizes non-traditional and non-genetic family arrangements. Thus, surrogacy arrangements are by definition permissive insofar as they move beyond traditional forms of family formation.

Legal scholar Erin Nelson (2013, 328) has aptly described Canadian provincial law concerning surrogacy arrangements as "unsettled," because validity and enforceability of those arrangements varies from province to province. The absence of legal clarity increases the likelihood of judicial involvement. While there have been several high-profile disputes between surrogates and intended parents abroad – most notably, the *Baby Cotton* and *Baby M* cases in the United States and the United Kingdom in the 1980s (*Re Baby M* 1988; *Re C (A Minor) (Wardship: Surrogacy)* 1985) – there is only one known contested case involving the enforceability of a surrogacy arrangement in Canada: *H.L.W. and T.H.W. v. J.C.T. and J.T.* (2005) in the Supreme Court of British Columbia. In this case, H.L.W. (the surrogate) agreed to act as a traditional surrogate for Mr and Mrs T. (the intended parents) using the male parent's sperm, meaning the surrogate was genetically related to the child (traditional surrogacy). The intended parents also agreed to compensate the surrogate. After disputes concerning both the extent of compensation and the contact she would have with the child, the surrogate opted not to consent to the child's adoption, instead deciding that she and her husband, T.H.W., would raise the child. Despite the fact that H.L.W. was genetically related to the child and that she was listed as the birth mother on the child's registration, the court's preliminary pretrial decision refused the surrogate and her husband access to the child, pending trial. The judge's main rationale was that the child had to that point (aged three months) been raised by his intended parents, and that the child's best interests were served by continuing in the same care pretrial. A trial decision was not reported, suggesting that the outstanding issues were resolved out of court (Boyd 2007, 79; Busby and Vun 2010, 31–2).

As Susan Boyd (2007, 79) notes, in this case two factors "seemed to carry weight": the pre-birth surrogacy arrangement, and "the genetic father's wish to complete his family by having children, whereas the genetic/birth mother and her husband already had four children." Because the decision was made pretrial and the judge's primary concern was the child's best interests, the decision cannot be construed simply as enforcing a surrogacy arrangement as if it were a contract. There are several additional reasons this case is unlikely to act as a precedent. First, it involved traditional (genetic) surrogacy, which is very rare in Canada. Second, the surrogacy arrangement was commercial, insofar as the surrogate was paid – indeed, part of the dispute centred on payment. This would be illegal in Canada today, but because the arrangement took place before the passage of the *AHR Act* in 2004, it was legal at the time. Third, and most importantly, British Columbia subsequently amended its *Family Law Act* in 2011. This legislation accepts the validity of surrogacy arrangements and does not necessarily render them unenforceable; however, it explicitly states that the surrogacy arrangement cannot, by itself, satisfy the conditions for transfer of parentage. In the future, the enforceability of surrogacy arrangements in British Columbia will depend much more on judicial interpretation of the *Family Law Act* (described below) than the *H.L.W.* case.

Other surrogacy cases have arisen in Canada, but these have not dealt with the enforceability of surrogacy arrangements; instead they have concerned birth registration, declarations of parentage, and access disputes between intended parents, all of which fit more properly into the parentage policy subfield.[19] Moreover, because many (if not most) surrogacy declarations are sealed to ensure privacy, there may be additional cases involving disputes between surrogates and the intended parent(s) about which there is no public knowledge. The above case demonstrates the importance of legislation for providing courts with guidance regarding surrogacy arrangements. A lack of legal clarity leaves considerable room for judicial interpretation about enforceability in the case of a dispute. In this vein, many Canadian provinces have recently moved to add legal clarity to rules for parentage, including regarding the validity and enforceability of surrogacy arrangements.

---

19 A different Quebec case, which also predates the *AHR Act*, involved a dispute in which a traditional surrogate was awarded custody and the intended parents were not. In this particular case, the surrogate was the biological mother of the *intended* mother, further complicating matters (Boyd 2007, 79).

Parentage Policy: A Framework for Measurement and Comparison

Because of long-standing common-law rules based on a heteronormative family framework, in most jurisdictions the traditional legal assumption has been that a child's legal parents are the woman giving birth and, if applicable, her husband or male partner. As Harder (2015, 111) notes, prior to genetic testing, "the formal status of marriage and husband served as a proxy for biological proof of paternity" (see also Busby 2013, 289; Mykitiuk 2001, 779–80; Nelson 2013, 335). The advent of assisted reproduction and growing social acceptance of LGBTQ families mean these traditional assumptions are no longer always valid. It is in this context that governments have created parentage policy, which I define as *the rules concerning the procedures and eligibility requirements used to determine legal parenthood for children born through assisted conception or surrogacy*. The purpose of parentage policy is to avoid formal adoption and accelerate the process for transferring or adding legal parenthood. This process can occur through various mechanisms, such as statutory recognition or, more commonly, after-the-fact orders made by a court or government agency (known as "parental orders" or "parentage orders"). Fundamentally, parentage policy is designed increase the range of possible parental arrangements to keep up with the reality of assisted reproduction and new family structures.

In order to create a framework to measure parentage policy variation, I adopt a continuum ranging from "permissive" to "restrictive." Legislation permitting parentage is by definition permissive because it rejects traditional biological rationales of family formation: as parentage policy involves the "potential disengagement of biology from parenting," legislation is *required* to increase permissiveness: the law becomes a vehicle for permitting new families, enabling jurisdictions to "adapt their legal regimes to changing modes of family formation that flow from the availability" of assisted reproduction (Nelson 2013, 335). Hence, parentage policy becomes more permissive as governments introduce fewer legal barriers for the intended parent(s).

Table 5.1 sets out a framework that identifies ten ways governments can reduce barriers for legal parents. The parental status of the woman giving birth is normally assumed, even if she is not genetically related to the child. As such, parentage policy is typically implicated in two instances: assisted conception and surrogacy. In the context of assisted conception, the woman giving birth intends to *add* other parents to the child's birth certificate, as opposed to surrogacy, when the woman

Table 5.1
Ten Measures of Parentage Permissiveness

1	Assisted Conception: Female Partner
2	Assisted Conception: More Than Two Parents
3	Surrogacy: Heterosexual Parents
4	Surrogacy: Two Female Parents
5	Surrogacy: Two Male Parents
6	Surrogacy: Single Female Parent
7	Surrogacy: Single Male Parent
8	Surrogacy: No Genetic Relation Requirement
9	Gestational Surrogacy as Contract
10	Traditional Surrogacy as Contract

giving birth intends to *transfer* responsibility to other parents. The first two rows of Table 5.1 concern assisted conception. If the woman giving birth intends to raise a child conceived via assisted conception alone, the issue of parentage addition obviously does not arise. Nor does it arise if the woman giving birth intends to raise the child with her male partner, who is traditionally deemed the child's other parent through law. There are only two instances in which parentage policy becomes relevant in the case of assisted conception: if the woman giving birth intends to parent her child with a single female partner (row 1), or with two or more other parents (row 2).

Unlike assisted conception, surrogacy occurs when the woman giving birth, at least at the time of conception, does not intend to parent the child. With surrogacy, parentage is *transferred* from the surrogate to the intended parent(s). Typically, this involves a written pre-birth agreement – a surrogacy arrangement – which states that the intended parent(s) will raise the child. To recognize the legal validity of such agreements, jurisdictions can take five courses of action in order to increase parentage permissiveness in the context of surrogacy arrangements. In Table 5.1, rows 3–7 concern the eligible types of parents to whom parentage can be transferred: a heterosexual couple (row 3); a lesbian couple (row 4); a gay male couple (row 5); a single female parent (row 6); and a single male parent (row 7). Many jurisdictions across the world make distinctions based on these five categories. However, when a law permits parentage transfer in general and does not expressly exclude any of these parental arrangements, I assume they are all permitted.

The final three rows in Table 5.1 concern three additional permissiveness possibilities. The first of these concerns genetic relatedness. Many jurisdictions – such as Alberta and Nova Scotia – stipulate that parentage transfer can only occur following a surrogacy arrangement if at least one parent shares a genetic relation to the child. Because the genetic relation requirement is an additional burden for the intended parent(s), jurisdictions are more permissive if this requirement is absent (row 8). Jurisdictions can also deem surrogacy arrangements legally enforceable, making it easier for the intended parent(s) to achieve parentage if a surrogate changes her mind after signing the arrangement. In such instances, the surrogate would be given no authority to decide to keep the child. As Snyder and Byrn (2005, 634) note, with such a pre-birth "contract," the intended parent(s) "are determined to be the legal parents of the child before the child's birth, thereby giving them immediate and sole access to and control over the child and its postnatal care and medical treatment when it is born." Although legal enforceability of surrogacy arrangements is uncommon – no Canadian province provides for this possibility – it does exist in certain jurisdictions, such as in Ukraine and in the American states of Florida and Nevada (Busby 2013, 293). Because jurisdictions that permit legal enforceability often distinguish between traditional and gestational surrogacy, rows 9 and 10 reflect the two types of surrogacy that involve parental transfer. In each case, the existence of enforceable surrogacy arrangements would render a jurisdiction more permissive, insofar as enforceability creates fewer legal barriers for the intended parent(s). Although legal enforceability does not currently exist in any Canadian province, these rows remain in the table for the purposes of comparative measurement.

Collectively, the ten categories in Table 5.1 provide an analytical framework by which to measure parentage permissiveness across jurisdictions. The more categories that apply to a jurisdiction, the more permissive its parentage policy. Permissiveness is described in ordinal rather than interval terms: each category is treated as quantitatively equal, with a higher number of categories reflecting higher permissiveness. The framework is not all-encompassing. Other requirements – such as age, residency, criminal background checks, and counselling

– do exist for parentage in certain jurisdictions,[20] and others could be introduced. For clarity and simplicity, the framework is limited to the most common requirements: the type and number of the intended parent(s), their genetic relation to the child, and the enforceability of surrogacy contracts. The following discussion occurs in the context where there is no dispute among the parties concerning parentage transfer, whether between surrogates and the intended parent(s), gamete donors and the intended parent(s), or the intended parents themselves. This framework considers only those situations when all parties agree about who should be parents, but must navigate legislation, regulations, and common law in order to achieve their desired outcome.

Parentage Policy in the Canadian Provinces

In Canada, parentage policy has been almost entirely created by provincial governments, with the exception of policies for issuing passports to children born to a surrogate outside of Canada for Canadian intended parent(s) (Citizenship and Immigration Canada 2014). Provinces have jurisdiction over the regulation of contracts, all parenting issues, adoption, birth registration, and custody/access excluding situations involving divorce. Moreover, each province and territory has a law stating that decisions regarding custody and access are made with the "best interests of the child" in mind (Busby and Vun 2010, 28). While some have argued that the federal government should take a leadership role to drive uniformity,[21] Ottawa has left parentage policy

20 Millbank (2011) identifies the following conditions for successful parentage transfer, alone or in combination, in the Australian states and territories: the surrogate must be over a certain age; the surrogate has already given birth to a child; the intended parent(s) must be over a certain age; the intended parent(s) must be married or in a de facto relationship for a certain period of time; the intended parent(s) must be "classified" as infertile; they must be "fit and proper" parents; the intended parent(s) must reside within the jurisdiction; all or some parties must undergo a criminal record check; and all parties must have undergone counselling and/or received legal advice (179–83). In part because Canada's federal government has already made surrogacy policy in relation to age and compensation, there are far fewer requirements in Canada.

21 The Uniform Law Conference of Canada, an organization made up of delegates from the federal, provincial, and territorial governments, was part of a joint working group that reviewed federal, provincial, and territorial legislation pertaining to parentage with the goal of creating a template for a *Uniform Child Status Act*. The draft legislation was prepared for consideration in 2010. The working group's

up to the provinces. As a result, parentage policy varies considerably across the country.

Using the framework above, this section outlines each province's parentage policy, providing a basis for intra-Canadian comparison. I begin with provinces whose rules are clearest (Quebec, Alberta, and British Columbia), then move to provinces with less clear policy (Newfoundland and Labrador, Nova Scotia, Manitoba, and Prince Edward Island), and then to provinces whose parentage policy is, in whole or in part, governed by decisions resulting from litigation (Saskatchewan and New Brunswick).[22] I conclude with Ontario, a province that had long been governed by judicial rulings before it passed the country's most comprehensive legislation in December 2016. Describing provinces in this order highlights the importance of differences between legislative and judicial rules.

Parentage in Quebec

Quebec was the first jurisdiction in Canada to introduce permissive rules for parentage in the case of assisted conception. In 2002, Quebec extended the presumption of paternity to a spouse of either sex (married or civil union), thereby recognizing that a child can have two female parents (Nelson 2013, 339). Quebec's legislation also stipulates that merely contributing genetic material (sperm or eggs) for a "third-party parental project" does not create any parental obligation, and its legislation does not permit more than two parents. This "filiation" system revolves around the concept of a "parental project," which begins at the moment the intended parent(s) decide to have a child using third-party reproductive material. Effectively, the system confers the same presumptions, rights, and obligations on parents of children conceived through assisted conception as those conceived through coital

---

principles and approach were approved by the federal minister and deputy minister responsible for justice, and representatives from the (now defunct) federal agency Assisted Human Reproduction Canada were consulted. The federal government has not moved to introduce this template as an actual bill, but Alberta's, British Columbia's, and Ontario's parentage legislation, as well as Manitoba's failed *Family Law Reform Act*, reflect the *Uniform Child Status Act* in many respects.

22 Of the territories, only the Yukon has any rules for parentage transfer. Its provisions are similar to those of Prince Edward Island.

reproduction (*Civil Code of Québec*, LRQ, c. C-1991). When passed in 2002, the legislation made Quebec the most permissive province in the country regarding parentage.

This permissiveness with assisted conception contrasts sharply with Quebec's rules for surrogacy. Article 541 of Quebec's *Civil Code* makes surrogacy arrangements null and void. The surrogate retains legal custody over the child, and parentage cannot be transferred from her to another woman, regardless of whether that woman is genetically related to the child. Courts have interpreted this provision quite strictly: in *X, sub. nom Adoption –091* (2009), a Quebec court refused to recognize the validity of a surrogacy arrangement. In an attempt to get around the *Civil Code* provision, the surrogate had left the "mother" line on the birth registration blank, had named the intended father as the child's father, and did not oppose an application by the intended mother to adopt the child. However, the court held that "the child does not have the right to a maternal affiliation at any price" and that permitting the adoption would "require willful blindness" to the attempt to skirt the letter of the law (paras. 77–8; cited in and translated by Busby and Vun 2010, 29–30). The situation was not helped by the fact that the intended parents had agreed to pay $20,000 to the surrogate, which was technically a criminal violation of the federal *AHR Act*. No federal criminal charges were laid against the intended parents, and it is unclear how the adoption was subsequently resolved.

There are signs that Quebec may soon change: the government recently created a committee to examine recognizing surrogacy arrangements (Canadian Press 2015). In the absence of legal reform, however, Quebec's surrogacy ban means that the province – fifteen years ago a national leader in parentage permissiveness – is a restrictive province overall, with legal rules in place for parentage only in the context of assisted conception. Indeed, in a confidential interview, one fertility lawyer said that Quebec's policy has contributed to many Quebec-based parties completing surrogacy arrangements in Ontario, as the province of birth determines legal parentage on the birth certificate (Interview 2011d).

Parentage in Alberta

In 2005, two lesbian co-mothers successfully challenged Alberta's *Family Law Act*, which limited the default parentage presumption in the case of assisted conception to the "male partner" of the woman giving birth.

In *Fraess v. Alberta (Minister of Justice and Attorney General)* (2005), Justice Clarke of the Alberta Court of Queen's Bench found the legislation violated section 15 (equality rights) of the *Canadian Charter of Rights and Freedoms* and that it could not be justified as a "reasonable limit" under section 1 of the *Charter*. He read in changes to make the legislation gender neutral, permitting the presumption of lesbian parentage. Alberta subsequently overhauled its legislation to make it consistent with this ruling.

Alberta's parentage legislation is, along with British Columbia's and Ontario's, the most comprehensive in Canada, although it relies more heavily on court orders than those provinces. With respect to assisted conception, Alberta presumes that the parents are the woman giving birth and the man who provided sperm or an embryo, provided it was for his own reproductive use. This prevents third-party donors from having parental obligations. When the woman giving birth has a female partner, they are both presumed to be parents of the child provided her partner was in a "conjugal relationship of interdependence of some permanence with the woman giving birth at the time of the child's conception" and consented to assisted conception; in such instances, no application for parentage needs to be made (*Family Law Act*, S.A. 2003, ch. F-4.5). This is the remedy that was sought by the parents in *Fraess*. Finally, Alberta's legislation prohibits courts from transferring or adding parentage if the child would have more than two parents.

With respect to surrogacy, Alberta's legislation presumes that the legal parents are the woman giving birth (the surrogate) and the child's *genetic* father – not the surrogate's partner. The *Family Law Act* then permits transfer of parentage, whereby the genetically related intended father's partner can be declared the parent of the child and the surrogate can be declared not to be the child's parent. This transfer of parentage is also possible for a female intended parent who can prove that the eggs of an embryo used in surrogacy came her from own genetic material. If the court is satisfied that the child is genetically related to an intended parent and the surrogate consents post-birth, it will grant the application that the intended parent(s) are the child's parents (Nelson 2013. 339–40). Because the surrogate agrees to relinquish her parental rights, parentage transfer can occur in five of the six possible surrogacy scenarios. However, genetic relation matters: if a child is born to a surrogate and no intended parent is genetically related to that child, the surrogate and her partner (if the partner consented) are the child's legal parents.

Although Alberta's legislation states that once an application is granted the intended parent(s) will be deemed legal parents "at and from the time of the birth of the child," the requirement that the surrogate must consent means all parentage transfers occur post-birth, and surrogacy is not treated as a contract. Surrogacy arrangements are valid but not enforceable in Alberta; if the surrogate does not consent to the parentage order and decides to keep the child, then she is listed as the sole parent. Even if the surrogate consents pre-birth to transfer parentage, this consent cannot be used as post-birth consent, although it can be used as consent for the non-genetic parent (Busby and Vun 2010, 30; Nelson 2013, 340).

Parentage in British Columbia

In 2011, British Columbia amended its *Family Law Act* to include provisions for surrogacy and assisted conception, and the law fully came into force in March 2013. For assisted conception, the woman giving birth and her consenting partner are parents provided they are in a "marriage-like relationship," regardless of whether they have a genetic relation to the child (*Family Law Act*, S.B.C, ch. 25). The legislation also contains a provision saying that a donor is not a parent merely by donating genetic material.

For surrogacy, the intended parent(s) – regardless of sex or genetic relation – are deemed parents if there is a written agreement that the surrogate does not wish to parent the child, that she intends to surrender the child, and that the intended parent(s) wish to parent the child. The surrogate must also consent post-birth. Unlike Quebec and Alberta, British Columbia does not declare surrogacy arrangements invalid; while a pre-conception surrogacy arrangement alone cannot satisfy the requirements for parentage transfer, it can be used as "evidence of the parties' intentions with respect to the child's parentage if a dispute arises after the child's birth" (*Family Law Act*, S.B.C, ch. 25, ss. 34–5). Thus, the legislation acknowledges the possibility that a dispute can arise and that judicial discretion will play a significant role. Although British Columbia permits immediate post-birth parental registration without the need to go to court, the fact that the surrogate must continue to consent means the surrogacy arrangement is not treated as a contract. This diminished reliance on courts – something since emulated by Ontario in 2016 – marks a difference from the other provinces, insofar as parentage is typically established administratively rather than judicially.

British Columbia's *Family Law Act* also permits courts to declare three parents in two situations: when the woman giving birth and two intended parents have an agreement to raise the child together; or when a donor, the woman giving birth, and her partner have an agreement to raise the child together (ss. 27, 29[2]). Although section 30 of the legislation does use the word "donor," as long as all three parties agree to the order, there is no requirement for DNA testing; hence, no genetic relation is required. In February 2014, the first such three-parent case was reported after a lesbian couple and a known sperm donor were all named on a child's birth certificate (Subdhan 2014).

Perhaps one reason the *Family Law Act* was designed to reduce the reliance on courts in parentage proceedings was the heavy influence of the courts in the pre-*Family Law Act* years. Two cases from the 2000s are particularly illustrative. In *Rypkema v. H.M.T.Q. et al.* (2003), Justice Gray of the Supreme Court of British Columbia granted the intended parents – both genetically related to the child born through an unpaid surrogacy arrangement – legal parentage over a child born to a surrogate, who consented throughout the process. Subsequently, in *B.A.N. v. J.H.*, (2008), Justice Metzger of the same court granted parentage to intended parents. In *B.A.N*, the child was genetically related to the intended father, but not the intended mother. According to the intended parents' affidavit, British Columbia's Vital Statistics Agency had set out rules for registering a birth following a surrogacy arrangement, which involved getting a post-birth court declaration. Thus, in the five-year interim between *Rypkema* and *B.A.N.* – what Karen Busby (2013, 296) calls the "*Rypkema* regime" – without any legislative initiative, the bureaucracy had drafted internal policy to be consistent with the *Rypkema* judgment. British Columbia's 2011 amendments to the *Family Law Act* have effectively superseded these common-law cases, but those amendments, like Alberta's, came in no small part because of litigation. The permissive factors with respect to parentage for both surrogacy and assisted conception, in addition to no requirement for genetic relation and the possibility of more than two parents, mean that until Ontario passed similar legislation in 2016 (see Table 5.2), British Columbia had the most permissive legislation in Canada.

Parentage in Newfoundland and Labrador

Newfoundland and Labrador's legislation permits parentage orders in the case of both surrogacy and assisted conception. According to the *Vital Statistics Act*, in the case of "artificial insemination" (which likely encompasses other forms of assisted conception), the birth mother's

Table 5.2
Parentage Policy in Canada (Legislation Only)

	BC	AB	SK	MB	ON	QC	NB	NS	PE	NL
Assisted Conception: Female Partner	x	x	x	x	x	x		x	x	x
Assisted Conception: More Than Two Parents	x				x					
Surrogacy: Heterosexual Parents	x	x			x			x		x
Surrogacy: Two Female Parents	x	x			x			x		x
Surrogacy: Two Male Parents	x	x			x			x		x
Surrogacy: Single Female Parent	x	x			x			x		x
Surrogacy: Single Male Parent	x	x			x			x		x
Surrogacy: No Genetic Relation Requirement	x				x					x
Gestational Surrogacy as Contract										
Traditional Surrogacy as Contract										
PERMISSIVENESS TOTAL	8	6	1	1	8	1	0	6	1	7

partner will be deemed the "father or other parent" provided there is written consent of both parents (*Vital Statistics Act*, ch. V, 6.01).

When a child is born through a surrogacy arrangement, the registrar general will register the child's intended parent(s) provided a court issues a parentage order under the *Children's Law Act* or an adoption order under the *Adoption Act*. The language is gender neutral, and nothing in either the *Children's Law Act* or the *Vital Statistics Act* suggests there must be two intended parents. However, the exclusion of any mention of more than two parents means that courts are not given authority to issue declarations of parentage for more than two parents. Parentage orders can be sought before the child is born and, as Busby and Vun (2010, 30) note, "the consent of the surrogate mother is not expressly required." Nor does the legislation require a genetic relation in the case of surrogacy. For its relative permissiveness, however, surrogacy in the sparsely populated province is rare. In a 2010 magazine article, surrogacy lawyer Nancy Lam wrote that she was not aware of any declarations of parentage that had actually occurred in Newfoundland and Labrador (Lam 2010).

Parentage in Nova Scotia

In 2007, Nova Scotia created the *Birth Registration Regulations*, which concern both assisted conception and surrogacy, pursuant to its *Vital Statistics Act*. For assisted conception, if the woman giving birth is married, her spouse is the child's other parent; if she is unmarried but has a partner who wishes to be the parent, her partner must file a statutory declaration with the birth registrar acknowledging that he/she wishes to parent the child with the woman giving birth. The regulations permit this form of parentage addition either before or after the birth. Like Newfoundland and Labrador, Nova Scotia's legislation does not include a provision to allow more than two parents.

With respect to surrogacy, the regulations enable a court to make a declaration of parentage registering the intended parent(s) and removing the surrogate as long as the agreement was made pre-conception, was initiated by the intended parent(s), and one of the parents has a genetic link to the child. Section 5(2)(c) states that a condition for parentage transfer is that "the woman who is to carry and give birth to the child does not intend to be the child's parent" (*Birth Registration Regulations*, O.I.C. 2007–498, N.S. Reg. 390/2007). This suggests if the surrogate decides she does want to raise the child, the transfer will not go through, and the surrogate (and her partner, if applicable) will remain the child's legal parent(s).[23] Thus, surrogacy arrangements are likely not enforceable.

---

23 Busby and Vun (2010, 30) differ in their interpretation of the requirement for post-birth surrogate consent. They contend that "the regulation does not expressly require the surrogate's post-delivery consent to the order or even that she be given notice that an order is being sought," suggesting that in Nova Scotia, surrogacy arrangements may be enforceable (see also Busby 2013, 298). I believe theirs is an incorrect reading of the regulation: because the condition in section 5(2)(c) is that the surrogate "does not intend to be the child's parent," and it is not limited to a pre-birth agreement, the surrogate must still consent post-birth.

Parentage in Manitoba

Manitoba's parentage legislation does not currently contain surrogacy provisions. However, section 3(6) of the *Vital Statistics Act* states that when a child is born as a result of "artificial insemination" (which, like Newfoundland and Labrador, likely applies to other forms of assisted conception), the birth registration will list the woman giving birth and her spouse (defined as "cohabiting with her in a conjugal relationship of some permanence") as the "father or other parent," thus permitting two female parents (*Vital Statistics Act*, ch. V, C.C.S.M. c. V60). There is currently no provision for more than two parents, although the failed *Family Law Reform Act* (described below) would have changed this.

In Manitoba, litigation to change surrogacy procedures was unsuccessful. In *J.C. v. The Queen (Dept. of Vital Statistics)* (2000), Manitoba's Court of Queen's Bench rejected an application that would have compelled hospital staff to recognize the intended parents as the child's legal parents following a surrogacy birth. Even though the surrogate and her husband supported the application, Justice Keyser held that the legislature had deliberately excluded pre-birth declaratory orders for maternity from the *Manitoba Family Maintenance Act*. The judge did, however, indicate that a declaration of parentage with respect to the genetic mother could be made after the birth was registered, although he did not make that declaration, as the case facts preceded birth of the child.

In 2015, Manitoba looked set for considerable policy change. In June 2015, the NDP government introduced Bill 33, the *Family Law Reform Act* (*FLRA*). The legislation sought to overhaul Manitoba's parentage policy and bring it more into line with policy in Alberta and British Columbia. In addition to changing the wording from "artificial insemination" in the *Vital Statistics Act* to "assisted reproduction," the bill would have confirmed that a donor is not a parent simply by virtue of donating reproductive material. It also stipulated a procedure whereby a court order for parentage transfer must be made in the case of surrogacy, provided there is a pre-birth surrogacy agreement, the surrogate consents post-birth, and one or both of the intended parent(s) "provided reproductive material or the embryo used in the assisted reproduction" (Manitoba 2015, s. 16(2)). Like Alberta, a genetic relation would have been required in order for parentage transfer to occur.

The *FLRA* also contained a provision that would have permitted a child to have three parents if born through assisted reproduction, but as with surrogacy, a genetic relation would have been required. Notably, while the bill stated that a court "must" grant the parentage order if it is satisfied certain conditions are met in the case of surrogacy, in the case of three parents the court "may" grant the order – providing judges with greater discretion in the latter situation (Manitoba 2015, ss. 16–19). However, the bill died on the order paper when an election was called in 2016. The Progressive Conservatives won a majority on 19 April 2016, and the NDP were reduced to opposition. Although the *FLRA* was not an election issue and the NDP has called on the new government to revive certain elements of the legislation (CBC News 2016), as of January 2018, no new bill has been introduced into the Manitoba legislature.

Parentage in Prince Edward Island

In Prince Edward Island, the *Child Status Act* contains provisions for assisted conception but not surrogacy. The law stipulates that when a child is conceived via assisted conception, the partner of the woman giving birth is the other legal parent. It also states that the woman giving birth will be the mother of the child regardless of whether she is the genetic mother, thus effectively precluding surrogacy arrangements (*Child Status Act*, ch. C-6.). No known legal challenges have occurred to change Prince Edward Island's parentage policy.

Parentage in Saskatchewan

Saskatchewan amended its *Vital Statistics Act* in 2009 to include the term "other parent" as someone "cohabiting with the mother or father of the child in a spousal relationship at the time of the child's birth and who intends to participate as a parent in the upbringing of the child" (*Vital Statistics Act*, S.S., ch. V-7.21). This allows the female partner of the woman giving birth to be a legal pre-birth parent in cases involving assisted conception. However, Saskatchewan legislation does not recognize parentage with respect to surrogacy, and there is no provision for more than two parents.

Litigation has affected parentage policy for surrogacy in Saskatchewan. In *W.J.Q.M. v. A.M.A.* (2011), a gay male couple who had engaged in a third-party surrogacy arrangement sought a declaration to remove the name of the woman giving birth from the child's birth registration and have their names included. The child was conceived using donor sperm from one of the men and an anonymous egg donor. The surrogate did not dispute the order. There were no prior precedents in Saskatchewan, but drawing from other provincial cases in Canada, Justice Ryan-Froslie was satisfied that the surrogate was not the child's "biological mother" based on the *Children's Law Act*, and that "neither the applicants nor [the surrogate] ever intended that [she] would assume any parental rights or obligations" (para. 25). She granted a declaration that the two men were the legal parents, and the surrogate was not.

Because the case involved statutory interpretation, it will likely serve as a precedent. However, the importance given to the lack of genetic relationship between the surrogate and the child suggests that this might not apply in cases of traditional surrogacy; following the case, the men's lawyer claimed that "there would have been a greater risk for us" had the surrogate been genetically related to the child (Brean 2011). The extent to which the case would apply in other parentage scenarios is unclear.

Parentage in New Brunswick

There is no legislation regarding surrogacy or assisted conception in New Brunswick. Neither the *Vital Statistics Act* nor the *Family Services Act* provides for parentage transfer in either procedure although, like other provinces, same-sex parents have been able to adopt in New Brunswick since 2004, when it became the last province to permit same-sex adoption. Instead, movement in parentage policy has occurred because of case law. The first relevant case was a Labour and Employment Board decision regarding assisted conception: *A.A. v. New Brunswick* (2004). In this case, a woman had a child after artificial insemination from an anonymous sperm donor, but the Department of Health and Wellness would not register her female partner as the second parent.[24] The board found that the couple had faced discrimination according to section 5(1) of New Brunswick's *Human Rights Act* and awarded damages.

In the 2010 case *J.A.W. v. J.E.W.*, the Court of Queen's Bench allowed a parentage order in the case of surrogacy, where the birth mother had

---

24 This case preceded *Reference re Same-Sex Marriage* (2004) and the federal *Civil Marriage Act* (2005) and, as such, the legal recognition of same-sex marriage in New Brunswick.

carried a child to term for her sister and sister's husband. The judge noted that the child was genetically related to both of his intended parents, claiming "the Legislature intended to vest [the court with] jurisdiction so as to allow for declarations of parentage based on biology" (para. 18). It is unclear whether the same judge would have permitted a parentage order to other (non-heterosexual) intended parent(s), or to those without a genetic connection to the child. New Brunswick has not amended its legislation to reflect either decision.

Parentage in Ontario

When discussing parentage law in Ontario, it is important to distinguish between three aspects: Ontario's limited law until 2016; the litigation that produced policy change; and the sweeping new Bill C-28, the *All Families Are Equal Act*, which received Royal Assent in December 2016.

Before December 2016, Ontario law regarding parentage was quite restrictive. The *Vital Statistics Act* was amended in 2009 to recognize that the woman giving birth and the "other parent" could be presumed to be parents by default in scenarios involving assisted conception. As in Alberta, this change occurred in response to a *Charter* challenge to the legislation, where two lesbian mothers sought parental recognition through birth registration (*Rutherford v. Ontario (Deputy Registrar General)* 2006). Although Ontario did not have any legislation permitting surrogacy until 2016, it was a fairly common (if legally complicated) practice. In a 2011 interview, one Ontario surrogacy lawyer suggested that her firm wrote four surrogacy arrangements each month, and estimated that there were fifteen legal surrogacy arrangements per month provincewide. Navigating surrogacy contracts was a complicated process in which the intended parent(s) would make an application for a legal declaration of parentage in court via affidavits, after which "the Deputy Registrar with Births, Deaths, and Marriages, has to take a [positive] position" in order to have parentage approved (Interview 2011d).

However, Ontario proves that a legislative vacuum does not necessarily mean a legal vacuum. The Ontario Superior Court of Justice case *M.D. et al. v. L.L. et al.* (2008) involved a situation in which two heterosexual intended parents used their own genetic material and entered into a surrogacy arrangement with a surrogate and her husband. The surrogate's name had to be placed on the birth certificate, and all four parties sought a declaration that the intended parents were the only parents of the child. Justice Nelson granted the declaration of parentage, ruling that there was a "gap" in the *Vital Statistics Act* "that does not operate in the child's best interests, insofar as the inferential definition of 'mother' impedes the court's jurisdiction to declare a person not to be the mother of a child" (para. 61). Justice Nelson did not mandate genetic testing, even though both intended parents claimed a biological connection to the child (para. 46). Because the legislature did not amend the *Vital Statistics Act* in response to this specific case, it was unclear whether it would apply in other parentage arrangements where the intended parents were not a heterosexual couple.

The Ontario Court of Appeal case *A.A. v. B.B.* (2007) also set a precedent until the law was changed in 2016. In this case, a lesbian couple (A.A. and C.C.) used their male friend B.B.'s sperm to impregnate C.C. Subsequently, the couple raised the child recognizing that B.B. would play a smaller parental role. However, under Ontario law, the woman giving birth and the genetic father were the child's legal parents (the child was born before the 2009 amendments to the *Vital Statistics Act*). When the child was two, A.A. applied for a declaration that she was the child's parent in addition to B.B. and C.C. On appeal, Justice Rosenberg also held that there was a gap in the *Children's Law Reform Act* (*CLRA*), and added A.A. as the child's third parent. His rationale is worth quoting at length:

> Present social conditions and attitudes have changed. Advances in our appreciation of the *value of other types of relationships and in the science of reproductive technology* have created gaps in the *CLRA*'s legislative scheme. Because of these changes the parents of a child can be two women or two men. They are as much the child's parents as adopting parents or "natural" parents. The *CLRA*, however, does not recognize these forms of parenting and thus the children of these relationships are deprived of the equality of status that declarations of parentage provide. (para. 35, emphasis added)

Interestingly, Justice Rosenberg rejected the argument that the legislative gap was deliberate, holding that "the Legislature did not foresee for the possibility of declarations of parentage for two women," which was "a product of the social conditions and medical knowledge at the time" (para. 38). He thus granted that a child can have three parents, making Ontario the first jurisdiction (prior to British Columbia's 2011 legislation) to allow this. However, as Fiona Kelly (2009) notes, it was not clear whether this applied "beyond the individual facts of the case"; as with

M.D., the legislation was not amended after the case. Presumably, to have a legally recognized three-parent family in Ontario prior to 2016, one would have needed to go through litigation. Moreover, the case did not "address legal parentage at birth," and instead "require[d] parents to initiate a legal process after the child is born" (193).

Thus, prior to 2016, all the permissive features of Ontario's parentage policy stemmed from judicial decisions. *Rutherford* enabled lesbian mothers to be presumed as "other parents" and eventually led the government to amend its legislation; *M.D.* granted parentage to intended parents genetically related to a child born through surrogacy; and *A.A.* allowed a child born through assisted conception to have three parents. Yet the reliance on the discretion of individual judges produced legal uncertainty. In January 2014, Ontario fertility lawyer Sara Cohen (2014) lamented the fact that one judge had been moved to another court and thus would no longer be granting parentage declarations. Her observation suggests that an individual judge or group of judges with a permissive approach to parentage, particularly in a province with unclear public policy, can make a sizeable difference.

In response to mounting criticism of the existing regime, Ontario introduced comprehensive legislation, which received Royal Assent in December 2016. Bill C-28, the *All Families Are Equal Act* (*AFAE Act*), amends the *Children's Law Reform Act* (*CLRA*), the *Vital Statistics Act*, and other legislation. Ontario's Liberal government created the bill in response to a court order in *Grand v. Ontario* (2016), in which a judge in the Ontario Superior Court of Justice found that the *Children's Law Reform Act* violated section 15 of the *Charter*, as it did not accord "equal recognition and the equal benefit and protection of the law to all children, without regard to their parents' sexual orientation, gender identity, use of assisted reproduction or family composition" (*Grand v. Ontario* 2016, 1–2). The *Grand* case also contained Minutes of Settlement, in which Ontario's Attorney General agreed to create *Charter*-compliant legislation by 31 August 2016. The *AFAE Act* drew heavily from NDP member of provincial Parliament (MPP) Cheri DiNovo's 2015 private member's bill, *Cy and Ruby's Act*, which had died on the order paper. Notably, DiNovo's bill drew explicitly from British Columbia's experience, as noted by one of the bill's architects, lawyer Jennifer Mathers McHenry: "We took a look at a number of jurisdictions. British Columbia in particular has had much more expansive parental recognition for a number of years and that was one of the jurisdictions that we took a look at. The bill that we drafted was not modelled after it necessarily, but inspired by it. We took steps to have the legislation be a little bit smoother and a little bit broader" (TVO 2016, 13:35).

The *AFAE Act* is easily the most comprehensive parentage policy in Canada. In a press release, the Attorney General's office highlighted three goals of the legislation: to "provide greater clarity and certainty for parents who use assisted reproduction," to "provide a streamlined process for the legal recognition of parents who use a surrogate," and to "reduce the need for parents who use assisted reproduction to have to go to court to have their parental status recognized in law" (Ontario 2016b). The legislation is also more inclusive of LGBTQ families, gender identity, and gender fluidity: it replaces references to "father" and "mother" with "parent" in the *CLRA* and the *Vital Statistics Act*, and removes references to "natural parents" and relations "by blood." The *CLRA* now states that, except in cases of surrogacy, the "birth parent" (the person who gives birth to the child) is the child's parent. Moreover, amendments made at committee stage removed the few remaining references to "biological father"; the final version amends the *CLRA* to state that when a child is conceived through sexual intercourse, the "person whose sperm resulted in the conception of a child through sexual intercourse" is the parent of the child. This does not apply if, before conception, the "birth parent" and "person whose sperm resulted in the conception of a child" had a written agreement that the donor of sperm did not intend to parent the child (Ontario 2016c).

The *AFAE Act* also amends the *CLRA* to clarify that, if a child is conceived through assisted conception, the birth parent's spouse at the time of conception is the other parent. It also stipulates that if the birth parent enters into a pre-conception agreement with up to three other intended parent(s), they are all presumed to be the child's parents. If the parentage agreement included more than four total parents, however, they must apply for a judicial declaration of parentage. Thus, the new *CLRA* makes possible four-parent families without the need for judicial intervention, regardless of whether the child was conceived through assisted conception, sexual intercourse, or surrogacy.

The movement away from court orders in the *AFAE Act* is most pronounced with respect to surrogacy. The intended parent(s) are recognized as the child's legal parents if the following conditions are met: there are no more than four intended parents; each party has received independent legal advice before signing the surrogacy agreement; the child is conceived through assisted reproduction; and the surrogate gives written consent relinquishing her parental rights. The surrogate cannot relinquish her rights until the child is at least seven days old; before she does so, she and the intended parent(s) share parental responsibilities for and rights over the child. Surrogacy agreements can be used as evidence of parental intent but are "unenforceable in law" (Ontario 2016c).[25] Like British Columbia's *Family Law Act*, the goal of Ontario's new policy is to reduce the use of the courts through legal certainty. However, the legislation does allow a judicial safety valve: section 13 of the *CLRA* now states that "any person having an interest may apply to the court for a declaration that a person is or is not a parent of the child."

Trends in Parentage Policy

Table 5.2 combines information about provincial parentage policy with the above framework to enable comparison and deduce several conclusions. First, most provinces have some sort of legislation in place regarding parentage. New Brunswick remains the only province without any legislation for assisted conception or surrogacy. Second, legislation in certain provinces – particularly in Alberta, Quebec, British Columbia, and Ontario – provides clarity for surrogates and the intended parent(s). Legal clarity does not always mean permissiveness, however: Quebec's legal clarity restricts parentage transfer by declaring surrogacy arrangements null and void.

Third, courts have been prominent in shaping parentage policy. In Alberta, British Columbia, and Ontario, challenges to parentage provisions provided the impetus for legislative reform. In Saskatchewan and New Brunswick, the outcome of litigation operates as the status quo in the absence of legislative responses. Moreover, litigation strategies have typically nudged policy towards permissiveness, particularly in the absence of legislation. True, not all judicial challenges result in permissive reform: in *J.C. v. The Queen* (2000), a Manitoba judge rejected a parentage claim, and in *X, sub. nom Adoption –091* (2009), a Quebec court reaffirmed Quebec's restrictive approach to surrogacy. Overall, however, Table 5.3 demonstrates that in the two provinces for which litigation

---

25 The *AFAE Act* also amends the *CLRA* to stipulate that merely donating reproduction material or an embryo does not make someone a parent, and includes a provision that if an intended parent dies before the child's birth, the surviving spouse can apply to a court for a posthumous declaration of parentage.

Table 5.3
Parentage Policy in Canada (Legislation and Judicial Decisions)

	BC	AB	SK	MB	ON	QC	NB	NS	PE	NL
Assisted Conception: Female Partner	x	x	x	x	x	x	x*	x	x	x
Assisted Conception: More Than Two Parents	x				x					
Surrogacy: Heterosexual Parents	x	x			x		x*	x		x
Surrogacy: Two Female Parents	x	x			x			x		x
Surrogacy: Two Male Parents	x	x	x*		x			x		x
Surrogacy: Single Female Parent	x	x			x			x		x
Surrogacy: Single Male Parent	x	x			x			x		x
Surrogacy: No Genetic Relation Requirement	x									x
Gestational Surrogacy as Contract										
Traditional Surrogacy as Contract										
PERMISSIVENESS TOTAL	8	6	2*	1	8	1	2*	6	1	7

* Because of judicial decisions.

currently acts as the policy status quo, the result has been more permissive policy. The same was also true in British Columbia, Alberta, and Ontario before their legislative overhauls. This general trend of courtroom success with respect to parentage policy is consistent with the comparative (and Canadian) evidence on judicial policymaking, which suggests that courts will promote legal change by "asserting individual rights and liberties against traditional social values" in "moral" conflicts (Tatalovich and Daynes 2005, xxvii).

Fourth, parentage policy change in the last decade has reflected a movement away from restrictive policy, regardless of which institution has made those changes. In some provinces this was secured through legislative action, in others a judicial decision, and in some provinces

Table 5.4
Parentage Policy Permissiveness in Canada

Restrictive < – – – – – – – – – – – – – – – – – > Permissive					
1	2	3	6	7	8
MB	SK* (2)		AB	NL	BC
QC	NB* (0)		NS		ON
PE					

* In part because of judicial decisions (legislative total in parentheses).

both. The most recent provinces to change their policy (Alberta, British Columbia, and Ontario) have done so through comprehensive legislation. Quebec's recent committee to examine surrogacy and Manitoba's *Family Law Reform Act*, which died on the order paper due to a provincial election, are a continuation of this trend. Finally, Table 5.4 shows that parentage policy in Canada is subject to considerable provincial variation, with provinces scoring anywhere from one to eight on the 10-point parentage permissiveness scale.

Conclusion

As the federal government slowly moved forward with making assisted reproduction policy in the 1990s and 2000s, parentage policy, including parentage rules in cases of surrogacy, was the one subfield deliberately left to the provinces. The development of surrogacy and parentage policy both before and after the Supreme Court's 2010 *Reference re Assisted Human Reproduction Act* is thus a crucial part of Canada's assisted reproduction story that has too often been ignored by scholars. Surrogacy policy and parentage policy have considerable implications for families and individuals considering the use of assisted reproduction. The rules in place – whether by legislation or judicial decisions – can inhibit or promote the creation of new families. They can provide legal certainty for parents, create security for surrogates, and prevent legal disputes. Canada's provincial diversity in this regard is also instructive for comparative analysis, insofar as the ten different frameworks illustrate the various ways in which legislation can inhibit or promote policy permissiveness.

In addition to its comparative utility, the above analysis adds nuance to understanding Canada's overall assisted reproduction policy mix. At least in terms of surrogacy and parentage, assisted reproduction policy in Canada is not "unregulated," nor does it resemble the "Wild West." All provinces have some form of a legal status quo regarding parentage, whether by legislation or common law. Laws in several provinces, particularly Alberta, Quebec, British Columbia, and Ontario, achieve some measure of clarity for surrogates, their partners, and the intended parent(s). Most of this policy change has occurred in the last decade, and it has moved in a permissive direction. It is fair to say that policy is gradually catching up with the reality of assisted reproduction. Canada's permissiveness is especially striking compared with other common-law jurisdictions such as the United Kingdom and Australia; Canada has attached comparatively "few evidentiary, substantive, or procedural requirements to surrogacy-related parentage applications," whereas those other jurisdictions have implemented "expensive, invasive, time-consuming, and ineffective post-delivery processes" (Busby 2013, 300, 289).

This analysis also shows that legislation – whether permissive (British Columbia and Ontario) or restrictive (Quebec) – can set clear rules and boundaries for prospective parents, decreasing the potential for expensive litigation. Regardless of whether one desires permissive or restrictive policy, legislation seems far more desirable than piecemeal judicial change. As Nelson (2013, 336) notes, statutory rules for parentage afford a "significant advantage" because of the "clarity they afford"; without clear rules, the intended parent(s) must resort to the courts, where "judges are placed in the position of applying rules that were not fashioned to deal with" assisted reproduction. The result is legal uncertainty. Ontario and British Columbia, the most recent provinces to introduce parentage legislation, have each focused in large part on limiting judicial involvement in this regard.

Irrespective of this permissive policy movement, some of the Royal Commission's fears have been realized. While the Commission recognized that parentage was provincial jurisdiction, it nevertheless urged interprovincial collaboration to "clarify and standardize in all provinces the parentage of children born as a result of donor insemination" (Royal Commission on New Reproductive Technologies 1993, 489). "Matters so important to women and children," the Commission argued, "in terms not only of their health but of their legal status and how they are viewed, cannot differ from province to province" (xxxvi). Over twenty years later, there is considerable variation between provinces with respect to the legal status of children born through assisted reproduction, and there have been no substantive intergovernmental attempts to harmonize policy between provinces. While legislative momentum seems to have occurred recently, and certain provincial legislatures have amended legislation to address the growing use of assisted reproduction, the policy movement has certainly been uneven. Because this is a result of the structure of the *Constitution Act, 1867*, this uneven policy movement and provincial policy variation is here to stay.

Chapter 6

Many Actors, Many Policies:
Clinical Intervention Policy in Canada

When commentators criticize the lack of assisted reproduction policy in Canada, this criticism is typically aimed at the governance of fertility clinics. Françoise Baylis (2011, 318), Canada's most prominent critic of government inaction over assisted reproduction, has been especially critical of lax rules regarding multiple embryo transfer, which can lead to health consequences associated with multiple births. Legal scholars Vanessa Gruben and Angela Cameron (2011) stress that such health problems could include "pre-eclampsia, gestational diabetes, anemia and premature labour" for pregnant women, and "low birth weight and prematurity" for their children. They have made similar claims regarding the collection and management of health-reporting information, which is "vital to ensuring that these children receive important genetic health information about their biological heritage." All of these features – rules for fertility treatments, donors, information collection, and licensing requirements – fall into the subfield of clinical intervention policy, which I define as rules that cover the use of technology to enhance the prospects of reproductive success.

When a majority of Supreme Court justices found unconstitutional the provisions in the federal *AHR Act* that had the effect of regulating "a specific type of health services provided in health-care institutions by health-care professionals to individuals who for pathological or physiological reasons need help to reproduce," they were referring primarily to clinical intervention policy (*Reference re Assisted Human Reproduction Act* 2010, para. 227). This chapter examines who regulates clinical intervention in Canada and how they regulate it in the wake of the Supreme Court reference. In terms of government institutions, I find that the federal government, provincial governments, and even the judiciary have each been involved in some form of policymaking, albeit to different degrees. While the federal government's involvement is largely limited to criminal prohibitions, Ontario and Quebec demonstrate that provinces have the capacity to regulate clinical intervention policy. Yet provinces outside of Quebec have been reluctant to make policy – even Ontario's policies have been primarily limited to IVF coverage and rules for embryo transfer. As a result, the majority of policymaking is done by national specialist medical associations, with some minor policy being set by provincial regulatory colleges. The Canadian experience thus deviates from the experience in France, Germany, and the United Kingdom, where "the state has progressively played a more pivotal role in the field over time" (Engeli and Rothmayr Allison 2016, 249).

I offer two explanations for this. First, the decentralization of Canadian health-care policy, which the Supreme Court's *Reference re Assisted Human Reproduction Act* intensified, has created incentives for provinces to defer to the medical profession. By accepting the medicalized framing of assisted reproduction, the Supreme Court majority opinion helped solidify the view, long held by medical professionals, that policymaking for the clinical aspect of assisted reproduction is best left to the experts. Because of the privileged position and epistemic authority granted to medical professionals, provincial governments remain reluctant to intervene in any aspect of clinical intervention; indeed, the only occasions when provincial governments have created restrictions for clinical intervention policy have been when Quebec and Ontario simultaneously introduced some public coverage for IVF, a policy generally supported by fertility physicians.

Second, and relatedly, medical professionals in Canada have continued to self-regulate as a strategy to influence and prevent state intervention. Relatively few major controversies have occurred, and the emergence of best practices – such as the recent decline in multiple birth rates – provides even less incentive for provincial governments to act in this subfield. However, the reliance on opaque professional guidelines and best practices could produce one unintended consequence: an increasingly assertive judiciary might mandate government intervention. As the *Pratten v. British Columbia* (2011) trial decision shows, judges are willing to use the *Canadian Charter of Rights and Freedoms* to require governments to act to protect those affected by assisted reproduction. While the decision was ultimately overturned on appeal, it nevertheless indicates that the judiciary could become an important player in clinical intervention, just as it has with surrogacy and parentage policy.

Defining Clinical Intervention

Public policy in the clinical intervention subfield can be subdivided into three overlapping categories. First, *clinical policies* are designed to affect the behaviour of one particular target group: medical professionals. These include licensing and inspection requirements, rules for the use and transfer of human reproductive material, and rules regarding clinical practice. These rules cover the permissibility of all assisted conception procedures, including but not limited to artificial insemination, IVF, and intracytoplasmic sperm injection (ICSI). Second, *donor policies* are designed to affect the behaviour of another target group: donors, patients, and, by implication, children born through assisted reproduction. These policies primarily include rules for the storage and donation of human gametes (egg and sperm), such as screening requirements, limits on payment, limits on the number of donations permitted, rules for the identification of donors, and the maintenance of databases. Included in this category are rules for egg freezing and donor identification. Third, *coverage policies* concern patient health-insurance coverage. The target group is primarily patients, but these policies also affect the behaviour of medical professionals. This category includes the coverage of costs associated with assisted reproduction treatments and fertility drugs. Governments can make policy for this category through direct coverage of a particular type of assisted reproduction and/or drugs in a public system (as in Ontario with IVF), or through rules that mandate private insurers to cover assisted reproduction procedures and/or drugs (as in some American states).

There is considerable overlap between these three components of clinical intervention, which is why they comprise an integrated subfield. Clinical policies mandating the creation or maintenance of patient databases will affect the behaviour of both medical professionals and patients, while rules extending patient coverage encourage patients to access assisted reproduction services and provide medical practitioners with a steady supply of patients. Moreover, donor policies limiting the donation of human reproductive material will have a direct impact on the fertility industry: a complete ban on multiple sperm donations, for example, would decrease the supply of reproductive material and affect private practice. While the policy subcategories can be separated in part by the target group they seek to affect, physician and patient interests are typically intertwined with clinical intervention policy.

Historically and comparatively, medical organizations have been hostile to state intervention with respect to clinical intervention policy. In Western European countries, for example, the initial method of governance was voluntary self-regulation, which consisted of "full control over rulemaking by stakeholders, even without that power being explicitly delegated to them" (Engeli and Rothmayr Allison 2016, 250). This was also true in Canada. During hearings for Canada's Royal Commission on New Reproductive Technologies, most scientists, medical practitioners, and legal organizations "strongly opposed the creation of a regulatory body and the use of criminal sanctions" and "depicted professional self-regulation as the panacea for any potential misuse of reproductive technologies" (Scala 2007, 220). However, when testifying during the Brown Committee hearings in 2001, many physicians had grown to accept that federal legislation would happen. Dr Michael Rudnicki said the legislation was "timely and prudent, and brings a necessary level of oversight and regulation" (Canada 2001c, 1135), and Dr Roger Godsen from the Canadian Fertility and Andrology Society (CFAS) claimed "on behalf of my colleagues throughout Canada that we do welcome legislation in this area" (Canada 2001c, 1135). Dr Ronald Worton, while admitting he had some reservations about the criminal prohibitions (as most physicians, researchers, and lawyers did), agreed that "there is a need for legislation, a need for regulation, and a need for a regulatory body to oversee it" (Canada 2001f, 1230).

Some Canadians physicians continued to oppose the legislation, even as it became obvious it would pass. Dr Calvin Greene told the Senate Standing Committee on Social Affairs, Science and Technology in 2004 that the position of CFAS was that the bill "does more harm than good ... It compromises the care of our patients, and our patients tell us they do not want it." Dr Clifford Librach told the same committee that the legislation was "seriously flawed and will have devastating consequences for the infertile population" (Canada 2004a, 2004b). Several years after the legislation had passed, physicians interviewed for this study were less concerned. One Canadian fertility specialist said in 2012 the legislation "reflected the feelings of most people," and that there was "nothing there [physicians] couldn't live with"; another observed in 2011 that the legislation "hasn't made that much of an impact" on physicians' day-to-day dealings with infertile individuals, suggesting the *AHR Act* did not interfere a great deal with clinical practice (Interview 2012b, 2011b). Many medical professionals recognized, and recognize today, that some legislation was inevitable, and that collaboration through federal institutions might be the optimal way to retain professional autonomy.

Federal Clinical Intervention Policy

The 2004 *AHR Act* gave Health Canada sweeping authority to create regulations pertaining to clinical intervention, and included a framework for licensing and monitoring fertility clinics. This capacity was significantly reduced by the 2010 *Reference re Assisted Human Reproduction Act*, which found much of this regulatory and licensing power unconstitutional. However, the federal government retains a minor role in clinical intervention policy. For example, several of the criminal prohibitions contained in the *AHR Act* pertain to clinical intervention: Section 7 of the *Act* bans any "offer to purchase or advertise for the purchase of" sperm, eggs, or embryos; sections 8(1) and 8(3) ban the "use of human reproductive material for the purpose of creating an embryo" and "the use of an *in vitro* embryo for any purpose" without a donor's written consent; and section 9 bans the use of such material from a minor. In 2007, Health Canada passed the *Assisted Human Reproduction (Section 8 Consent) Regulations*, which outline the required consent procedures for the donation and use of reproductive material (*Assisted Human Reproduction (Section 8 Consent) Regulations*, SOR/2007–137). Collectively, these prohibitions and regulations primarily target the behaviour of prospective patients and donors. In 2017, Health Canada released a set of policy proposals after consulting with stakeholders to introduce additional regulations that would add specificity and bring into force sections of the *AHR Act* related to processing and importation of human reproductive material, reimbursement of expenditures, and enforcement. However, these policy proposals have yet to become enshrined in law.

Under the Harper Conservatives (2006–15), the federal government was criticized for inaction on assisted reproduction (see Snow, Baylis, and Downie 2015). However, it did make one potentially significant change to clinical intervention policy in 2012. In *Reference re Assisted Human Reproduction Act*, the Supreme Court had found section 10 – which banned the use, importation, and distribution of human reproductive material without regulations and a license – to be an unconstitutional violation of provincial jurisdiction. Parliament subsequently amended the *AHR Act* in 2012. This amendment, created to "reduce the risks to human health and safety," prohibits the use, distribution, and importation of human reproductive material unless it meets a series of health requirements and is done in accordance with a regulation. As regulations have not yet been created, the new section 10 has not yet come into force (Bill C-38; see chapter 4).

There are additional federal provisions regarding clinical intervention, all of which fall under the category of clinical policies. The *Processing and Distribution of Semen for Assisted Conception Regulations* prohibit the importation and distribution of semen unless it has undergone rigorous testing, screening, and a period of quarantine. Health Canada also inspects fertility clinics every three years, in a process one fertility physician claimed is fairly rigorous; as this physician said in an interview, "they come here looking for trouble" (Interview 2012b). Overall, the federal government's role in clinical intervention is essentially limited to a directive regarding the processing of semen, mandatory inspection of fertility clinics by Health Canada, regulations concerning consent for reproductive material, not-yet-in-force prohibitions on the use of human reproductive material, and prohibitions on payment for human gametes. After the 2010 Supreme Court reference, provinces have jurisdiction over the vast majority of the clinical intervention subfield.

Provincial Clinical Intervention Policy

In spite of the Supreme Court's wide grant of provincial jurisdiction in 2010, only Quebec and Ontario have implemented clinical intervention policy in any significant manner. Several other provinces include artificial insemination (AI) or intrauterine insemination (IUI) under their health insurance plans, including British Columbia, Saskatchewan, Prince Edward Island, and Newfoundland and Labrador. Certain medical procedures related to IVF such as blood tests, ultrasounds, and diagnostic tests may also be covered. However, the more costly components of clinical intervention – such as IVF, ICSI, fertility drugs, gamete and embryo storage, and preimplantation genetic diagnosis (PGD) – are not covered in these provinces. Other provinces offer grants and tax relief: In 2010, Manitoba introduced the Fertility Treatment Tax Credit, which permits patients to claim up to $20,000 in eligible expenses from fertility drugs and treatment for a maximum credit of $8,000. New Brunswick offers a one-time grant of 50 per cent of fertility treatment costs for patients, up to a maximum of $5,000 (Manitoba 2013; New Brunswick 2014). Most provinces cover some form of infertility testing, including sperm counts and ultrasounds.

There was also a study to explore the possibility of clinical intervention policy in Alberta. In February 2013, the Government of Alberta commissioned a nearly 500-page study from the School of Public Health at the University of Alberta to examine whether the province should regulate and fund assisted reproduction procedures (Alberta Health 2014). The government has yet to officially respond with any policy. In 2013, Guichon, Mitchell, and Doig (2013, 232) conducted email correspondence with government officials in Ontario, British Columbia, Alberta, Manitoba, and Nova Scotia, and concluded at the time that "none has plans to regulate assisted human reproduction or is prepared to report that it has such plans." Ontario has since introduced policy, although the first province to do so was Quebec.

Quebec's Clinical Intervention Policy

In June 2009, Quebec's National Assembly passed Bill C-26, *An Act respecting Clinical and Research Activities relating to Assisted Procreation*. This legislation covered much of clinical intervention by combining clinical policies and coverage policies. It provided that assisted reproduction must occur in licensed centres that provide annual reports, with licenses issued by the provincial Minister of Health and Social Services. The legislation also granted licensing and general regulatory powers to the Minister, and mandated that centres must be accredited by a body recognized by the Minister. Although the law requires clinics to produce annual reports and maintain databases, it does not contain any policies specifically targeting donors. As a result, donor identification remains governed by internal rules from the Collège des médecins du Québec, which, like other provincial colleges, maintains donor anonymity due to concerns about the privacy of patients' health information (*An Act respecting Clinical and Research Activities relating to Assisted Procreation*; see also Ogbogu 2011, 180).

In 2010, Quebec passed the *Regulation respecting Clinical Activities related to Assisted Procreation*, which provided additional clinical intervention policies by defining acceptable clinical practices. The regulation limited PGD to the identification of serious diseases and abnormalities and mandated free and informed consent for donors and patients, thus adding a small policy to the primarily federally regulated subfield of screening/enhancement policy. Most notably, it contained conditions for single embryo transfer during IVF by mandating single embryo transfer for women thirty-five and under, permitting up to two embryos for women aged thirty-six, and up to three for women thirty-seven years or older (*Regulation Respecting Clinical Activities Related to Assisted Procreation*, s. 17). In the same year, Quebec amended its *Regulation respecting the Application of the Health Insurance Act*, which stipulates the procedures covered under Quebec's public health insurance, to include comprehensive fertility coverage. The regulation covered the costs for clinical intervention procedures such as artificial insemination, and it covered the full costs for up to three stimulated cycles of IVF or six non-stimulated cycles for all women of childbearing age, whether at a private clinic or a public hospital (Bissonnette et al. 2011). Quebec's Public Prescription Drug Insurance Plan, which is only available to Quebec citizens who are ineligible for a private plan, also covers fertility drugs.

Proponents of Quebec's legislation linked the two primary aspects – clinical policies mandating single embryo transfer and coverage policies that paid for fertility treatment – as a single package, inseparable aspects of the same plan. The logic was essentially presented as follows: first, because IVF is so expensive, patients will want as many embryos transferred as possible to ensure success, and this increases the likelihood of multiple births. Second, multiple births, because of complications that arise and the likelihood of premature birth, are an expensive drain on the public health-care system, and therefore ought to be limited. The most efficient way to reduce multiple births is through public funding of IVF. If patients do not actually pay for IVF, there will be fewer incentives to transfer multiple embryos. For both ethical reasons (fewer multiple births) and financial ones (stemming from fewer multiple births), IVF should be funded by the state. Quebec's multiple pregnancy rate immediately dropped from 25.6 per cent to 3.7 per cent for the three months after the program's initiation, an outcome touted by many as proof of increased savings (Bissonnette et al. 2011).

The argument connecting funding to reduced multiple births was championed by fertility physicians, for whom the policy undoubtedly increased the supply of patients. As one physician noted in response to a question about whether the government should fund IVF, "I think the government should do it; it's not only the right thing to do to help build families, but it's also the smart thing to do because you can make safer pregnancies and healthier babies" (Interview 2012b). Yet as Erin Nelson (2013, 288) notes, "the profession is in essence asking the government to pay to solve a problem that the profession is responsible for creating." If medical associations or regulatory colleges were truly convinced that anything other than single embryo transfer were unethical, they would create internal regulations mandating strict single embryo transfer, as indeed they have begun to do. Moreover, if Quebec were truly concerned that rogue physicians would continue multiple embryo transfer in spite of clinical guidelines, then the government could mandate single embryo transfer regardless of whether it also included public funding. As Cattapan (2015) argues, "Single-embryo transfer is widely recognized as the best practice for IVF, and should be practiced everywhere, regardless of who foots the bill."[26]

Not long after it was introduced, the financial prudence of Quebec's policy was questioned. In 2013, Quebec's Minister of Health announced the government was reviewing the policy, which was costing the province roughly $60 million per year. In November 2014, Quebec introduced Bill 20, which removed public funding for IVF. The initial bill proposed to restrict access to IVF treatment to women between the ages of eighteen and forty-two; require women undergoing IVF to take a psychological evaluation; and impose fines on physicians who advised their patients to receive IVF in other provinces. The bill also introduced the provisions for single embryo transfer, which were previously regulatory, into formal legislation. Overall, the bill maintained or introduced restrictions on physician practice but removed the carrot of publicly funded IVF. Unsurprisingly, it was criticized by physicians, not just for its coverage policies, but also for the restrictive new clinical policies that would fine physicians and require women to undertake a psychological evaluation. In November 2015, an amended bill was passed with two key changes: first, women over the age of forty-two would be permitted to receive privately funded IVF; second, the government introduced a sliding tax credit for IVF, permitting citizens with less than $50,000 in family income to receive up to 80 per cent of treatment costs (higher earners can still receive up to 20 per cent). Coverage for artificial insemination remains, as does the controversial requirement

---

26 Some fertility physicians were not even aware that provinces could introduce restrictions unrelated to funding. I asked one physician about what would happen if his/her province introduced regulations for clinical care (such as limiting embryo transfer) without introducing simultaneous health-insurance coverage. This physician answered, "I don't think [the province] can do that," at least when it came to private IVF clinics. This statement says as much about the extent to which provinces have stayed out of clinical policymaking as it does about physician attitudes, as this particular physician erroneously thought governments simply could not legislate for clinical practice (Interview 2012a).

for psychological evaluations for women undergoing IVF (CBC News 2015a). While Quebec's IVF funding policy experiment lasted only five years, its rules for clinical practice remain, proving that provinces can legislate single embryo transfer without funding IVF – albeit while running the risk of angering physicians.

Ontario's Clinical Intervention Policy

Until recently, Quebec was the only province to experiment with funding IVF in the new millennium. However, Ontario had fully covered IVF under public insurance from 1985 to 1994 – well before its use became mainstream – provided it was performed in a hospital or a clinic associated with a hospital. Ontario amended its policy in 1994 by limiting public funding to three IVF cycles only for women with completely blocked or absent fallopian tubes, and for intrauterine insemination (IUI) for all women. In 2009, an Expert Panel on Infertility and Adoption recommended that Ontario fund three cycles of IVF for all women under the age of forty-two, as well as fund ICSI and the freezing and storage of surplus embryos. Like Quebec, it made the case based on the connection between IVF funding and reduced embryo transfer. The panel claimed that funding IVF would "save the Province money by reducing the financial burden that high-risk pregnancies and multiple births have on the health care system," and justified the claim with rhetorical flourish: "Ontario cannot afford NOT to fund assisted reproduction" (Ontario Ministry of Children and Youth Services 2009, 118).

The panel's recommendation sat on the shelf for five years, but in April 2014, the Health Minister announced that the provincial government would "contribute to the costs" of one cycle of IVF for patients, and would establish an advisory body to "provide advice on the establishment of a quality framework to promote safe and high quality infertility services, including single embryo transfer" (Ontario 2014). In October 2015, the government announced the details of program, which would fund a single cycle of IVF for all women with Ontario health insurance under the age of forty-three. The funding would be tied to single embryo transfer, and the transfer of any surplus embryos would also be funded in subsequent cycles. Beginning in December 2015, the province began funding eligible clinics across the province at an estimated cost of $50 million per year, with the goal of offering funding to 5,000 patients; this was set to rise to $100 million per year and 9,000 patients in 2017. The program also covers artificial insemination, intrauterine insemination, and one cycle of fertility preservation, which includes egg/sperm freezing for medical purposes. Clinics are responsible for managing wait lists (Cattapan 2015; CBC News 2015c; Ontario 2016a; Racco 2016).

Ontario's IVF funding is similar to Quebec's in certain ways. It contains both clinical policies (single embryo transfer) and coverage policies (funding one cycle of IVF for women under the age of forty-three). However, in each respect it is less extensive. Ontario's rules for embryo transfer and age limits apply only to publicly funded procedures; physicians can still use multiple embryo transfer for IVF that is not being funded by the province, and can also provide for-profit IVF to women forty-three and older. With respect to the funding itself, Ontario's single cycle differs from Quebec's, which had covered three stimulated and six unstimulated cycles of IVF. Moreover, the funding is channelled through individual contracts with fertility clinics rather than through the Ontario Health Insurance Plan (Ontario 2016a). Ontario also does not fund fertility drugs. Finally, by setting a cap of 5,000 cycles – set to rise to 9,000 in 2017 – Ontario's program does not risk the cost overruns that plagued Quebec's system. However, it has set up "an almost instant logjam": in May 2016, it was reported that clinic caseloads have nearly doubled, and in November 2016 one physician reported having a five-year wait list for publicly funded treatment (Blackwell 2016; Racco 2016).

One other element of Ontario's clinical intervention policy is notable: the extent to which it engaged in selective "policy learning" based on the Quebec experience. On the one hand, one could argue that Ontario did not learn anything from Quebec's experience: just as Quebec was scaling down its funding, Ontario introduced its program. On the other hand, Ontario's decision to limit funding to $50 million per year by funding a maximum of one cycle for 5,000 patients suggests it learned from Quebec's experience, deliberately deciding to constrain supply and reduce access compared with Quebec. While many have criticized the policy for turning IVF access into a lottery (CBC News 2015b; Racco 2016), its cap on patients should prevent costs from escalating as Quebec's policy did.

Medical Self-Regulation of Clinical Intervention

Compared with other policy fields, government involvement in medical practice tends to be minimal due to the level of technical expertise and the high social status accorded to physicians. In Canada, provinces have primary authority to create health and medical policy, but they delegate a range of powers over rulemaking, education, licensure, monitoring, enforcement, and sanctions to provincial colleges of physicians and surgeons. Provinces take one of two approaches to health-care delegation. Under "umbrella" legislation, such as Ontario's *Regulated Health Professions Act*, a single piece of legislation provides a framework for all self-governing health professions and enumerates the professions to which it applies. Under the "traditional" approach, each health profession is regulated through a separate piece of legislation; Saskatchewan, for example, has over twenty statutes regulating the different health professions, including the *Medical Practitioners Act* for physicians. In either case, statutory self-regulation means medical colleges are the primary policymakers for the clinical intervention subfield of assisted reproduction in every Canadian province; they issue licenses to allow physicians to practise medicine, maintain and monitor standards of practice, inspect clinics, produce ethical and clinical guidelines, and conduct disciplinary hearings for professional misconduct (Epps 2011). One physician noted that inspections performed by provincial colleges tend to be less arduous than Health Canada's: when the provincial college inspects clinics, it is "more of an accreditation; it makes sure you're doing your documentation properly, you're getting your ultrasound machines updated on a regular basis, that the things you're reporting are actually happening, that your employees are trained" (Interview 2012b).

However, the main professional guidelines governing assisted reproduction do not come from provincial medical colleges. Many colleges do have policies that affect fertility centres; the College of Physicians and Surgeons of British Columbia runs an accreditation program for fertility centres, and the College of Physicians and Surgeons of Ontario revised its Out-of-Hospital Premises Inspection Policy (OHPIP) in December 2016 (College of Physicians and Surgeons of Ontario 2016; Scotti 2016). However, only the College of Physicians and Surgeons of Alberta (2011) and the College of Physicians and Surgeons of Saskatchewan (2015) have created actual guidelines for assisted reproduction. These guidelines outline qualifications for medical directors, physicians performing IVF, and support staff. They also stipulate screening tests for patients, mandate written rules for surgical and non-surgical procedures, and describe the details regarding patient records, including consent forms and the number of gametes and embryos retrieved. At only 5–6 pages long, however, the guidelines are far from comprehensive; they "lack any description of process and values" and do not even reference the *AHR Act* (Guichon, Mitchell, and Doig 2013, 327, 330). Physicians interviewed for this study confirmed this. One physician claimed that "my experience with the colleges is that they try not to get too involved with policy things, they see themselves as policing good practices" (Interview 2011b). A physician from a different province similarly said that his college recently "got out of the policy business," preferring to rely on national specialist guidelines for clinical intervention (Interview 2012a).

Unlike most provincial colleges, the Society of Obstetricians and Gynaecologists of Canada (SOGC) and the Canadian Fertility and Andrology Society (CFAS), two national specialist associations, have created guidelines that inform clinical practice for assisted reproduction. Relying on such organizations does not necessarily mean professional abdication. Between SOGC and CFAS, there are many guidelines related to assisted reproduction, including but not limited to advanced reproductive age and fertility, elective single embryo transfer following IVF, diagnosis and management of ovarian hyperstimulation syndrome, fertility preservation in women of reproductive age, and the number of embryos transferred. These organizations also have several guidelines on prenatal screening (including PGD) and embryonic research. In May 2016, CFAS provided an extensive update to its third-party reproduction guidelines, which include sections on the law, legal counsel, infectious disease screening, surrogacy, and gamete donation, among others (Canadian Fertility and Andrology Society 2016b; Society of Obstetricians and Gynaecologists of Canada 2016).

These guidelines – which cover all health professionals involved with assisted reproduction – are comprehensive, specific, and frequently updated. They date back to the late 1990s, when SOGC and CFAS produced a joint assisted reproduction policy statement that outlined clinical guidelines for sperm sorting, egg donation, ICSI, PGD, donor screening, embryonic research, and surrogacy (Canadian Fertility and Andrology Society and Society of Obstetricians and Gynaecologists of Canada 1999). Moreover, most private clinics voluntarily adhere to accreditation standards set by Accreditation Canada, a non-profit health accreditation organization (Scotti 2016). Fertility clinics have become increasingly (though by no means fully) transparent in terms of data collection; Canadian clinics offering IVF, intracytoplasmic sperm injection (ICSI), and frozen embryo transfer (FET) voluntarily contribute detailed information on children born through assisted reproduction to the Canadian Assisted Reproductive Technologies Register Plus (CARTR Plus), with thirty-four out of thirty-six Canadian IVF centres voluntarily submitting data in 2015 (Canadian Fertility and Andrology Society 2016b). CARTR Plus data on aspects such as live birth rates, multiple pregnancy rates, and overall success rates are published on the CFAS website, and frequently in academic journals such as the *Journal of Obstetrics and Gynaecology Canada*.

The existence of clinical guidelines and the CARTR Plus register has not assuaged critics of self-regulation in Canada because such reporting remains entirely voluntary and is not subject to government oversight, and the register does not identify individual clinics. These critics stress how self-regulating physicians could be inclined towards under-regulation, as the motivation for profits in the fertility industry may outweigh ethical concerns in the absence of criminal sanctions. American scholar Aaron D. Levine (2010, 49), for example, has compiled evidence that donor agencies and wealthy recipients often ignore the American Society for Reproductive Medicine (ASRM) guidelines regarding compensation for egg donors, in part because "violating the ethical guidelines has few serious consequences." In the Canadian context, Erin Nelson (2013, 264–5) notes an obvious tension between the physicians' obligation "to protect their patients' confidences" and "the need to regulate the use of these technologies in the interests of patients and the wider public." Similarly, Guichon, Mitchell, and Doig (2013, 335–6) stress that "physician colleges ought not to be placed in the position of being the only regulators of assisted human reproduction" because of "inherent conflicts of interest between the physician as caregiver and physician as manager of an economic enterprise" (see also Downie and Baylis 2013). Health Canada's 1996 report that many physicians were not following the voluntary moratorium on certain practices demonstrates that public policy cannot always rely on professional goodwill with respect to clinical intervention (see chapter 3).

By contrast, proponents of self-regulation in general stress that it can create a more flexible, adaptable, and financially efficient governance structure compared with outright state regulation, as administrative costs are often internalized by self-regulating professions (Ogus 1995, 97–8; Vrielink, van Montfort, and Bokhorst 2011, 490). As Gunningham and Rees (1997, 380) note, when a self-regulated profession develops an "industrial morality" – part of which includes an expectation of obedience – non-statutory guidelines can be "remarkably effective in guiding and controlling industry conduct," even when they lack the sanctioning power associated with statutory law. Others favour self-regulation in clinical intervention precisely because the policies produced by medical professionals are more likely to be permissive. As Rogerio A. Lobo of the ASRM wrote in 2011, comparative government regulations often include "prohibiting in vitro fertilization, allowing its use only for married couples, prohibiting treatments for single or gay patients, and denying a woman compensation for the effort, pain and inconvenience associated with being an oocyte donor" (652). Whether because of the desire for profits, the Hippocratic oath, or some combination of the two, when barriers to assisted reproduction exist, those barriers tend to be produced by governments, not professional organizations.[27]

Certainly, medical self-regulatory guidelines are not as effective as government policy. The criminal law is the most effective, albeit the bluntest, instrument to deter behaviour: fertility specialists are highly unlikely to go underground or openly perform activities that would put them in jail. Non-criminal policy changes can also have an important impact on clinical practice, as shown by Quebec's rapid drop in multiple pregnancies following the regulation of single embryo transfer (Bissonnette et al. 2011). Fertility physicians interviewed for this study recognized that certain clinics and physicians do not always abide by professional guidelines. One physician claimed, "You'd be hard pressed in Canada not to follow the guidelines; you get into trouble with the lawyers." But this physician also admitted, "There are a few guys who are pushing the envelope, that's for sure," attributing this to both "competition" between clinics and "personalities" of individual clinicians (Interview 2012b). Another physician echoed the recognition that "in a place like Canada ... we have competition, not just between provinces but between clinics within provinces. So there will always be those clinics that don't follow the recommendations" (Interview 2011b).

On the other hand, there is evidence that voluntary guidelines can be effective. One American study (Stern et al. 2007) attributed a dramatic

---

27 While rare, it is not unheard of that medical organizations will come out in favour of stricter legislation. In 2001, the Slovenian government introduced an amendment to liberalize assisted reproduction policy by making single women eligible for fertility services. The National Organization of Physicians opposed the law. The law was passed, but was subsequently subject to a referendum. Again, the National Organization of Physicians – along with the Professional College for Gynecology and several religious organizations – opposed the law, which was eventually struck down by popular vote (Rothmayr Allison and Varone 2009, 442–3).

decrease in multiple pregnancies through IVF to the introduction of the ASRM's voluntary guidelines, while Australia's non-statutory ethical guidelines coincided with the highest proportion of singleton deliveries ever reported (Cook et al. 2011, 164–5; National Health and Medical Research Council 2007; Williams 2011). Canada is no exception: the high rate of reporting for the CARTR Plus register indicates some professional buy-in has occurred, while multiple pregnancies following assisted reproduction have dropped – not as rapidly as in Quebec, but still significantly – from 32 per cent in 2009 to 13.3 per cent in 2014, a period that maps onto CFAS's 2013 guidelines for single embryo transfer (Canadian Fertility and Andrology Society 2016a; Min and Sylvestre 2013). While it is difficult to impute cause and effect given contemporaneous clinical and technological improvements, the evidence certainly suggests that an "industrial morality" may have developed in Canada, and that professional self-regulation ought not be ignored as a policy-making lever affecting clinical intervention.

Court-Ordered Clinical Intervention Policy?
The Case of Donor Anonymity

Much of Canada's assisted reproduction policy has been shaped by judicial decisions, both from the Supreme Court of Canada in 2010 and from several provincial court decisions related to parentage. Yet the judiciary also had a preliminary and nearly crucial influence on one aspect of clinical intervention policy: donor anonymity. Donor policies target the behaviour of donors, patients, and children born through assisted reproduction. Along with screening requirements for patients, the most important consideration for donors is whether their identifying information must be released to donor-conceived offspring. Without legislation, the default rules for patient-physician confidentiality typically apply, which tend to favour donor anonymity; if a sperm donor[28] does not wish his identifying information to be released to his offspring, then it will not be released unless legislation dictates otherwise. Currently, every province in Canada operates under conditions

---

28 Anonymous gamete donation occurs with both sperm and eggs. However, because of the expense, time, invasiveness, and health risks associated with egg donation, sperm donation is far more common.

that permit donor anonymity, and physicians typically destroy patient records for sperm donors after five or six years.

Olivia Pratten sought to end donor anonymity in Canada. Born in 1982, Pratten was conceived via artificial insemination at a Vancouver fertility clinic. In the absence of government legislation, internal rules from the College of Physicians and Surgeons of British Columbia (CPSBC) meant Pratten was unable to receive identifying information about the sperm donor, her biological father. She and others had lobbied for federal legislation to ban anonymity and mandate identifying donor information, which offspring would then be able to locate after a certain time. Initially, it seemed as if her efforts would be successful. Although the 2001 draft legislation presented to the Brown Committee originally contained a provision to maintain donor anonymity, Pratten appeared before the Committee to convince legislators otherwise, claiming that "there is no ethical, moral, or legal justification for allowing an anonymous sperm system to operate, or any other gamete donation system" (Canada 2001j, 1135). Barry Stevens, another donor offspring and member of the Alliance of People Produced by Assisted Reproductive Technology, articulated the threefold opposition to donor anonymity: "It deprives us of essential medical information; it promotes a culture of deception and secrecy; and it leaves a gap in the formation of a person's identity" (Canada 2001j, 1200).

The Committee was receptive to Pratten's and Stevens's claims. Liberal Committee chair Bonnie Brown reflected, "We pretty well all agreed we're against this anonymity thing … The whole committee, as a matter of fact, I think is unanimous." Canadian Alliance MP James Lunney noted that he and others on the Committee were "quite interested in making sure the needs of the children are adequately protected" (Canada 2001o, 1925). In the end, the Committee's final report argued that federal legislation should remove donor anonymity. The majority report stated, "Where there is a conflict between the privacy rights of a donor and the rights of a resulting child to know its heritage, the rights of the child should prevail … We want to end the current system of anonymous donation" (Canada 2001p, 21). The Canadian Alliance,[29]

29 In fact, the Canadian Alliance dissenting report claimed the majority was not emphatic enough in its rejection of anonymity; it called for "a clear statement to the effect that where the privacy rights of the donors of human reproductive materials conflict with the rights of children to know their genetic and social heritage, that the rights of the children shall prevail" (Canada 2001p, 81).

New Democratic Party, and Bloc Québécois all echoed the sentiment in their dissenting reports, although the Progressive Conservative dissenting statement had "extremely strong reservations about doing away with anonymity" (93).

However, this near-unanimous recommendation did not make its way into subsequent legislation, which maintained anonymity but allowed the disclosure of certain health-related information. Section 18(3) of the *AHR Act* permitted Assisted Human Reproduction Canada, "on request," to "disclose health reporting information relating to a donor" to offspring," but added that "the identity of the donor – or information that can reasonably be expected to be used in the identification of the donor – shall not be disclosed without the donor's written consent." The disconnect between the Committee recommendations and the legislation can be explained in a few ways. On the one hand, one pediatric physician noted that in committee hearings that took place after the Brown Report, certain committee members "brought in two infertile women to tell their sob stories, and [then] they got rid of the ... provision [to remove anonymity]" (Interview 2012c). While the explanation is likely not that straightforward, one member of Parliament did claim to have been "appalled" at the Standing Committee on Health's lack of consultation with patients: "They didn't hear properly from the infertility community; they hadn't heard what it meant from the people who it meant the most to" (Interview 2011f). This was rectified, in part, after the Brown Report by bringing in infertile individuals to testify about their experiences and the extent to which removing anonymity could reduce the supply of reproductive material.

While the influence of infertile witnesses likely played a part in removing the provisions that would have mandated the provision of donor information, federalism was also important. Ian Shugart, the Assistant Deputy Minister for Health, claimed at committee that "the conditions conducive to the mandatory release of donor identification are not yet in place in Canada," and that removing anonymity "gets very much into the domain of the federal-provincial environment," particularly regarding family law. Federal government lawyer Glenn Rivard similarly noted during C-56 hearings that regulating donor anonymity was "really not an authority that the federal government has" (Canada 2002b, 1220). Essentially, government officials argued that rules regarding the anonymity and identification of donors were provincial jurisdiction. In light of the Supreme Court reference in 2010, which found section 18 *ultra vires* the federal Parliament, they were correct.

Although the *AHR Act* provided for the establishment of a Personal Health Information Registry to create a national database for information pertaining to donors, patients, and donor-conceived offspring, this federal registry was never created. Following the *Reference re Assisted Human Reproduction Act* (2010), such registries, if they are to exist, must now be created and maintained by the provinces. Pratten was not content with a non-identifying registry; having failed to convince the federal and provincial governments, she turned to the courts, arguing that the *Canadian Charter of Rights and Freedoms* required permanent preservation of patient records in the case of sperm donation. Initially, Pratten launched her legal challenge against both the Province of British Columbia and the CPSBC, whose rules regarding donor anonymity and destruction of records were the default policy in the absence of legislation. In 2010, an agreement was reached between Pratten and the CPSBC, stating that the College would amend its bylaws in the case of a Pratten victory. Consequently, Pratten's action against the College was dismissed, and her case focused solely on the government (*Pratten v. British Columbia* 2011, para. 22).

In May 2011, Justice Elaine Adair of the Supreme Court of British Columbia found much of British Columbia's *Adoption Act* and *Adoption Regulation* unconstitutional. Justice Adair accepted Pratten's submission that the provincial government's adoption policy – which gave adopted children access to the medical history of their biological parents – was "underinclusive" for not giving similar protections to children born through assisted reproduction. Accordingly, this violated the equality rights of donor-conceived children by subjecting them to unfair discrimination (para. 251). Justice Adair gave the province fifteen months to rewrite the legislation to grant equal information access to donor-conceived offspring. She also granted a permanent injunction "prohibiting the destruction, disposal, redaction or transfer" of gamete donor records from British Columbia (para. 335).[30] Justice Adair effectively mandated provincial action, rejecting medical professional guidelines as insufficient: "I do not think that practices developed by private service providers, however excellent or thoughtful or thorough, can be a full answer to the circumstances of donor offspring"; she also added that "the circumstances of donor offspring ... are too important

---

30 Justice Adair rejected Pratten's argument that the *Charter's* section 7 guarantee of "life, liberty and security of the person" gave Olivia Pratten a "constitutional right to know where she comes from." Adair held that "the potential implications of a free-standing constitutional right to know one's biological origins are uncertain and may be enormous" (paras. 273, 290).

to leave unregulated" and that "the private sector cannot provide an adequate substitute for government protection and regulation" (paras. 177, 210). Although the records of Pratten's own biological father had been destroyed long before the case, the result was a victory for donor-conceived offspring in British Columbia.

However, this victory was short-lived. In 2012, the Court of Appeal for British Columbia overturned the decision. The Court found that the government's adoption legislation and regulation qualified under section 15(2) of the *Charter* as an ameliorative program that targeted a disadvantaged group (*Pratten v. British Columbia* 2012, paras. 34–43). Essentially, section 15(2) permits affirmative-action-type policies that are aimed at reducing the burdens of a historically disadvantaged group, even if that program discriminates against others. Because British Columbia's permissive adoption regime was designed to aid adopted children (who themselves had faced historical disadvantage), Justice Frankel found that it qualified "as an ameliorative program within the meaning of s. 15(2)" and was thus constitutional (para. 37). Pratten appealed this ruling to the Supreme Court of Canada, which in May 2013 denied her leave to appeal. For now, donor anonymity remains the default framework in every Canadian province.

While Olivia Pratten was ultimately unsuccessful, her initial victory at the trial level suggests that, in the absence of government policy, courts are not afraid to mandate state action with respect to clinical intervention. *Pratten* is not the only near miss in this regard: in 1999 the Nova Scotia Court of Appeal rejected an argument that Nova Scotia's failure to cover IVF and ICSI was an unconstitutional violation of the *Canadian Charter of Rights and Freedoms* (*Cameron v. Nova Scotia* 1999). Like *Pratten*, the case was ultimately unsuccessful, but a majority of justices did recognize that infertility constitutes a disability under section 15(1) of the *Charter*; a similar case could conceivably arise in other provinces as infertility becomes a growing social concern. There will likely be disputes surrounding the ownership of human gametes and embryos as well. In 2012, the Supreme Court of British Columbia ruled that sperm obtained by a lesbian couple from an anonymous donor had to be split evenly in a custody case, holding that the sperm was "property" and that additional consent regulations did not need to be addressed (*J.C.M. v. A.N.A.* 2012; see also Gruben and Cameron 2013). As debates continue surrounding the limits of health insurance coverage, the use of human reproductive material, and the role of donors in the process of clinical intervention, the judiciary will remain front and centre in the subfield of clinical intervention.

Conclusion

In 1993, the Royal Commission on New Reproductive Technologies wrote that it was "unrealistic to expect self-regulating professional bodies, or the provinces, individually or together, to provide the necessary level of regulation and control" (12) for the governance of fertility clinics – what I have termed "clinical intervention" policy. Whether the Royal Commission was correct depends on how one defines "necessary." As with surrogacy and parentage, the 2010 Supreme Court reference means that the primarily provincial subfield of clinical intervention is subject to considerable variation depending on the province. In most provinces, provincial policy is non-existent; only Quebec and Ontario have engaged in any form of substantive policymaking by combining health insurance coverage for IVF with clinical rules for single embryo transfer, albeit with different approaches. Notably, both provinces initially implemented the "stick" of clinical policies (proscribing multiple embryo transfer in certain situations) at the same time as the "carrot" of coverage policy (paying for IVF and consequently increasing patient demand for fertility services). Although Quebec later restricted much of its IVF funding, these two provinces' clinical intervention policies, combined with their clear rules for surrogacy and parentage policy, demonstrate that provinces have the capacity to comprehensively regulate assisted reproduction policy.

Yet most provinces have opted not to act. More than six years after the Supreme Court reference, the policy subfield is subject to a myriad of policies from the federal government, provincial governments, and a variety of medical organizations, including provincial regulatory colleges and national specialist associations. For most aspects of clinical intervention in most provinces, policy is set by medical organizations. This is not unusual with policy affecting medical practice: because of the high degree of autonomy granted to the medical profession and the technical expertise required to make policy, provincial governments have long delegated regulatory power to provincial colleges of physicians and surgeons. Yet a closer look demonstrates that provincial colleges engage in minimal clinical intervention policymaking apart from brief, vague guidelines in Alberta and Saskatchewan. Instead, voluntary guidelines set by national specialist associations remain de facto policies governing clinical intervention. These guidelines lack the force of government intervention, and tend to be more permissive than government policy. Yet there is also evidence of growing professional buy-in, as demonstrated by a dramatic drop in multiple pregnancies in recent years and the high rate of reporting to the anonymized CARTR Plus register. While professional guidelines, sanctions, and monitoring are considerably more opaque than government policy, they nevertheless seem to constrain physician behaviour in important ways.

Why has there not been more government involvement in clinical intervention policy since the 2010 Supreme Court reference? One reason might be the medicalized frame accepted by a majority of Supreme Court justices. By characterizing assisted reproduction as "a burgeoning field of medical practice and research that ... brings benefits to many Canadians," and the day-to-day work at fertility clinics as "a specific type of health services provided in health-care institutions by health-care professionals" (*Reference re Assisted Human Reproduction Act* 2010, paras. 251, 227), the majority further entrenched the position, long held by medical organizations in Canada, that the most important thing the government can do to help patients build families is to leave clinical intervention rulemaking to the experts. Since the time of the Royal Commission, physicians and scientists have engaged in "boundary work" by "negotiat[ing] and maintain[ing] the boundaries that delineate their activities and spheres of influence and authority" over assisted reproduction (Scala 2007, 213). The Supreme Court's acceptance of the medical-scientific framing of the clinical intervention aspects of assisted reproduction – consistent with the way these aspects were framed by federal policymakers from 1993 to 2004 – has further entrenched the primacy of medical professional authority.

This produces a paradox of sorts. When the Supreme Court adopts a socially liberal approach to "moral issues" in division of power disputes, as a majority of justices did in the 2010 reference, provincial authority vis-à-vis the federal Parliament increases. Because provinces have primary authority over health and medicine, they have an incentive to frame legislation that straddles the health care/criminal line as "merely medical." However, by framing assisted reproduction as medical and clinical intervention as inherently beneficial, provinces strengthen the boundaries that medical and scientific communities have long drawn: that issues of health and medicine, particularly those that take place in the clinic, ought to be subject to minimal government regulation. Thus, in addition to limiting Parliament's legal authority to legislate for clinical intervention, one of the unintended consequences of the Supreme Court reference may have been to limit provincial legislatures' normative authority to legislate as well.

Chapter 7

Making Sense of Canadian Assisted Reproduction Policy

In describing the trajectory and development of Canadian assisted reproduction policy, this study has drawn from a Royal Commission, parliamentary debates, Supreme Court jurisprudence, lower court decisions, professional medical guidelines, and provincial and federal laws. This final chapter brings this information together to make sense of Canadian assisted reproduction policy, and to draw lessons for scholars, policymakers, and practitioners alike.

The first question this book sought to answer was, Why was the federal government so unsuccessful in its major attempt to create assisted reproduction policy? The answer stems from the framing strategy used by the 1993 Royal Commission on New Reproductive Technologies, which constitutes the critical juncture for Canadian policy development. The way the Royal Commission defined the emerging field and structured the debate – how it combined an ambivalent substantive frame with a national jurisdictional frame – explains much about the federal government's failed attempts at regulating assisted reproduction, and why a majority of Supreme Court justices found much of the *Assisted Human Reproduction Act* unconstitutional in 2010. This framing strategy has also influenced the second line of inquiry considered in this book: What exactly is Canadian assisted reproduction policy today? In comparative terms, how should it be classified? Using the restrictive-intermediate-permissive terminology from past comparative studies of assisted reproduction (Bleiklie, Goggin, and Rothmayr 2004; Engeli, Green-Pedersen, and Larsen 2012), I argue Canada's assisted reproduction policy remains comparatively "intermediate," as Éric Montpetit (2007) found prior to the Supreme Court reference. However, for a field as encompassing as assisted reproduction, a one-size-fits-all

characterization obscures important variation between the assisted reproduction subfields and among provinces. In the early part of this
chapter, I break down the content of assisted reproduction policy in
the six subfields when all policymakers have been taken into account,
and find that although there is variation between (and even within)
subfields, most can still be classified as comparatively intermediate.

The complexity of assisted reproduction policy in Canada provides
several lessons, many of which speak to the value of studying political
science from an institutional perspective. In Canada specifically, the big-
gest lesson is the enduring influence of federal institutional constraints
on policymakers, and the extent to which jurisdictional framing strategies can affect policy outputs in unanticipated ways. Comparatively,
the Canadian story provides valuable contributions for scholars using a
historical institutional lens. In particular, the interaction between policy
framing and institutional structures can provide fruitful explanation of
policy outcomes. Dominant frames can clearly influence the development of political institutions, especially during states of policy flux such
as the critical juncture period of Canada's Royal Commission. Finally,
for scholars of assisted reproduction specifically, the six-part typology
and the focus on additional policymakers can provide a more accurate
picture of a country's overall policy mix. As social scientists move forward with comparative measurement of assisted reproduction policy,
this framework demonstrates the value of disaggregating the subfields
of assisted reproduction policy and measuring them individually.

The Royal Commission: The First Mover of Assisted Reproduction Policy

To understand Canadian assisted reproduction policy, one must begin
with the 1993 Royal Commission on New Reproductive Technologies,
whose influence cannot be overstated even two and a half decades after
it issued its recommendations. To argue that the Royal Commission influenced the *AHR Act* is hardly controversial; however, it may seem
odd to say that its recommendations continue to influence Canadian
assisted reproduction policy to this day. The Commission's principal
recommendations were legislated but never institutionalized; its worst
fear – a lack of uniformity, with policy set by provincial governments
and medical professional organizations – best describes much of the
current status quo. Yet much of Canadian policy, including in policy subfields over which provinces have primary jurisdiction, stems

directly from the Royal Commission's recommendations and framing strategy. Although the Royal Commission did not get the outcome it wanted, that does not diminish its influence on that outcome.

The Commission's jurisdictional framing was especially important. Qualitative analysis of Commission's final report, parliamentary debates, and parliamentary committee hearings preceding the *AHR Act* demonstrates that the way the Royal Commission framed assisted reproduction policy had a lasting impact among policymakers. The work of the Royal Commission was not mere "policy analysis," as the Chief Justice of the Supreme Court of Canada claimed in 2010. Instead, the Commission constitutes the critical juncture for Canadian assisted reproduction policy for a number of interrelated reasons: it was given a wide latitude for action; its perceived expertise granted it considerable authority; and the field of assisted reproduction was most certainly a legislative (and largely medical) policy vacuum, with little in the way of concrete rules in 1993. The Royal Commission's work, consistent with the literature on critical junctures, occurred during a "relatively short" time period with "a substantially heightened probability that agents' choices [would] affect the outcome of interest" (Capoccia and Kelemen 2007, 38).

The Commission's subsequent influence was equally undeniable. Policy experts and parliamentarians referenced its final report approvingly and with great frequency throughout the parliamentary process. Its chief recommendations were reproduced in various bills, and eventually passed into law in the *AHR Act* in 2004. Its framing strategy – both substantive and jurisdictional – was also largely duplicated by government officials. While distinguishing between medically beneficial technologies and activities (which would be subject to regulation) and morally harmful technologies and activities (which would be subject to criminal prohibition), the Commission insisted that both ought to be administered by the federal government. In other words, while there may have been a "division of labour" between regulation and criminal prohibition, all the work was to be done by the same labourer: the federal government. The federal Liberal government embraced the Commission's frames, and maintained them in path-dependent ways.

This framing strategy, even more than the actual content of the legislation, explains much about the state of Canadian assisted reproduction policy today. Framing the regulation of medically beneficial assisted reproduction as of sufficient "national concern" to justify federal jurisdiction had always been constitutionally risky. It became even riskier throughout the legislative process, as the Supreme Court of Canada shifted away from the Constitution's "Peace, Order, and Good Government" clause's "national concern" doctrine as a support for federal legislation that impinged on provincial jurisdiction. This meant that Ottawa faced the much more difficult challenge of justifying medically beneficial assisted reproduction policy as legitimate criminal law. The persistent, path-dependent framing strategy established by the Royal Commission and maintained by Ottawa put the *AHR Act* on a collision course with the provinces in the Supreme Court of Canada.

When the institutional clash finally occurred in 2010, the Supreme Court of Canada found nearly every regulatory aspect of the federal *AHR Act* unconstitutional, leaving the federal government with little more than criminal prohibitions. A majority of Supreme Court justices agreed that the legislation contained a division of labour between beneficial and harmful activities, but insisted that the same labourer could not do both jobs. In their view, the regulation of medically beneficial activities could not plausibly be characterized as criminal law, and thus fell within the provincial health-care jurisdiction. The Royal Commission's initial constitutional gamble, reinforced throughout the years by a federal Liberal Party partial to national policy, had failed. While the Commission's recommendations had been successfully reproduced via legislation, the structure of Canadian federalism meant that these recommendations were never fully institutionalized. Reliance on provincial and medical-regulatory policies, feared by the Commission as a "patchwork," would come to constitute Canada's assisted reproduction policy framework going forward.

Assisted Reproduction Policy in Canada: The Six Subfields

Following the Supreme Court reference, Canadian commentators and policy experts have decried the current policy status quo. The most common criticisms are twofold: first, Canadian assisted reproduction policy is an unregulated "Wild West"; second, it represents a "patchwork." By examining the different subfields of assisted reproduction policy, chapters 4–6 demonstrate that these concerns are only partially justified. Using these subfields to analyse the state of current assisted reproduction policy in Canada shows that while it is indeed subject to provincial variation, it is a mistake to refer to Canadian policy as an unregulated "Wild West."

Human Cloning, Embryonic Research, and Screening/Enhancement

These three policy subfields are subject to minimal provincial policy, and relatively few rules from medical professionals. While the Canadian Fertility and Andrology Society (CFAS) does have internal guidelines regarding the treatment and use of embryos, these rules are effectively superseded by federal legislation. CFAS and the Society of Obstetricians and Gynaecologists of Canada (SOGC) also have rules regarding the "screening" component of screening/enhancement, rules that largely concern preimplantation genetics diagnosis (PGD). However, both because of their source (professional organizations) and their content, these rules only marginally increase overall policy restrictiveness.

The lack of policy by provinces or medical organizations in these subfields does not, however, mean that they are unregulated: these subfields are covered almost entirely by the federal government. Human cloning policy, which is subject to an unconditional criminal ban in the *AHR Act*, is restrictive. Criminalization of certain aspects of screening/enhancement makes Canada's law intermediate in this subfield. Most screening/enhancement prohibitions relate to genetic enhancement: the *AHR Act* prohibits germ-line engineering, a form of genetic manipulation that creates permanent genetic enhancements. It also prohibits ectogenesis, putting human reproductive material into a non-human life form for the purposes of reproduction, and the creation of chimeras and animal-human hybrids. Both prenatal screening and PGD are permitted in Canada, with rules primarily governed by medical guidelines. However, the *AHR Act* does contain one screening-related prohibition: the ban on non-medical sex selection after PGD. Thus, while screening is for the most part regulated loosely by CFAS and SOGC guidelines, as a whole the category of screening/enhancement is intermediate, stemming from the prohibitions in the *AHR Act*.

Embryonic research policy is slightly more complicated. The key concern in this subfield is the extent to which researchers are granted autonomy to conduct their research. On this issue, Canadian policy falls into the "intermediate" category insofar as the *AHR Act* and the *Assisted Human Reproduction (Section 8 Consent) Regulations* prohibit some forms of embryonic research, and prohibit the creation of embryos solely for research purposes. The *AHR Act* also prohibits the creation of animal-human chimeras and hybrids, creating an embryo from part of an embryo or fetus, and non-reproductive human cloning. These prohibitions have been subject to considerable criticism from several academic commentators, who claim the law inhibits scientific research (Caulfield 2004; Caulfield and Bubela 2007; Morris 2007; Rasmussen 2004). Nevertheless, Canada falls between more permissive countries like the United Kingdom (which permits the creation and destruction of embryos for research purposes) and restrictive countries like Austria (which prohibits embryonic research) and Italy (which prohibits embryo freezing). Because Canadian law permits some embryonic research – and lays out rules pertaining to federal funding of such research under the federal *Tri-Council Policy Statement on Ethical Conduct for Research Involving Humans* – I classify its embryonic research policy as intermediate. Overall, in each of the subfields of human cloning, screening/enhancement, and embryonic research, neither "Wild West" nor "patchwork" is an apt description.

Clinical Intervention Policy: Intermediate, with Provincial Variation

Of the six subfields, clinical intervention policy – the subfield most commonly associated with assisted reproduction as a whole – is the most encompassing, the most difficult to define, and involves the greatest number of policymakers. I have defined clinical intervention as including three overlapping policy areas: clinical policies that target medical professionals; donor policies that target donors, patients, and offspring; and coverage policies for assisted reproduction health insurance.

Past assessments of clinical intervention policy characterized permissive policies as those with high levels of physician autonomy and patient access (see Bleiklie, Goggin, and Rothmayr 2004; Engeli 2009). Using this rubric, Canada's clinical intervention policy should be classified as intermediate. Medical professionals are subject to light governmental policies such as Health Canada inspections, in-house licensing and accreditation requirements, and rules regarding the importation and freezing of human gametes. While national specialist associations have produced many clinical guidelines, these rules lack the force of the criminal law and fall on the permissive side of the spectrum. Patients are not restricted from accessing clinical intervention based on particular characteristics – indeed, section 2(e) of the *AHR Act* states that "persons who seek to undergo assisted reproduction procedures must not be discriminated against, including on the basis of their sexual orientation or marital status." However, outside of Ontario, coverage for costly clinical intervention procedures such as IVF is limited to minor policies such as tax credits and coverage of certain procedures and drugs. With respect to donor policies, patients currently retain the option of donor anonymity in every province, but the *AHR Act* includes a restrictive criminal prohibition on compensation for gametes, which likely limits supply for patients and intended parents.

Provincially, Alberta and Saskatchewan are the only two provinces whose medical colleges have published standards for testing and training for clinical intervention, while Quebec and Ontario are the only provinces to include insurance coverage for IVF (which Quebec largely rescinded and Ontario capped) and rules for embryo transfer. Even Ontario's IVF coverage, which is marginally more permissive than the rest of the provinces, is effectively a lottery, with lucky patients having their IVF covered and others receiving no funding at all. Quebec's policy framework is the broadest: it grants licensing powers to the Minister of Health and mandates the collection of patient information, with inspection and data gathering still largely carried out by the Collège des médecins du Québec. Every province's medical college maintains donor anonymity.

Those who favour legislation will rightly claim that the provinces could certainly be *more* regulated, but existing federal prohibitions and medical guidelines mean it is a mistake to call this policy area *un*regulated. Whether medical specialist guidelines can achieve substantial professional buy-in requires additional research. Overall, however, regulation varies significantly across the provinces – although whether the oft-used "patchwork" label is helpful will be discussed below.

Surrogacy and Parentage Policy: One Size Does Not Fit All

Like clinical intervention policy, surrogacy and parentage are subject to provincial variation. In these subfields, policy permissiveness is defined in terms of the absence of legal barriers for the intended parent(s), and provinces differ in how many barriers exist. Because of growing policymaking from provincial governments and even courts in recent years, the term "unregulated" is as unjustified here as in the other subfields.

Although surrogacy policy varies by province, that variation occurs largely with respect to the permissibility of surrogacy arrangements, which are best conceptualized as part of parentage policy. On the other two aspects of surrogacy – payment and the distinction between traditional and gestational surrogacy – there is actually uniformity throughout Canada. With respect to payment, the federal *AHR Act* prohibits payment to a surrogate or to an intermediary facilitating a paid surrogacy arrangement, and counselling someone under twenty-one to be a surrogate. It also includes a provision that allows reimbursement of surrogacy-related expenditures, although the full extent of that coverage has yet to be spelled out in federal regulations. With respect to the distinction between traditional/gestational surrogacy, neither Parliament nor the provincial legislatures have legislated on this distinction, apart from whether genetic relation to the surrogate plays a role in parentage considerations. On surrogacy, Canada is "intermediate," because it bans some (paid) but not all (unpaid) forms of surrogacy.

Chapter 5 also demonstrated, via a new framework for measurement, that parentage is subject to considerable variation among provinces – each of which, whether through legislative or judicial action (or a combination of both), have introduced policy over the last decade. It is impossible to refer to parentage policy in Canada as permissive, intermediate, or restrictive *as a whole*. It would be accurate to say it is quite restrictive in Quebec, New Brunswick, Prince Edward Island, Saskatchewan, and Manitoba; it is intermediate in Newfoundland and Labrador, Nova Scotia, and Alberta; and it is permissive in British Columbia and Ontario.

Summarizing Canada's Assisted Reproduction Policy

In each subfield of assisted reproduction policy, Canada has myriad regulations and prohibitions, which demonstrates that the "Wild West" characterization is far from accurate. In no subfield – apart from certain provinces' parentage policy – would I call Canada's regime "permissive," as Table 7.1 makes clear. In every single subfield except parentage, federal prohibitions exist. Provincial governments are active in surrogacy and parentage, and Quebec and Ontario have become more active in clinical intervention policy. Medical organizations, particularly national specialist associations, have a number of internal policies regarding clinical intervention, and a few related to screening.

The existence of multiple policymakers and provincial variation in certain subfields makes a "one-size-fits-all" definition of assisted reproduction policy especially difficult to determine for Canada, and likely for other federations. This further strengthens the case that simply defining assisted reproduction policy as a whole as permissive, intermediate, or restrictive overlooks important details of a given country's assisted reproduction framework. Even when analysing the subfields

Table 7.1
Assisted Reproduction Policy in Canada

	Federal Prohibitions	Federal Policy	Provincial Policy	Medical Regulations	Overall Restrictiveness
Clinical Intervention	x	x	Quebec Ontario	x	Intermediate
Surrogacy	x		x		Intermediate
Parentage			x		Varies by Province
Human Cloning	x				Restrictive
Screening/ Enhancement	x	x		x	Intermediate
Embryonic Research	x	x			Intermediate

themselves, a simple classification does not give the detail of a qualitative reading of, for example, Quebec's clinical intervention policy or
Alberta's parentage regime. For better or worse, Canadian assisted reproduction policy is undoubtedly subject to provincial variation.

Does this variation constitute a "patchwork"? In an obvious sense,
yes. Parentage, surrogacy, and clinical intervention are regulated un-
evenly across the provinces. Yet the term "patchwork" may send the
wrong message about this policy field. The patchwork metaphor stems
from the Royal Commission on New Reproductive Technologies,
which said in 1993 that Canada "depends on a patchwork of laws to
address the bewildering challenges of medically assisted procreation,"
and stressed that the issues were "too important ... to be left to be resolved by a fragmented and disjointed sector-by-sector or province-
by-province approach" (17). This national jurisdictional framing continued through parliamentary debates, as both the Brown Committee's
majority report and Health Minister Allan Rock lamented the possibility of a Canadian "patchwork." And it has continued to influence
media and academic commentary to describe Canada's assisted reproduction policy since the Supreme Court reference (Eggertson 2011;
Galloway 2015; Gruben and Cameron 2014, 146; Scotti 2016; Stechyson
2013), including my own (Snow 2016).

However, I now believe the patchwork metaphor is unhelpful for
a number of reasons. First, it is almost always used pejoratively: it

assumes that uniformity for uniformity's sake is a desirable outcome. Observers of Canada's nearly three-decade-long journey in policymaking should now be aware that federal intervention does not always benefit citizens and stakeholders. Critics of certain federal prohibitions in the *AHR Act* can attest that just because something is regulated by the federal government does not mean it is good public policy. Assisted Human Reproduction Canada (AHRC), the national agency created by the *AHR Act*, did virtually nothing during its six years of existence. AHRC's inactivity may be explained in part by anticipation of the Supreme Court reference, although one opposition MP involved with the health file noted that "the Court decision was a convenient way for the government to not have to do anything" (Interview 2011g). Overall, Françoise Baylis (2012, 511) is largely correct that "few (if any) will mourn the passing of this agency," which quite simply "did not deliver on its major responsibilities." Yet an assumption often inherent in the "patchwork" metaphor is that national policy, however ineffective or wrong-headed, is preferable to provincial variation.

Second, the "patchwork" metaphor assumes that provinces are unable to effectively regulate assisted reproduction. This assumption dates back to the Royal Commission, for whom "provincial inability" was a major theme. The above analysis shows that, if it were ever true, it is no longer the case. Quebec's experience with regulating single embryo transfer and funding IVF has provided the opportunity for policy learning, policy transfer, and the emergence of best practices. The same can be said for the British Columbia's and Alberta's parentage policies. Indeed, Ontario's 2015 and 2016 reform of clinical intervention and parentage policy shows clear evidence of policy learning from both Quebec and British Columbia. Whether provinces should make policy for assisted reproduction, and what the content of that policy should be, remains up for debate. But Quebec and Ontario show that, for parentage and clinical intervention policy, provinces have the capability to regulate virtually all the non-criminalized aspects of assisted reproduction.

Finally, provincial variation is a natural consequence of Canada's decentralized health-care structure. Even as organizations such as the Canadian Medical Association call for national standards in certain areas of assisted reproduction (O'Neill and Blackmer 2015), a patchwork, for better or worse, will be the status quo going forward. Health care remains provincial jurisdiction; apart from criminalizing certain activities, the *AHR Act* was never going to eliminate "fertility tourism" and differential access to fertility clinics between rural and urban areas. A 2017 list of fertility clinics in Canada shows that there are forty-eight clinics in Ontario – the city of Toronto alone has sixteen – compared with one each in Manitoba, Nova Scotia, and Prince Edward Island (Infertility Network 2017). Because procedures such as IVF require expensive equipment and medical expertise, assisted reproduction will always be more accessible in large urban centres, whether the policymaking authority falls under federal or provincial jurisdiction. Although patients can conceivably travel to provinces that provide more liberal procedures, this is no reason to disapprove of province-to-province variation in the provision of ethical procedures. And if something is considered unethical, Parliament retains the authority to criminally proscribe it. Like postsecondary education, municipal governance, and auto insurance policy, the non-criminalized aspects of assisted reproduction policy are primarily provincial jurisdiction. While these other policy fields certainly constitute a Canadian patchwork, few would advocate reforming them with a one-size-fits-all policy for a country as geographically and politically diverse as Canada.

As the influence of the Royal Commission on New Reproductive Technologies endures, its desire for uniformity remains a goal for many who care deeply about the future of assisted reproduction policy in Canada. While intergovernmental collaboration would be beneficial, scholars ought to be cognizant that for many of the subfields of assisted reproduction policy, provincial variation will continue to exist in Canada. There is no inherent reason that such variation must necessarily be dismissed as second best. Two and a half decades of failed policy at the national stage ought to lead us to reconsider whether uniformity for uniformity's sake is something to be desired.

A Policy Failure: Lessons for Canadian Politics

The recognition that provinces can (and in some instances perhaps should) take the lead in policy innovation should not take away from the fact that Canada's assisted reproduction policy is not what its creators intended. From the federal government's perspective, it is very evidently a policy failure, insofar as policymakers desired a national framework and got the opposite. And while many will lament the provincial variation that will characterize Canadian assisted reproduction policy going forward, Canada's history of assisted reproduction policy can also provide important lessons to students of Canadian politics. In particular, the story told here shows the need to pay attention to federalism, the judiciary, and different types of medical organizations.

Federal Institutions and Jurisdictional Framing Strategies

First and foremost, this study demonstrates the enduring influence of federal institutions in Canadian politics. Consider the following train of events: A federally appointed Royal Commission's framing strategies lead to federal legislation but limited institutionalization. A federal court strikes this legislation down, in the process granting provincial governments authority over several aspects of the field. Provincial government inaction means that rules produced by provincial regulatory colleges effectively govern other aspects. However, these rules stem from national specialist associations, which creates the ironic possibility of uniformity (albeit with far less enforcement) after a remarkably decentralized string of events. Quite simply, one cannot explain the Canadian assisted reproduction policy experience without taking account of federalism at every instance. And yet that is precisely what federal policymakers did from the beginning, and what much of the literature to date has generally replicated.

In chapter 1, I described Canadian assisted reproduction policy as a "tragedy" that can be traced back to its first act, the Royal Commission on New Reproductive Technologies. I mean tragedy in the literary sense of the term. In contrast to everyday understanding of tragedy,[31] which describes "situations where pain and suffering are mainly inexplicable," tragedy in the literary sense is "written by authors who seek to make the trials of life intelligible and instructive" (Ricci 1984, 20–1). As Ricci notes, "Tragedy is an affair of men and women choosing between ideals such as civic duty and family obligation, which are severely dear to them, when no one alternative is patently superior to rest, and where failure to compromise, if compromise is possible at all, leads to downfall and destruction" (22).

I do not claim that the stakes in Canadian assisted reproduction policy are always as high as life and death. Rather, I use Ricci's apt description

---

31 Elsewhere, Baylis and Downie (2013a) have described AHRC as a "tragedy," although it is clear that they are referring to tragedy in its colloquial sense – as an unfortunate turn of events and squandered opportunities – rather than the literary sense used here.

to demonstrate how the Royal Commission's initial choice between two ideals, and its failure to compromise, led to a tragic outcome. Here, the competing ideals were Canada's constitutional framework and the desire for national uniformity. No federal policymaker suggested that Canada ought to rewrite the constitutional division of powers; the commitment to Canada's constitutional order was never questioned. However, much of this commitment was actually lip service. The federal government suggested that it would consult with the provinces, but never did. It included equivalency agreements to placate the provinces, but these agreements were essentially dependent on federal discretion. It ignored opposition party concerns about constitutionality. While the federal government ostensibly wanted to avoid intruding on provincial jurisdiction, its commitment to a national program outweighed all other concerns. This process began with the Royal Commission, which did not adequately articulate the constitutional doctrine that would justify federal intervention. The Commission's jurisdictional framing strategy was sustained throughout by a federal government convinced – and at times galvanized by constitutional lawyers, almost all of whom argued the legislation was constitutional – that the need for a national framework outweighed constitutional concerns. As we now know, the federal government lost its gamble.

The assisted reproduction policy experience should also serve as a cautionary tale for those who favour a national strategy for seemingly every emerging policy issue. The call for national standards is a hallmark of Canadian politics, whether in the field of housing, health care, or postsecondary education. Yet such strategies cannot be undertaken without adequate provincial consultation. Assisted reproduction policy demonstrates that the constitutional division of powers can inhibit overzealous federal governments from overstepping their bounds, and that the Supreme Court of Canada is not afraid to enforce federal encroachments on provincial jurisdiction. The Royal Commission, the federal government, and most legal scholars dangerously underplayed the extent to which the Supreme Court would find federal assisted reproduction legislation unconstitutional. The result was, by the standards of almost everyone involved, a policy failure.

Canada's experience also emphasizes the importance of framing strategies. Had the *AHR Act* been portrayed throughout the legislative process using the "moral" substantive frame – as a piece of legislation that, in its entirety, was dedicated to limiting harmful behaviour – the courts would have found it much more difficult to strike down the impugned provisions. In the end, the federal government relied on ambivalent framing because the legislation truly did have two purposes, and the federal government could not fathom that its role was limited only to eliminating harmful behaviour. Future policymakers cannot and should not underplay the importance of constitutional law and Supreme Court jurisprudence, as the Royal Commission and subsequent federal policymakers undoubtedly did. As Thomas Posyniak (2011, 3) notes, "Comprehensive legislative responses to new social phenomena, apart from exceptional and exigent circumstances, should remain reflective of our constitutional history and our incrementally developed and judicially influenced regime of divided legislative powers." Future policymakers will need to pay careful attention to what constitutes "exceptional and exigent circumstances."

The Canadian assisted reproduction policy experience also demonstrates the extent to which federal institutions can, intentionally or unintentionally, delay policymaking. In 2004, prior to the passage of the *AHR Act*, Montpetit wrote that Canada's federal structure had "worked to prevent policy-makers from making decisions" about assisted reproduction, as the constitutional division of powers "discouraged the regulatory option in the short term, channelling policy-making efforts into criminal prohibitions" (81). Although this was true at the time, the imminent passage of the *AHR Act* would condition this argument slightly; it is more accurate to say that the division of powers delayed rather than prevented assisted reproduction policymaking, particularly given the federal government's ostensible desire to create policy. This is in keeping with other areas – such as pensions and the environment – where federal institutions have delayed policymaking (see Banting 2012; Harrison 1999).

A decade later, Montpetit's analysis rings true in an entirely different sense: Canadian assisted reproduction policy provides yet another highlight of the extent to which Canada's intergovernmental cooperation is poorly institutionalized. Both the federal government's failure to consult the provinces before the passage of the *AHR Act* and the lack of provincial collaboration after the 2010 Supreme Court reference have contributed to provincial variation in assisted reproduction policy. Absent strong federal government attempts at true collaboration, there are few existing institutional incentives for provinces to collaborate with one another, as is borne out by Canada's current assisted reproduction policy – particularly in the subfields of clinical intervention, surrogacy, and parentage, where policymaking has been anything but coordinated.

This raises one final aspect of the federal government's approach that remains something of a mystery: its lack of willingness to engage in substantive intergovernmental collaboration with the provinces. While the federal government's cuts to provincial transfers in the 1990s led to intergovernmental tensions, by the 2000s these tensions had diminished, to the extent that some scholars heralded a shift to "collaborative federalism" (Cameron and Simeon 2002). Such collaboration was most notable in the field of health-care funding, particularly the 2003 Accord on Health Care Renewal and the September 2004 *10-Year Plan to Strengthen Health Care*. Thus, during the period the federal government was engaging in long-term collaboration with the provinces on one aspect of health care (funding), it simultaneously failed to adequately consult the provinces on another aspect for which it was producing legislation (assisted reproduction). What explains the incongruity?

While there is no one single reason, the evidence suggests that the federal government simply did not perceive assisted reproduction as a field that involved shared jurisdiction. The most prominent areas of intergovernmental collaboration – the environment and climate change, internal trade, and health-care delivery – contain aspects over which provincial input is understood to be constitutionally required. They also have a significant financial dimension. By contrast, from the Royal Commission onward, the federal government viewed every aspect of assisted reproduction apart from parentage as federal jurisdiction. In documents such as Health Canada's 1996 *Setting Boundaries* and the 2001 Brown Report, the federal government nodded towards a need for collaboration with the provinces, but only on aspects pertaining to family law and parentage. And while consultation did occur following the 2000 release of an overview paper from Health Canada, provincial and territorial concerns about federal regulatory authority do not seem to have been treated with the seriousness they deserved (see Miller Chenier 2002, 8–9). Just as the federal government does not significantly collaborate with the provinces on military spending or the postal service, its actions concerning assisted reproduction demonstrate that it did not, ultimately, feel the need to consult with the provinces in any meaningful way.

Moreover, assisted reproduction did not contain enough of a financial dimension that would necessitate transfers between governments or put an undue burden on one level of government. Emboldened by legal experts about the law's constitutionality, and combined with provincial reticence outside of Quebec to engage in legislation, the federal government seems to have seen minimal need for collaboration. In recent years, many scholars have come to question whether the "collaborative turn" in Canadian federalism was truly that collaborative (Simmons and Graefe 2013; see also Bickerton 2010, 61; Schertzer 2016, 105–6). At least in the case of assisted reproduction, such collaboration was virtually non-existent.

The Judicialization of Assisted Reproduction Policy in Canada

Since the introduction of the *Canadian Charter of Rights and Freedoms* in 1982, Canadian courts have become more involved in policymaking. Even in such a relatively new policy area such as assisted reproduction, the judicial presence is striking. The Supreme Court's intervention in the 2010 case demonstrates both the enduring influence of Canada's constitutional constraints and the willingness of courts to strike down legislation. The Supreme Court of British Columbia's donor-anonymity decision in *Pratten*, although subsequently overturned on appeal, demonstrates that interested parties will continue to use the courts in order to achieve policy change with respect to assisted reproduction.

When read together, these two cases are an interesting example of policy results stemming from the intersection of federalism and *Charter* cases, particularly in conflicts involving health care and the criminal law. Over the last few decades, the Supreme Court has adopted a socially liberal approach to moral issues in *Charter* cases, including cases regarding LGBTQ rights, reproductive autonomy, and drug use (*Dobson (Litigation Guardian of) v. Dobson* 1999; *M. v. H.* 1999; *Canada (Attorney General) v. PHS Community Services Society* 2011). In the *Reference re Assisted Human Reproduction Act* (2010), the division between the majority and dissenting judgments effectively concerned different conceptions of morality: the majority's medicalized framework argued that much of the *AHR Act* sought to regulate a "good" (the medical-scientific frame), while the dissent claimed that the legislation was designed to eliminate an "evil" (the moral frame). Quebec was able to convince a majority of justices that the non-criminal components of the *AHR Act* fit under the "medical-scientific" frame and were fundamentally related to health rather than to the criminal law, and this led to an increase in provincial power. Thus, the medical-scientific (and socially liberal) view of morality in the courts has implications for the federal division of powers: while a socially liberal approach to morality in *Charter* cases often invalidates legislation by any level of government, the same approach in federalism cases increases provincial power (see Snow 2012). When provinces are reluctant to legislate, as they seem to be with clinical intervention policy, this medicalized framing de facto leads to increased power for medical organizations.

It is useful to read this judicial liberalism in concert with Justice Adair's *obiter* comment in *Pratten* (2011) that "practices developed by private service providers" could not "be a full answer to the circumstances of donor offspring" and were "too important to leave unregulated" (paras. 177, 210). This need for regulation reflects what Thomas M.J. Bateman calls "postliberal" constitutionalism, whereby positive state action is required to advance freedom (Bateman 1998). Under postliberal decision-making, judges are more likely to mandate, rather than restrict, government action in order to enhance individual liberty and opportunity. Thus, from these two constitutional rulings, a curious picture emerges. The medical-scientific frame in a federalism case, mixed with a postliberal approach in a *Charter* case, produced judicially mandated provincial action concerning clinical intervention. Private-sector inability mandated state action, while federalism mandated that such action be undertaken by provincial governments specifically. As Justice Adair herself said, the 2010 Supreme Court reference made clear that "the primary legislative response needed – and needs – to come from provincial legislatures" (*Pratten v. British Columbia* 2011, para. 211). The result of this decision would have been to mandate provincial intervention concerning clinical intervention. Although the case was overturned a year later, it is highly suggestive that challenges to the lack of provincial assisted reproduction policymaking may be successful in the courts, and that it could be judges who force provincial legislatures to act – as they did, in many provinces, with respect to parentage policy.

Yet Another Policymaker: The Role of Professional Medical Organizations

The role of physicians, especially in Canada, cannot be understated when it comes to assisted reproduction policymaking. Yet there is a dearth of Canadian political science literature on the role of medical professionals in health-care policy. Chapter 6 may only scratch the surface, but it makes the case that greater qualitative exploration of medical organizations is necessary. Such scholarship should include, at the very least, an exploration of the extent to which physicians feel constrained by regulatory college sanctions; the extent to which medical colleges and national specialist organizations have created internal norms and an "industrial morality"; how the views of private service providers at IVF clinics differ from those working in public hospitals; physicians' views on provincial and federal governments' ability to become involved in health-care policymaking, especially with respect to clinical practice; the role of provincial college policy-specific guidelines, such as those introduced in Saskatchewan and Alberta for assisted reproduction; the fear (if any) of punishment for not following such guidelines; and the correlation between physician behaviour and attitudes on the one hand with longitudinal data on the other, to measure the effectiveness of internal and external regulation. Well beyond assisted reproduction, we have a limited understanding of how medical practice actually works in Canada. Considering the enormous influence of physicians as healers, policymakers, and gatekeepers, more research is required.

The typical response to medical self-regulation within Canadian political science, and indeed other fields studying assisted reproduction, has been to assume that medical self-regulation effectively means no regulation. Before and after the *AHR Act* passed, scholars claimed that Canada represented the "Wild West" of assisted reproduction, where doctors could take risks and disregard patients' best interests with little fear of sanction. This view requires reconsideration. Canada certainly has a burgeoning for-profit fertility industry. As would be expected in a country without outright government regulation, until 2010 it had one of the highest assisted-reproduction-related multiple birthrates in the Western world (Cook et al. 2011). However, that rate has seen a substantial drop, from 32 per cent in 2009 to 9.7 per cent in 2016 (Canadian Fertility and Andrology Society 2017). Moreover, in a completely unregulated system, one might have expected that the introduction of a piece of federal legislation deemed one of the most comprehensive in the world would have had a noticeable effect on the industry, or that its winding down would have opened the floodgates to all sorts of fertility-related experimentation. Yet in practice, the *AHR Act* changed little. This speaks, at least in part, to the considerable degree of self-regulation that had taken place in Canada.

This book is not a defence of medical self-regulation as a panacea; it merely contains a preliminary articulation of its merits and limitations in the Canadian context. My more modest argument is that the existence of medical guidelines should lead us to reconsider claims that assisted reproduction is an "unregulated nightmare" that reflects the "Wild West." Assisted reproduction policy in Canada is not perfect, nor can self-regulatory bodies do everything. There are clearly subfields of assisted reproduction policy, such as parentage and reproductive human cloning, that cannot be adequately guided by medical organizations of any kind. However, as Canada and other countries move forward with assisted reproduction policies, scholars must pay greater attention to the scope and content of medical organizations' internal guidelines to gain a more complete understanding of this emerging field.

Two points in particular highlight the increased need for a focus on medical self-regulation in the Canadian context. The first relates to assisted reproduction specifically, and the utility of the six-part typology developed here. I have argued that a renewed emphasis on both federalism and medical self-regulation can, combined with this new typology, enable scholars to identify whether a given subfield of assisted reproduction policy is regulated, and perhaps whether it ought to be regulated. In Canada, clinical intervention takes place in public hospitals and private fertility clinics, and falls primarily under provincial jurisdiction. Since the regulation of these types of health services are typically delegated to provincial medical colleges, those colleges, along with national specialist associations composed of members of those colleges, may be the best place to create and implement certain components of clinical intervention policy. CFAS and SOGC have direct guidelines that govern only two subfields: clinical intervention and screening/enhancement – and guidelines for the latter are exclusively related to screening. However, in the absence of provincial and federal legislation, medical organizations can also develop indirect, and perhaps unintentional, policymaking authority. Consider the subfield of embryonic research: the *AHR Act* limits embryonic research to "surplus" embryos created during clinical intervention, but medical guidelines determine the number of embryos created during clinical intervention and, by implication, the number of embryos left over for research purposes. For scholars interested in the scope of medical self-regulation and for governments interested in reform, a closer look at such "policy creep" is especially relevant.

A second point about medical self-regulation requires explication: the role of federalism in, paradoxically, creating some level of national policy uniformity. Clinical intervention policy, as with much other policy related to clinical practice in Canada, is quite decentralized in theory. Provincial governments have authority, but they have delegated this policy authority to medical regulatory colleges through statutory self-regulation. However, because provincial colleges have increasingly "got out of the policy business" (Interview 2012a), most guidelines are effectively set by national specialist associations – in the case of clini-' cal intervention policy, the Canadian Fertility and Andrology Society and the Society of Obstetricians and Gynaecologists of Canada. As Dr Richard MacLachlan noted during Brown Committee hearings, rather than being "balkanized," national specialist associations and accreditors can have a unifying effect on Canada's seemingly decentralized assisted reproduction policy: "A large part of the world we operate in is meeting national standards ... when my hospital or my facility is accredited by the Canadian Council on Health Services Accreditation, a single standard is used nationally" (Canada 2001i, 1240). Given the specialist associations' national scope, these rules, if followed, could buck the trend of provincial variation. Greater qualitative evidence is required, but this process demonstrates a feedback loop of policy uniformity through decentralized institutions that has yet to be explored in studies of Canadian health policy.

Lessons for Comparative Assisted Reproduction

The three main areas of further study identified above for Canadian scholars – federalism and decentralization, judicialization, and the role of medical professionals – are of just as much interest for comparative assisted reproduction scholars. A few points require elaboration for those engaging in the comparative study of assisted reproduction.

One of my central arguments has been that comparative scholars of assisted reproduction policy have inadequately defined their scope of inquiry. There are two reasons for this: first, scholars rarely explicitly delineate what is included and excluded by the term "assisted reproduction policy"; and second, to a large degree there has been a failure to properly identify the extent to which actors other than federal governments engage in regulation in the absence of, or as a complement to, national policy in this area. The Canadian case study demonstrates the utility of the six-part typology for defining assisted reproduction policy, and of expanding the focus beyond national governments to other policy actors. Clarifying the definition of assisted reproduction policy and extending the definition of "state actor" to examine medical organizations with delegated authority can signal the beginning, for Canada and comparatively, of a more expansive research project.

Without examining policy produced by provincial governments, medical organizations, and courts, any description of Canadian assisted reproduction policy would be incomplete. I suggest the same is likely true for other jurisdictions, even those with centralized assisted reproduction policymaking. The typology used for assisted reproduction policy in this book can help explore policy divergence across regimes with greater clarity.

Within jurisdictional federations such as Australia and the United States, the role of subnational governments requires explication in order to get a proper understanding of comparative assisted reproduction policy. Likewise, a focus on judicialization is necessary – Canadian parentage policy in particular cannot be understood without reference to judicial decisions. Having said all this, the area most in need of study within assisted reproduction policy scholarship is medical self-regulation. There is a paucity of comparative literature on the subject, but the limited scholarship suggests avenues for future research. In a 2016 article on the governance of biotechnology in Europe, Isabelle Engeli and Christine Rothmayr Allison find that the type of regulation varies considerably within each polity studied: whereas the French government has "fully taken over" self-regulation and adopted a "command and control" approach to assisted reproduction, the United Kingdom has "mostly delegated regulatory power to an independent body." Germany's "hybrid" approach falls somewhere between the two. Overall, however, they find that "the state has progressively become a primary player in governing the field of human biotechnology, and its responsibility and steering capacity has strengthened over time" (249).

Their finding raises several important questions concerning assisted reproduction policy. The first is simply whether the growth of state power in the assisted reproduction field is true across jurisdictions beyond the three they examine. The evidence produced in this book suggests that outside of Quebec (and perhaps Ontario), the Canadian state's "steering capacity" has not grown over time. Compared with 1993, the year of the Royal Commission, there is more government involvement, particularly because of federal criminal prohibitions and provincial judicial decisions regarding parentage. However, there has been limited institutionalization at the federal level, with some (Downie and Baylis 2013) questioning the federal government's willingness and capacity even to enforce the criminal prohibitions. At the provincial level, meanwhile, there has been limited government involvement concerning clinical intervention policy outside Quebec and Ontario, even following a Supreme Court reference that opened the door for provinces to act. At least compared to its European counterparts, Canada seems to have bucked the statist trend.

Why has Canada had less government involvement in the clinical intervention subfield of assisted reproduction? One answer may be the federalized nature of Canada's own self-regulatory framework. The primary decision-making and licensing bodies are provincial regulatory colleges, not national medical associations. Another answer may be the fact that, as Engeli and Rothmayr Allison (2016, 259) note, "Comprehensive and well-followed voluntary self-regulation strengthens the medical community's position as expert and its credibility as a reliable partner in the regulatory process." In France, division among medical expert organizations was a catalyst for increased state intervention. In Canada, by contrast, this division never occurred. According to Montpetit (2004), Canadian physicians had an "unambiguous preference for self-regulation" of assisted reproduction; they opposed criminal prohibitions and favoured an independent regulatory body provided that it "complement, not duplicate, the work already accomplished through so called self-regulation" (64, 75). While some physicians eventually welcomed the *AHR Act*, they uniformly opposed its criminal prohibitions and showed no sign of organizational strife regarding the federal government's proposed national regulatory policy. And while Montpetit cautions that "the sheer power of the medical profession ... does not constitute a sufficient explanation" (81) for the lack of legislation prior to the *AHR Act*, the profession's homogeneity of beliefs likely helped to delay the legislation and its eventual implementation.

One final point regarding comparative studies of medical self-regulation is worth noting: the Canadian case shows that scholars must recognize the important distinction between policy capacity and policy content. Clearly, provincial medical colleges and national specialist associations in Canada have the regulatory capacity to create clinical guidelines for certain subfields of assisted reproduction, particularly clinical intervention. They have been doing this for decades. Yet it is likely that the content of policies offered through medical self-regulation tends to be more permissive than that put forward by governments. This seems true in Canada, where Quebec's stricter policy on single embryo transfer resulted in a contemporaneously lower multiple birth rate than the rest of Canada. The distinction between capacity and content should be kept in mind, insofar as self-regulation seems to be more permissive.

Conclusion: Taking a Closer Look

While this book's main goal was to assess the state of assisted reproduction policy in Canada, it has also suggested a framework by which to assess and measure policy in other countries going forward. By adopting a typology to define the six subfields of assisted reproduction policy, it has produced a model for comparative scholars that can be used to measure variation across and within regimes with greater clarity. Put simply, without exploring these other actors and disaggregating the assisted reproduction policy subfields, we would have an impoverished view of the overall state of assisted reproduction policy in Canada. The same is likely true for other countries, especially federal ones.

One qualitative case study does not make the case for a general theory, but small-N studies can help the process of theory building. For comparative scholars more broadly, this book demonstrates the utility of adopting a historical institutional framework when undertaking qualitative analysis. Particularly in fields such as assisted reproduction policy, where a legislative vacuum and policy initiation can be identified, the literature on critical junctures helps explain the Royal Commission's enormous and continued influence in Canada today. Historical institutionalism's attention to the importance and fluidity of ideas shows how the embeddedness of initial choices can often lead to unintended consequences over time. Canada's unique situation from 2004 to 2010 – a robust federal framework in theory, with little actual policymaking done by the federal government – also provides an important lesson about the difficulty of moving from the realm of ideas to outright institutionalization.

From the enduring influence of Canadian federalism to the need for precise definition and measurement of emerging policy fields, this book makes the case that qualitative historical analysis can provide considerable analytical weight to explaining policy outcomes and that small-N studies can contribute to theory building within comparative political science. Channelling Paul Pierson (2004, 47), I firmly believe that the most important first step political scientists can take is to "go back and look," and to do so in as much detail as possible, when seeking to understand political outcomes. It is my hope that this book can play some part in adding to that overall understanding.

Appendix – List of Interviews

Interview. 2011a. Confidential author interview with former civil servant at Health Canada.

Interview. 2011b. Confidential author interview with Canadian physician specializing in fertility.

Interview. 2011c. Confidential author interview with parliamentary librarian who worked on the *Assisted Human Reproduction Act*.

Interview. 2011d. Confidential author interview with Ontario-area lawyer specializing in fertility law.

Interview. 2011e. Confidential author interview with member of the Evangelical Fellowship of Canada.

Interview. 2011f. Confidential author interview with member of Parliament and member of the Standing Committee on Health.

Interview. 2011g. Confidential author interview with member of Parliament involved with the health-care dossier in 2010.

Interview. 2011h. Confidential author interview with member of Parliament and member of the Standing Committee on Health.

Interview. 2012a. Confidential author interview with Canadian physician specializing in obstetrics and gynaecology.

Interview. 2012b. Confidential author interview with Canadian physician specializing in fertility.

Interview. 2012c. Confidential author interview with Canadian physician specializing in pediatrics and member of the Canadian Medical Association committee on ethics.

Cases Cited

A.A. v. B.B. [2007] O.N.C.A. 2.

A.A. v. New Brunswick [2004] HR-004–03.

B.A.N. v. J.H. [2008] BCSC 808, 294 D.L.R. (4th) 564.

Canada (Attorney General) v. PHS Community Services Society [2011] 3 S.C.R. 134.

Cameron v. Nova Scotia (Attorney General) [1999] CanLII 7243 (NS CA).

Dobson (Litigation Guardian of) v. Dobson [1999] 2 S.C.R 753.

Fort Frances Pulp & Power Co. v. Manitoba Free Press [1923] A.C. 695.

Fraess v. Alberta (Minister of Justice and Attorney General) [2005] A.B.Q.B. 889.

General Motors of Canada Ltd. v. City National Leasing [1989] 1 S.C.R. 641.

Grand et al. v. Ontario (Attorney General) [2016]. (Ontario Superior Court
   of Justice Interim order and minutes of settlement; FS-16–20779)

H.L.W. and T.H.W. v. J.C.T. and J.T. [2005] B.C.S.C. 1679.

J.A.W. v. J.E.W. [2010] N.B.Q.B 414.

J.C. v. The Queen (Dept. of Vital Statistics) [2000] 2000 M.B.Q.B. 173.

J.C.M. v. A.N.A. [2012] B.C.S.C. 584.

Labatt Breweries of Canada Ltd. v. Canada (Attorney General) [1980] 1 S.C.R. 114.

M. v. H. [1999] 2 S.C.R. 3.

M.D. et al. v. L.L. et al. [2008] 90 O.R. (3d) 127.

Munro v. National Capital Commission [1966] S.C.R. 663.

Ontario Hydro v. Ontario (Labour Relations Board) [1993] 3 S.C.R. 327.

Pratten v. British Columbia (Attorney General) [2011] B.C.S.C. 656.

Pratten v. British Columbia (Attorney General) [2012] B.C.C.A. 480.

Quebec (Attorney General) v. Canada (Attorney General) [2015] 1 S.C.R. 693.

R. v. Crown Zellerbach [1988] 1 S.C.R. 401.

R. v. Hydro-Québec [1997] 3 S.C.R. 213.

R. v. Malmo-Levine; R. v. Caine [2003] 3 S.C.R. 571, 2003 SCC 74.

Re Baby M 537 A 2d 1227 [1988].

Re Board of Commerce Act [1922] 1 A.C. 191.

Re C (A Minor) (Wardship: Surrogacy) [1985] F.L.R. 846.

Reference re Anti-Inflation Act [1976] 2 S.C.R. 373.

Reference re Assisted Human Reproduction Act [2008] Q.C.C.A. 1167 (CanLII), 298 D.L.R. (4th) 712.

Reference re Assisted Human Reproduction Act [2010] 3 S.C.R. 457.

Reference re Firearms Act [2000] 1 S.C.R. 783.

Reference re Same-sex Marriage [2004] 3 S.C.R. 698.

Reference re Securities Act [2011] 3 S.C.R. 837.

Reference re Senate Reform [2014] 1 S.C.R. 704.

Reference re Supreme Court Act, ss. 5 and 6 [2014] 1 S.C.R. 433.

RJR-MacDonald Inc. v. Canada (A.G.) [1995] 3 S.C.R 199.

Rutherford v. Ontario (Deputy Registrar General) [2006] 81 O.R. (3d) 81.

Rypkema v. H.M.T.Q. et al. [2003] B.C.S.C. 1784.

Toronto Electric Commissioners v. Snider [1925] A.C. 396.

W.J.Q.M. v. A.M.A. [2011] S.K.Q.B. 317.

X, sub. nom Adoption –091 [2009] S.Q., c. 30.

Statutes and Regulations Cited

An Act respecting Clinical and Research Activities Relating to Assisted Procreation. R.S.Q., c. A-5.01. http://www.canlii.org/en/qc/laws/stat/cqlr-c-a-5.01/ 83889/cqlr-c-a-5.01.html (Accessed 7 January 2017).

Assisted Human Reproduction Act. S.C. 2004, c. 2 (Bill C-6).

Assisted Human Reproduction (Section 8 Consent) Regulations. SOR/2007–137. http://laws-lois.justice.gc.ca/PDF/SOR-2007-137.pdf (Accessed 7 January 2017).

Bill C-38, An Act to Implement Certain Provisions of the Budget Tabled in Parliament on March 29, 2012 and Other Measures, 1st Sess, 41st Parl.

Birth Registration Regulations. O.I.C. 2007–498, N.S. Reg. 390/2007. https:// www.novascotia.ca/just/regulations/regs/visbirthreg.htm (Accessed 7 January 2017).

Child Status Act. Ch. C-6. https://www.princeedwardisland.ca/sites/default/ files/legislation/C-06-Child%20Status%20Act.pdf (Accessed 7 January 2017).

Civil Code of Québec. L.R.Q., c. C-1991. http://legisquebec.gouv.qc.ca/en/ showdoc/cs/CCQ-1991 (Accessed 7 January 2017).

Family Law Act. S.A., 2003, Ch. F-4.5. http://www.qp.alberta.ca/documents/ acts/f04p5.pdf (Accessed 7 January 2017).

Family Law Act. S.B.C., Ch. 25. http://www.bclaws.ca/civix/document/id/ complete/statreg/11025_01 (Accessed 7 January 2017).

Processing and Distribution of Semen for Assisted Conception Regulations. SOR/96–254. https://www.canlii.org/en/ca/laws/regu/sor-96-254/ latest/sor-96-254.html (Accessed 7 January 2017).

Regulation respecting Clinical Activities Related to Assisted Procreation. Ch. A-5.01, r. 1. http://legisquebec.gouv.qc.ca/en/ShowDoc/cr/A-5.01,%20r.%201 (Accessed 7 January 2017).

Vital Statistics Act. Ch. V, C.C.S.M. c. V60. http://web2.gov.mb.ca/laws/statutes/ccsm/v060e.php (Accessed 7 January 2017).

Vital Statistics Act. S.S., Ch. V-7.21. http://www.qp.gov.sk.ca/documents/English/Statutes/Statutes/V7-21.pdf (Accessed 7 January 2017).

Vital Statistics Act. Ch. V-6.01. http://www.assembly.nl.ca/legislation/sr/annualstatutes/2009/v06-01.c09.htm (Accessed 7 January 2017).

Works Cited

Alberta Health. 2014. *Assisted Reproductive Technologies (ARTs): Final Report (Revised February 2014)*. Health Technology & Policy Unit. https://open.alberta.ca/dataset/f635b529-8ab5-4f69-9895-4c357fbc167c/resource/5f401c83-e31f-4f63-8083-a84fe3dd65a2/download/AHTDP-Assisted-Reproductive-Technologies-2014.pdf (Accessed 7 January 2017).

Ariss, Rachel. 1996. "The Ethic of Care in the Final Report of the Royal Commission on New Reproductive Technologies." *Queen's Law Journal* 22 (1): 1–50.

Baier, Gerald. 2006. *Courts and Federalism: Judicial Doctrine in the United States, Australia, and Canada*. Vancouver: UBC Press.

Baier, Gerald. 2012. "The Courts, the Constitution, and Dispute Resolution." In *Canadian Federalism: Performance, Effectiveness, and Legitimacy*, 3rd ed., edited by Herman Bakvis and Grace Skogstad, 79–95. Don Mills: Oxford University Press.

Baker, Dennis. 2014. "The Temptation of Provincial Criminal Law." *Canadian Public Administration* 57 (2): 275–94. https://doi.org/10.1111/capa.12068.

Banting, Keith G. 2012. "The Three Federalisms Revisited: Social Policy and Intergovernmental Decision-Making." In *Canadian Federalism: Performance, Effectiveness, and Legitimacy*, 3rd ed., edited by Herman Bakvis and Grace Skogstad, 141–64. Don Mills: Oxford University Press.

Bateman, Thomas M.J. 1998. "Rights Application Doctrine and the Clash of Constitutionalisms in Canada." *Canadian Journal of Political Science* 31 (1): 3–29. https://doi.org/10.1017/S0008423900008660.

Bauer, Martin W. 2005. "Distinguishing Red and Green Biotechnology: Cultivation Effects of the Elite Press." *International Journal of Public Opinion Research* 17 (1): 63–89. https://doi.org/10.1093/ijpor/edh057.

Baylis, Françoise. 2011. "Supreme Court of Canada Decision on the *Assisted Human Reproduction Act* Creates Urgent Need for Action." *Journal of Obstetrics and Gynaecology Canada* 33 (4): 317–19. https://doi.org/10.1016/S1701-2163(16)34845-9.

Baylis, Françoise. 2012. "The Demise of Assisted Human Reproduction Canada." *Journal of Obstetrics and Gynaecology Canada* 34 (6): 511–13. https://doi.org/10.1016/S1701-2163(16)35264-1.

Baylis, Françoise, and Jocelyn Downie. 2013a. "The Tale of Assisted Human Reproduction Canada: A Tragedy in Five Acts." *Canadian Journal of Women and the Law* 25 (2): 183–201. https://doi.org/10.3138/cjwl.25.2.183.

Baylis, Françoise, and Jocelyn Downie. 2013b. "Wishing Doesn't Make It So." *Impact Ethics*, 17 December. https://impactethics.ca/2013/12/17/wishing-doesnt-make-it-so/ (Accessed 15 February 2017).

Baylis, Françoise, and Matthew Herder. 2009a. "Policy Design for Human Embryo Research in Canada: A History (Part 1 of 2)." *Journal of Bioethical Inquiry* 6 (1): 109–22. https://doi.org/10.1007/s11673-009-9135-8.

Baylis, Françoise, and Matthew Herder. 2009b. "Policy Design for Human Embryo Research in Canada: An Analysis (Part 2 of 2)." *Journal of Bioethical Inquiry* 6 (3): 351–65. https://doi.org/10.1007/s11673-009-9145-6.

Béland, Daniel. 2005. "Ideas and Social Policy: An Institutionalist Perspective." *Social Policy and Administration* 39 (1): 1–18. https://doi.org/10.1111/j.1467-9515.2005.00421.x.

Béland, Daniel, and Robert Henry Cox. 2011. "Introduction: Ideas and Politics." In *Ideas and Politics in Social Science Research*, edited by Daniel Béland and Robert Henry Cox, 3–20. Oxford: Oxford University Press.

Bickerton, James. 2010. "Deconstructing the New Federalism." *Canadian Political Science Review* 4 (2–3): 56–72.

Bissonnette, F., S.J. Phillips, J. Gunby, H. Holzer, N. Mahutte, P. St-Michel, and I.J. Kadoch. 2011. "Working to Eliminate Multiple Pregnancies: A Success Story in Québec." *Reproductive Biomedicine Online* 23 (4): 500–4. https://doi.org/10.1016/j.rbmo.2011.05.020. Medline:21840757

Blackwell, Tom. 2012. "Fertility Raid a Mystery to Owner." *National Post*, 2 March, A1.

Blackwell, Tom. 2013a. "Rare Fertility Charges Expose Lax Oversight of Baby Making Industry." *National Post*, 16 February, A1.

Blackwell, Tom. 2013b. "Surrogacy Agency Still Active Despite RCMP Charges." *National Post*, 18 March, A2.

Blackwell, Tom. 2013c. "Fertility Case Tied to 'Baby Selling.'" *National Post*, 16 December, A1.

Blackwell, Tom. 2016. "'Huge' Demand for IVF Treatment in Ontario – Where It's Fully Funded – Has Wait Lists Stretching to 2018." *National Post*, 20 May.http://nationalpost.com/health/huge-demand-for-ivf-treatment-in-ontario-where-its-fully-funded-has-wait-lists-stretching-to-2018.

Bleiklie, Ivar, Malcolm L. Goggin, and Christine Rothmayr, eds. 2004. *Comparative Biomedical Policy: Governing Assisted Reproductive Technologies*. London: Routledge.

Boyd, Susan B. 2007. "Gendering Legal Parenthood: Bio-Genetic Ties, Intentionality and Responsibility." *Windsor Yearbook of Access to Justice* 25 (1): 63–94.

Boyd, Susan B., and Cindy Baldassi. 2009. "Marriage or Naught? Unmarried Cohabitation in Canada." In *Changing Contours of Domestic Life, Family and Law: Caring and Sharing*, edited by Anne Bottomley and Simone Wong, 111–29. Oxford: Hart Publishing.

Boyle, Theresa. 2016. "New Standards Will Tighten Rules Governing Egg and Sperm Banks." *Toronto Star*, 7 October. https://www.thestar.com/news/canada/2016/10/07/new-standards-will-tighten-rules-governing-sperm-and-egg-banks.html (Accessed 7 January 2017).

Braun, Dietmar, ed. 2000. *Public Policy and Federalism*. Aldershot, UK: Ashgate.

Brean, Joseph. 2011. "Surrogate Not Legally a Baby's Mother, Judge Rules." *National Post*, 13 September. http://news.nationalpost.com/2011/09/13/surrogate-not-legally-a-babys-mother-judge-rules/ (Accessed 7 January 2017).

Broschek, Jörg. 2010. "Federalism and Political Change: Canada and Germany in Historical-Institutionalist Perspective." *Canadian Journal of Political Science* 43 (1): 1–24. https://doi.org/10.1017/S0008423909990023.

Broschek, Jörg. 2012. "Historical Institutionalism and the Varieties of Federalism in Germany and Canada." *Publius* 42 (4): 662–87. https://doi.org/10.1093/publius/pjr040.

Brouillet, Eugénie. 2011. "Canadian Federalism and the Principle of Subsidiarity: Should We Open Pandora's Box?" *Supreme Court Review* 54: 601–32.

Busby, Karen. 2013. "Of Surrogate Mother Born: Parentage Determinations in Canada and Elsewhere." *Canadian Journal of Women and the Law* 25 (2): 284–314. https://doi.org/10.3138/cjwl.25.2.284.

Busby, Karen, and Delaney Vun. 2010. "Revisiting *The Handmaid's Tale*: Feminist Theory Meets Empirical Research on Surrogate Mothers." *Canadian Journal of Family Law* 26 (1): 13–94.

Cairns, Alan C. 1971. "The Judicial Committee and Its Critics." *Canadian Journal of Political Science* 4 (3): 301–45. https://doi.org/10.1017/S0008423900026809.

Cameron, David, and Richard Simeon. 2002. "Intergovernmental Relations in Canada: The Emergence of Collaborative Federalism." *Publius* 32 (2): 49–72. https://doi.org/10.1093/oxfordjournals.pubjof.a004947.

Campbell, John T. 1998. "Institutional Analysis and the Role of Ideas in Political Economy." *Theory and Society* 27 (3): 377–409. https://doi.org/10.1023/A:1006871114987.

Canada. Parliament. House of Commons. 1996. *Debates*, 35th Parliament, 2nd Session. No. 96. 4 November. http://www.parl.gc.ca/HousePublications/Publication.aspx?Language=E&Mode=1&Parl=35&Ses=2&DocId=2332634&File=0 (Accessed 6 February 2017).

Canada. Parliament. House of Commons. 2001a. Standing Committee on Health. *Evidence*. Meeting 13, 3 May. 37th Parliament, 1st Session. http://www.parl.gc.ca/HousePublications/Publication.aspx?DocId=1040776&Language=E&Mode=1&Parl=37&Ses=1 (Accessed 6 February 2017).

Canada. Parliament. House of Commons. 2001b. Standing Committee on Health. *Evidence*. Meeting 15, 10 May. 37th Parliament, 1st Session. http://www.parl.gc.ca/Committees/en/MeetingPublication?publicationId=1040806&parl=37&session=1 (Accessed 6 February 2017).

Canada. Parliament. House of Commons. 2001c. Standing Committee on Health. *Evidence*. Meeting 16, 17 May. 37th Parliament, 1st Session. http://www.parl.gc.ca/Committees/en/MeetingPublication?publicationId=1040839&parl=37&session=1 (Accessed 6 February 2017).

Canada. Parliament. House of Commons. 2001d. Standing Committee on Health. *Evidence*. Meeting 19, 5 June. 37th Parliament, 1st Session. http://www.parl.gc.ca/HousePublications/Publication.aspx?Language=e&Mode=1&Parl=37&Ses=1&DocId=1040891 (Accessed 6 February 2017).

Canada. Parliament. House of Commons. 2001e. Standing Committee on Health. *Evidence*. Meeting 23, 25 September. 37th Parliament, 1st Session. http://www.parl.gc.ca/HousePublications/Publication.aspx?Language=e&Mode=1&Parl=37&Ses=1&DocId=1040918 (Accessed 6 February 2017).

Canada. Parliament. House of Commons. 2001f. Standing Committee on Health. *Evidence*. Meeting 25, 27 September. 37th Parliament, 1st Session. http://www.parl.gc.ca/Committees/en/MeetingPublication?publicationId=1040920&parl=37&session=1 (Accessed 6 February 2017).

Canada. Parliament. House of Commons. 2001g. Standing Committee on Health. *Evidence*. Meeting 31, 18 October. 37th Parliament, 1st Session. http://www.parl.gc.ca/HousePublications/Publication.aspx?DocId=1041012&Language=E&Mode=1&Parl=37&Ses=1 (Accessed 6 February 2017).

Canada. Parliament. House of Commons. 2001h. Standing Committee on Health. *Evidence*. Meeting 33, 24 October. 37th Parliament, 1st Session.

http://www.parl.gc.ca/HousePublications/Publication.aspx?DocId=10410
51&Language=E&Mode=1&Parl=37&Ses=1 (Accessed 6 February 2017).

Canada. Parliament. House of Commons. 2001i. Standing Committee on Health. *Evidence*. Meeting 32, 23 October. 37th Parliament, 1st Session. http://www.
parl.gc.ca/HousePublications/Publication.aspx?Language=
e&Mode=1&Parl=37&Ses=1&DocId=1041030 (Accessed 6 February 2017).

Canada. Parliament. House of Commons. 2001j. Standing Committee on
Health. *Evidence*. Meeting 34, 25 October. 37th Parliament, 1st Session.
http://www.parl.gc.ca/HousePublications/Publication.aspx?Language=
e&Mode=1&Parl=37&Ses=1&DocId=1041040 (Accessed 6 February 2017).

Canada. Parliament. House of Commons. 2001k. Standing Committee on
Health. *Evidence*. Meeting 39, 7 November. 37th Parliament, 1st Session.
http://www.parl.gc.ca/HousePublications/Publication.aspx?Language=
e&Mode=1&Parl=37&Ses=1&DocId=1041143 (Accessed 6 February 2017).

Canada. Parliament. House of Commons. 2001l. Standing Committee on
Health. *Evidence*. Meeting 40, 8 November. 37th Parliament, 1st Session.
http://www.parl.gc.ca/HousePublications/Publication.aspx?Language=
e&Mode=1&Parl=37&Ses=1&DocId=1041144 (Accessed 6 February 2017).

Canada. Parliament. House of Commons. 2001m. Standing Committee on
Health. *Evidence*. Meeting 43, 22 November. 37th Parliament, 1st Session.
http://www.parl.gc.ca/HousePublications/Publication.aspx?DocId=
1041185&Language=E&Mode=1&Parl=37&Ses=1 (Accessed 6 February
2017).

Canada. Parliament. House of Commons. 2001n. Standing Committee on
Health. *Evidence*. Meeting 44, 26 November. 37th Parliament, 1st Session.
http://www.parl.gc.ca/HousePublications/Publication.aspx?DocId=10411
99&Language=E&Mode=1&Parl=37&Ses=1 (Accessed 6 February 2017).

Canada. Parliament. House of Commons. 2001o. Standing Committee on
Health. *Evidence*. Meeting 46, 28 November. 37th Parliament, 1st Session.
http://www.parl.gc.ca/HousePublications/Publication.aspx?Language=
e&Mode=1&Parl=37&Ses=1&DocId=1041220 (Accessed 6 February 2017).

Canada. 2001p. *Assisted Human Reproduction: Building Families*. Report of the
Standing Committee on Health. Ottawa: Public Works and Government
Services Canada.

Canada. Parliament. House of Commons. 2002a. *Debates*, 37th Parliament,
1st Session. No. 188. 21 May. http://www.parl.gc.ca/HousePublications/
Publication.aspx?Pub=Hansard&Doc=188&Parl=37&Ses=1&Language=
E&Mode=1 (Accessed 6 February 2017).

Canada. Parliament. House of Commons. 2002b. Standing Committee on
Health. *Evidence*. Meeting 86, 4 June. 37th Parliament, 1st Session.

http://www.parl.gc.ca/HousePublications/Publication.aspx?Language=
e&Mode=1&Parl=37&Ses=1&DocId=606621 (Accessed 6 February 2017).

Canada. Parliament. House of Commons. 2002c. Standing Committee on Health.
Evidence. Meeting 88, 11 June. 37th Parliament, 1st Session. http://www.
parl.gc.ca/HousePublications/Publication.aspx?DocId=606619&
Language=E&Mode=1&Parl=37&Ses=1 (Accessed 6 February 2017).

Canada. Parliament. House of Commons. 2002d. Standing Committee on
Health. *Evidence*. Meeting 89, 12 June. 37th Parliament, 1st Session. http://
www.parl.gc.ca/Committees/en/MeetingPublication?publicationId=
585757&parl=37&session=1 (Accessed 6 February 2017).

Canada. Parliament. House of Commons. 2002e. Standing Committee on
Health. *Evidence*. Meeting 2, 19 November. 37th Parliament, 2nd Session.
http://www.parl.gc.ca/HousePublications/Publication.aspx?DocId=
573074&Language=E&Mode=1&Parl=37&Ses=2 (Accessed 6 February
2017).

Canada. Parliament. House of Commons. 2002f. Standing Committee on
Health. *Evidence*. Meeting 3, 20 November. 37th Parliament, 2nd Session.
http://www.parl.gc.ca/HousePublications/Publication.aspx?DocId=
573074&Language=E&Mode=1&Parl=37&Ses=2 (Accessed 6 February
2017).

Canada. Parliament. House of Commons. 2003a. *Debates*, 37th Parliament,
2nd Session. No. 49. 30 January. http://www.parl.gc.ca/HousePublications/
Publication.aspx?Language=E&Mode=1&Parl=37&Ses=2&DocId=666656
(Accessed 6 February 2017).

Canada. Parliament. House of Commons. 2003b. *Debates*, 37th Parliament,
2nd Session. No. 85. 7 April. http://www.parl.gc.ca/HousePublications/
Publication.aspx?Language=E&Mode=1&Parl=37&Ses=2&DocId=819536
(Accessed 6 February 2017).

Canada. Parliament. Senate. 2004a. Standing Committee on Social Affairs,
Science and Technology. *Evidence*. Issue No. 1, 18 February. 37th Parliament,
3rd Session. https://sencanada.ca/en/Content/SEN/Committee/373/
soci/pdf/01issue.pdf (Accessed 28 May 2018).

Canada. Parliament. Senate. 2004b. Standing Committee on Social Affairs,
Science and Technology. *Evidence*. Issue No. 2, 25 February. 37th Parliament,
3rd Session. https://sencanada.ca/en/Content/SEN/Committee/373/
soci/pdf/02issue.pdf (Accessed 28 May 2018).

Canada. 2016. "Government Notices – Department of Health: Assisted
Human Reproduction Act." *Canada Gazette* 150 (40): 1 October. http://www
.gazette.gc.ca/rp-pr/p1/2016/2016-10-01/html/notice-avis-eng.php#ne1
(Accessed 7 January2017).

Canadian Fertility and Andrology Society. 2016a. "CFAS – Canadian ART
    Register." https://cfas.ca/public-affairs/canadian-art-register/ (Accessed
    7 January 2017).
Canadian Fertility and Andrology Society. 2016b. "Clinical Practice Guidelines."
    https://cfas.ca/clinical-practice-guidelines/ (Accessed 27 June 2017).
Canadian Fertility and Andrology Society. 2017. "Multiple Pregnancy
    Rate Resulting from IVF at an All-Time Low of 9.7% in Canada." *Cision*,
    2 November. http://www.newswire.ca/news-releases/multiple-pregnancy-
    rate-resulting-from-ivf-at-an-all-time-low-of-97-in-canada-654686493.html
    (Accessed January 7, 2018).
Canadian Fertility and Andrology Society and Society of Obstetricians and Gyn-
    aecologists of Canada. 1999. "Joint Policy Statement: Ethical Issues in Assisted
    Reproduction." *Journal of Obstetrics and Gynaecology Canada* 21 (1): 1–42.
Canadian Press. 2015. "Quebec Surrogacy Contracts May Soon Be Recognized."
    CBC News, 8 March. http://www.cbc.ca/news/canada/montreal/quebec-sur-
    rogacycontracts-may-soon-be-recognized-1.2986424 (Accessed 7 January 2017).
Capoccia, Giovanni, and R. Daniel Kelemen. 2007. "The Study of Critical
    Junctures: Theory, Narrative, and Counterfactuals in Historical Institu-
    tionalism." *World Politics* 59 (3): 341–69. https://doi.org/10.1017/
    S0043887100020852.
Carter, Mark. 2011. "Federalism Analysis and the Charter." *Saskatchewan Law
    Review* 74 (1): 5–20.
Cattapan, Alana. 2015. "Why Ontario's IVF Funding Structure Is Not the
    Answer." *TVO*, 26 October. http://tvo.org/article/current-affairs/shared-
    values/why-ontarios-ivf-funding-structure-is-not-the-answer (Accessed
    7 January 2017).
Caulfield, Timothy. 2004. "Scientific Freedom and Research Cloning: Can a
    Ban Be Justified?" *Lancet* 364 (9429): 124–6. https://doi.org/10.1016/S0140-
    6736(04)16653-1. Medline:15246714.
Caulfield, Timothy, and Tania Bubela. 2007. "Why a Criminal Ban? Analyzing
    the Arguments against Somatic Cell Nuclear Transfer in the Canadian
    Parliamentary Debate." *American Journal of Bioethics* 7 (2): 51–61. https://
    doi.org/10.1080/15265160601109655.
CBC News. 2011. "Surrogate Mom of Twins Unfazed after Baby Deal Falls
    Apart." *CBC News*, 13 September. http://www.cbc.ca/news/canada/
    new-brunswick/surrogate-mom-of-twins-unfazed-after-baby-deal-falls-
    apart-1.1086273 (Accessed 7 January 2017).
CBC News. 2014. "Canadians Pay Egg Donors on the Grey Market." *CBC News*,
    26 March. http://www.cbc.ca/news/canada/montreal/canadians-pay-egg-
    donors-on-the-grey-market-1.2587853 (Accessed 15 February 2017).

CBC News. 2015a. "Quebec's Controversial Health Care Bill Passes at National Assembly." *CBC News*, 11 November. http://www.cbc.ca/news/canada/montreal/bill-20-ivf-healthcare-quebec-passes-national-assembly-1.3313705 (Accessed 7 January 2017).

CBC News. 2015b. "Some Fertility Doctors Will Use Lottery to Prioritize Ontario IVF Patients." *CBC News*, 16 December. http://www.cbc.ca/news/health/fertility-ivf-lottery-1.3368426 (Accessed 7 January 2017).

CBC News. 2015c. "Ontario Offering 50 Government-Funded Fertility Treatment Clinics." *CBC News*, 21 December. http://www.cbc.ca/news/canada/toronto/ontario-fertility-clinics-1.3374634 (Accessed 7 January 2017).

CBC News. 2016. "Law to Name and Shame Deadbeat Parents Dies Leaving Millions in Unpaid Support." *CBC News*, 5 October. http://www.cbc.ca/news/canada/manitoba/iteam/deadbeat-bill-manitoba-child-support-1.3788833 (Accessed 7 January 2017).

Citizenship and Immigration Canada. 2014. "Who Is a Parent for Citizenship Purposes Where Assisted Human Reproduction (AHR), Including Surrogacy Arrangements, Are Involved." 26 March. http://www.cic.gc.ca/english/resources/tools/cit/admin/id/parent-assist.asp (Accessed 7 January 2017).

Cohen, Sara. 2014. "Justice Czutrin No Longer Hearing Applications for Declarations of Parentage in Ontario." *Fertility Law Canada*, 9 January. http://www.fertilitylawcanada.com/fertility-law-canada-blog/justice-czutrin-no-longer-hearing-applications-for-declaration-of-parentage-in-ontario (Accessed 7 January 2017).

College of Physicians and Surgeons of Alberta. 2011. "In Vitro Fertilization (IVF): Standards and Guidelines." http://cpsa.ca/wp-content/uploads/2015/03/NHSF_IVF_Standards_-_December_2011.pdf?x91570 (Accessed 7 January 2017).

College of Physicians and Surgeons of Ontario. 2016. "Out-of-Hospital Premises Inspection Program (OHPIP) Program Standards." http://www.cpso.on.ca/CPSO/media/documents/CPSO%20Members/OHPIP/OHPIP-standards.pdf (Accessed 27 June 2017).

College of Physicians and Surgeons of Saskatchewan. 2015. "Standards: Assisted Reproductive Technologies." https://www.cps.sk.ca/imis/Documents/Legislation/Policies/STANDARD%20-%20Assisted%20Reproductive%20Technology.pdf (Accessed 7 January 2017).

Cook, Jocelynn L., John Collins, William Buckett, Catherine Racowsky, Edward Hughes, and Keith Jarvi. 2011 "Assisted Reproductive Technology-Related Multiple Births: Canada in an International Context." *Journal of Obstetrics and Gynaecology Canada* 33 (2): 159–67. https://doi.org/10.1016/S1701-2163(16)34803-4.

Daviter, Falk. 2011. *Policy Framing in the European Union*. London: Palgrave Macmillan. https://doi.org/10.1057/9780230343528.

Doern, G. Bruce. 1967. "The Role of Royal Commissions in the General Policy Process and in Federal-Provincial Relations." *Canadian Public Administration* 10 (4): 417–33. https://doi.org/10.1111/j.1754-7121.1967.tb00994.x.

Downie, Jocelyn, and Françoise Baylis. 2013. "Transnational Trade in Human Eggs: Law, Policy, and (In)Action in Canada." *Journal of Law, Medicine & Ethics* 41 (1): 224–39. https://doi.org/10.1111/jlme.12015.

Eichler, Margrit. 1993. "Frankenstein Meets Kafka: The Royal Commission on New Reproductive Technologies." In *Misconceptions: The Social Construction of Choice and the New Reproductive and Genetic Technologies*, edited by Gwynne Basen, Margrit Eichler, and Abby Lippmann, 196–222. Hull: Voyageur Publishing.

Eggertson, Laura. 2011. "Patchwork Regulations Likely Outcome of Reproductive Technology Ruling." *Canadian Medical Association Journal* 183 (4): E215–16. http://www.cmaj.ca/content/cmaj/183/4/E215.full.pdf.

Engeli, Isabelle. 2009. "The Challenges of Abortion and Assisted Reproductive Technologies Policies in Europe." *Comparative European Politics* 7 (1): 56–74. https://doi.org/10.1057/cep.2008.36.

Engeli, Isabelle, Christoffer Green-Pedersen, and Lars Thorup Larsen, eds. 2012. *Morality Politics in Western Europe: Parties, Agendas and Policy Choices*. New York: Palgrave Macmillan. https://doi.org/10.1057/9781137016690.

Engeli, Isabelle, and Christine Rothmayr Allison. 2016. "When Doctors Shape Policy: The Impact of Self-Regulation on Governing Human Biotechnology." *Regulation & Governance* 10 (3): 248–61. https://doi.org/10.1111/rego.12078.

Epps, Tracey. 2011. "Regulation of Health Care Professionals." In *Health Law and Policy in Canada*, 4th ed., edited by Jocelyn Downie, Timothy Caulfield, and Coleen Flood, 75–114. Markham, ON: LexisNexis.

Evans, John H. 2006. "Religious Belief, Perceptions of Human Suffering, and Support for Reproductive Genetic Technology." *Journal of Health Politics, Policy and Law* 31 (6): 1047–74. https://doi.org/10.1215/03616878-2006-019.

Galloway, Gloria. 2015. "No Mandatory Standards for In Vitro Fertilization Clinics." *Globe and Mail*, 30 July. http://www.theglobeandmail.com/news/politics/no-mandatory-standards-for-in-vitro-fertilization-clinics/article19868390/ (Accessed 7 January 2017).

Gaudreault-DesBiens, Jean-François. 1999. "The Quebec Secession Reference and the Judicial Arbitration of Conflicting Narratives about Law, Democracy, and Identity." *Vermont Law Review* 23 (4): 793–843.

Gruben, Vanessa, and Angela Cameron. 2011. "Assisted Human Reproduction in Canada: A Call to Action." *Blogging for Equality*. http://www.blogging forequality.ca/2011/09/assisted-human-reproduction-in-canada.html (Accessed 7 January 2017).

Gruben, Vanessa, and Angela Cameron. 2013. "Sperm Is Property: So Says the Court." *Impact Ethics*, 22 August. https://impactethics.ca/2013/08/22/sperm-is-property-so-says-the-court/.

Gruben, Vanessa, and Angela Cameron. 2014. "Quebec's Constitutional Challenge to the Assisted Human Reproduction Act: Overlooking Women's Reproductive Autonomy?" In *Fertile Ground: Exploring Reproduction in Canada*, edited by Stephanie Paterson, Francesca Scala, and Marlene K. Sokolon, 125–51. Montreal: McGill-Queen's University Press.

Guichon, Juliet, Michelle Giroux, and Ian Mitchell. 2008. "Once More, an Unregulated Nightmare." *Globe and Mail*, 24 June. [Originally published online, article no longer available. Cited in Snow and Knopff 2012.]

Guichon, Juliet, Ian Mitchell, and Christopher Doig. 2013. "Assisted Human Reproduction in Common Law Canada after the Supreme Court of Canada Reference: Moving beyond Regulation by Colleges of Physicians and Surgeons." *Canadian Journal of Women and the Law* 25 (2): 315–39. https://doi.org/10.3138/cjwl.25.2.315.

Gunningham, Neil, and Joseph Rees. 1997. "Industry Self-Regulation: An Institutional Perspective." *Law & Policy* 19 (4): 363–414. https://doi.org/10.1111/1467-9930.t01-1-00033.

Harder, Lois. 2015. "Does Sperm Have a Flag? On Biological Relationship and National Membership." *Canadian Journal of Law and Society* 30 (1): 109–25. https://doi.org/10.1017/cls.2014.24.

Hall, Peter A. 1986. *Governing the Economy: The Politics of State Intervention in Britain and France*. New York: Oxford University Press.

Hall, Peter A. 2003. "Aligning Ontology and Methodology in Comparative Politics." In *Comparative Historical Analysis in the Social Sciences*, edited by James Mahoney and Dietrich Rueschemeyer, 373–404. Cambridge: Cambridge University Press. https://doi.org/10.1017/CBO9780511803963.012.

Harrison, Kathryn. 1999. *Passing the Buck: Federalism and Environmental Policy*. Vancouver: UBC Press.

Harvison Young, Alison. 2005. "Let's Try Again ... This Time with Feeling: Bill C-6 and New Reproductive Technologies." *UBC Law Review* 38 (1): 123–45.

Health Canada. 1996. *New Reproductive Technologies: Setting Boundaries, Enhancing Health*. Ottawa: Minister of Supply and Services Canada.

Health Canada. 2013. "Prohibitions Related to Surrogacy." 18 July. https://
www.canada.ca/en/health-canada/services/drugs-health-products/
biologics-radiopharmaceuticals-genetic-therapies/legislation-guidelines/
assisted-human-reproduction/prohibitions-related-surrogacy.html.

Health Canada. 2017. *Toward a Strengthened Assisted Human Reproduction Act:
A Consultation with Canadians on Key Policy Proposals.* 11 July. https://www
.canada.ca/content/dam/hc-sc/documents/programs/consultation-
assisted-human-reproduction/ahr-white-paper-2017-07-07-eng.pdf
(accessed 8 August 2017).

Healy, Patrick. 1995. "Statutory Prohibitions and the Regulation of New Reproductive Technologies under Federal Law in Canada." *McGill Law Journal
/ Revue de Droit de McGill* 40 (4): 905–46.

Hogg, Peter W. 1979. "Is the Supreme Court of Canada Biased in Constitutional
Cases?" *Canadian Bar Review* 57 (4): 721–39.

Hogg, Peter W. 2012. *Constitutional Law of Canada.* 5th ed. (annually
supplemented). Toronto: Carswell.

Infertility Network. 2017. "Fertility Clinics: Canada." https://www
.infertilitynetwork.org/fertility_clinics_cda (Accessed 10 August 2017).

Ivison, John. 2009. "Bernier Still a Thorn to PMO; MP Thinks Single Securities
Office Unconstitutional." *National Post*, 10 November, A1.

Jones, Mavis, and Brian Salter. 2010. "Proceeding Carefully: Assisted Human
Reproduction Policy in Canada." *Public Understanding of Science (Bristol,
England)* 19 (4): 420–34. https://doi.org/10.1177/0963662509104722.

Kelly, Fiona. 2009. "(Re)Forming Parenthood: The Assignment of Legal Parentage within Planned Lesbian Families." *Ottawa Law Review* 40 (2): 185–222.

Kirkey, Sharon, and Janice Tibbetts. 2010. "Ruling Creates Regulation Gap."
Edmonton Journal, 23 December, A3.

Lam, Nancy. 2010. "Getting Your Name on the Birth Certificate after a
Surrogacy Birth." *Oh Baby Magazine.* http://www.ohbabymagazine.com/
prenatal/getting-your-name-on-the-birth-certificate-after-a-surrogacy-
birth/ (Accessed 7 January 2017).

Leclair, Jean. 2003. "The Supreme Court of Canada's Understanding of
Federalism: Efficiency at the Expense of Diversity." *Queen's Law Journal* 28
(2): 411–53.

Lederman, W.D. 1976. "Unity and Diversity in Canadian Federalism: Ideals
and Methods of Moderation." *Alberta Law Review* 14 (1): 34–49.

Lee, Ian B. 2012. "The *Assisted Human Reproduction Act Reference* and the
Criminal Law Power." *Canadian Bar Review* 90 (2): 471–93.

Levi, Margaret. 1997. "A Model, a Method, and a Map: Rational Choice in
Comparative and Historical Analysis." In *Comparative Politics: Rationality,*

Culture, and Structure, edited by Mark Irving Lichbach and Alan S. Zuckerman, 19–41. Cambridge: Cambridge University Press.

Levine, Aaron D. 2010. "Self-Regulation, Compensation, and the Ethical Recruitment of Oocyte Donors." *Asian Bioethics Review* 40 (2): 25–36.

Lobo, Rogerio A. 2011. "Recognizing Existing Framework for Regulation of Assisted Reproductive Technologies in the United States." *Contraception* 84 (6): 652, author reply 654–5. https://doi.org/10.1016/j.contraception .2011.03.020.

Maioni, Antonia. 2012. "Health Care." In *Canadian Federalism: Performance, Effectiveness, and Legitimacy*, 3rd ed., edited by Herman Bakvis and Grace Skogstad, 165–82. Don Mills: Oxford University Press.

Manitoba. 2013. "Fertility Treatment Tax Credit." Manitoba Finance. https:// www.gov.mb.ca/finance/personal/pcredits.html#fertility (Accessed 7 January 2017).

Manitoba. Legislative Assembly. 2015. *Family Law Reform Act*. https:// web2.gov.mb.ca/bills/40-4/b033e.php (Accessed 7 January 2017).

Millbank, Jenni. 2011. "The New Surrogacy Parentage Laws in Australia: Cautious Regulation or '25 Brick Walls'?" *Melbourne University Law Review* 35 (1): 165–207.

Miller Chenier, Nancy. 2002. *Intergovernmental Consultations on Health: Toward a National Framework on Reproductive Technologies*. Ottawa: Library of Parliament.

Min, Jason, and Camille Sylvestre. 2013. "Guidelines on the Number of Embryos Transferred." Canadian Fertility and Andrology Society. https:// cfas.ca/wp-content/uploads/2016/03/CFAS_CPG_Embryo_Transfer_2013 .pdf (Accessed 7 January 2017; Membership required to view.)

Mitchell, Graeme B. 2011. "Not a General Regulatory Power – A Comment on *Reference re Assisted Human Reproduction Act*." *Supreme Court Review* 43 (1): 633–70.

Montpetit, Éric. 2004. "Policy Networks, Federalism and Managerial Ideas: How ART Non-Decision in Canada Safeguards the Autonomy of the Medical Profession." In *Comparative Biomedical Policy: Governing Assisted Reproductive Technologies*, edited by Ivar Bleiklie, Malcolm L. Goggin, and Christine Rothmayr, 64–81. London: Routledge.

Montpetit, Éric. 2007. "The Canadian Knowledge Economy in the Shadow of the United Kingdom and the United States." In *The Politics of Biotechnology in North America and Europe*, edited by Éric Montpetit, Christine Rothmayr, and Frédéric Varone, 83–102. Lanham: Lexington Books.

Montpetit, Éric, Christine Rothmayr, and Frédéric Varone. 2005. "Institutional Vulnerability to Social Constructions: Federalism, Target Populations, and

Policy Designs for Assisted Reproductive Technologies in Six Democracies." *Comparative Political Studies* 38 (2): 119–42. https://doi.org/10.1177/0010414004271080.

Montpetit, Éric, Christine Rothmayr, and Frédéric Varone, eds. 2007. *The Politics of Biotechnology in North America and Europe: Policy Networks, Institutions and Internationalization.* Lanham: Lexington Books.

Morris, Stephen G. 2007. "Canada's Assisted Human Reproduction Act: A Chimera of Religion and Politics." *American Journal of Bioethics* 7 (2): 69–70. https://doi.org/10.1080/15265160601109846.

Motluk, Alison. 2010. "The Human Egg Trade." *The Walrus* (April). https://thewalrus.ca/the-human-egg-trade/ (Accessed 15 February 2017).

Motluk, Alison. 2014. "First Prosecution under Assisted Human Reproduction Act Ends in Conviction." *Canadian Medical Association Journal* 186 (2): E75–6. http://www.cmaj.ca/content/cmaj/186/2/E75.full.pdf.

Mykitiuk, Roxanne. 2001. "Beyond Conception: Legal Determinations of Filiation in the Context of Assisted Reproduction Technologies." *Osgoode Hall Law Journal* 39 (4): 771–815.

National Health and Medical Research Council. 2007. *Ethical Guidelines on the Use of Assisted Reproductive Technology in Clinical Practice and Research.* Canberra: Government of Australia. https://www.nhmrc.gov.au/_files_nhmrc/file/publications/synopses/e78.pdf.

Nelson, Erin. 2013. *Law, Policy, and Reproductive Autonomy.* Portland, OR: Hart Publishing.

New Brunswick. 2014. "Infertility Treatment – Special Assistance Fund." https://www.pxw1.snb.ca/snb7001/e/1000/infoTe.asp (Accessed 7 January 2017).

Norris, Sonya, and Marlisa Tiedemann. 2015. *Legal Status at the Federal Level of Assisted Human Reproduction in Canada.* Ottawa: Library of Parliament.

O'Neill, Shannon, and Jeff Blackmer. 2015. "Assisted Reproduction in Canada: An Overview of Ethical and Legal Issues and Recommendations for the Development of National Standards." Canadian Medical Association. https://www.cma.ca/Assets/assets-library/document/en/advocacy/assisted-reproduction-in-canada-e.pdf (Accessed 7 January 2017).

Ogbogu, Ubaka. 2011. "*Reference re Assisted Human Reproduction Act* and the Future of Technology-Assisted Reproduction and Embryo Research in Canada." *Health Law Journal* 19 (1): 153–87. Medline:23185905.

Ogus, Anthony. 1995. "Rethinking Self-Regulation." *Oxford Journal of Legal Studies* 15 (1): 97–108. https://doi.org/10.1093/ojls/15.1.97.

Ontario. 2014. "Improving Access to Safe Fertility Treatments." 10 April. https://news.ontario.ca/mohltc/en/2014/4/improving-access-to-safe-fertility-treatments.html (Accessed 7 January 2017).

Ontario. 2016a. "Fertility Services." Ministry of Health and Long-Term Care. https://www.ontario.ca/page/get-fertility-treatments.

Ontario. 2016b. "Ontario Passes Law Ensuring Equal Recognition for All Parents and Children." 29 November. https://news.ontario.ca/mag/en/2016/11/ontario-passes-law-ensuring-equal-rights-for-all-parents-and-children.html (Accessed 7 January 2017).

Ontario. Legislative Assembly. 2016c. *All Families Are Equal Act (Parentage and Related Registrations Statute Law Amendment), 2016.* http://www.ontla.on.ca/web/bills/bills_detail.do?locale=en&BillID=4176 (Accessed 7 January 2017).

Ontario. Legislative Assembly. 2016d. Official Report of Debates (Hansard). Standing Committee on Social Policy. 18 October. 41st Parliament, 2nd Session. *Bill 28, All Families Are Equal Act (Parentage and Related Registrations Statute Law Amendment), 2016.* http://www.ontla.on.ca/committee-proceedings/transcripts/files_pdf/18-OCT-2016_SP003.pdf.

Ontario Ministry of Children and Youth Services. 2009. *Raising Expectations: Recommendations of the Expert Panel on Infertility and Adoption.* Toronto: Ontario Ministry of Children and Youth Services. www.children.gov.on.ca/htdocs/english/documents/infertility/raisingexpectationsenglish.pdf (Accessed 22 May 2013).

Peters, B. Guy. 2005. *Institutional Theory in Political Science: The "New Institutionalism."* 2nd ed. London, New York: Continuum.

Pierson, Paul. 2004. *Politics in Time: History, Institutions, and Social Analysis.* Princeton: Princeton University Press. https://doi.org/10.1515/9781400841080.

Posyniak, Thomas. 2011. "Assisted Human Reproduction and the Constitution: Introduction and Background to the Four-Part Commentary." *Saskatchewan Law Review* 74 (1): 1–4.

Privy Council Office. 2001. *Guide to Making Federal Acts and Regulations.* 2nd ed. Ottawa: National Library of Canada.

Racco, Marilisa. 2016. "Here's What You Need to Know about Ontario's Fertility Program, One Year Later." *Global News,* 16 November. http://globalnews.ca/news/3066040/heres-what-you-need-to-know-about-ontarios-fertility-program-one-year-later/ (Accessed 7 January 2017).

Rasmussen, Colin. 2004. "Canada's *Assisted Human Reproduction Act*: Is It Scientific Censorship, or a Reasoned Approach to the Regulation of Rapidly Emerging Reproductive Technologies?" *Saskatchewan Law Review* 67 (1): 97–135.

Ricci, David M. 1984. *The Tragedy of Political Science: Politics, Scholarship, and Democracy.* New Haven: Yale University.

Roberts, Janet Hatcher. 1999. "Coalition Building and Public Opinion: New Reproductive Technologies and Canadian Civil Society." *International Journal of Technology Assessment in Health Care* 15 (1): 15–21. https://doi .org/10.1017/S0266462399015147.

Rocher, François, and Miriam Smith. 2003. "The Four Dimensions of Canadian Federalism." In *New Trends in Canadian Federalism,* 2nd ed., edited by François Rocher and Miriam Smith, 21–44. Peterborough, ON: Broadview.

Rothmayr Allison, Christine, and Frédéric Varone. 2009. "Direct Legislation in North America and Europe: Promoting or Restricting Biotechnology?" *Journal of Comparative Policy Analysis* 11 (4): 425–49. https://doi.org/10.1080/ 13876980903222864.

Royal Commission on New Reproductive Technologies. 1993. *Proceed with Care: Final Report of the Royal Commission on New Reproductive Technologies.* Ottawa: Minister of Government Services Canada.

Russell, Peter H. 1985. "The Supreme Court and Federal-Provincial Relations: The Political Use of Legal Resources." *Canadian Public Policy* 11 (2): 161–70. https://doi.org/10.2307/3550698.

Saywell, John T. 2002. *The Lawmakers: Judicial Power and the Shaping of Canadian Federalism.* Toronto: University of Toronto Press. https://doi.org/10.3138/ 9781442681613.

Scala, Francesca. 2002. "Experts, Non-experts, and Policy Discourse: A Case Study of the Royal Commission on New Reproductive Technologies." Doctoral dissertation, Carleton University.

Scala, Francesca. 2007. "Scientists, Government, and 'Boundary Work': The Case of Reproductive Technologies and Genetic Engineering in Canada." In *Critical Policy Studies,* edited by Michael Orsini and Miriam Smith, 211–31. Vancouver: UBC Press.

Scala, Francesca. 2008. "Feminist Ideals versus Bureaucratic Norms: The Case of Feminist Researchers and the Royal Commission on New Reproductive Technologies." In *Gendering the Nation-State: Canadian and Comparative Perspectives,* edited by Yasmeen Abu-Laban, 97–119. Vancouver: UBC Press.

Schertzer, Robert. 2008. "Recognition or Imposition? Federalism, National Minorities, and the Supreme Court of Canada." *Nations and Nationalism* 14 (1): 105–26. https://doi.org/10.1111/j.1469-8129.2008.00324.x.

Schertzer, Robert. 2016. *The Judicial Role in a Diverse Federation: Lessons from the Supreme Court of Canada.* Toronto: University of Toronto Press.

Schneider, Anne Larason, and Helen Ingram. 1997. *Policy Design for Democracy.* Lawrence: University of Kansas Press.

Scotti, Monique. 2016. "Oversight of Fertility Clinics Still Lacking across Canada." *Global News,* 23 November. http://globalnews.ca/news/3070555/

oversight-of-fertility-clinics-still-lacking-across-canada/ (Accessed 7 January 2017).

Simmons, Julie, and Peter Graefe. 2013. "Assessing the Collaboration That Was 'Collaborative Federalism' 1996–2006." *Canadian Political Science Review* 7 (1): 25–36.

Smith, Kevin B. 2002. "Typologies, Taxonomies, and the Benefits of Policy Classification." *Policy Studies Journal: The Journal of the Policy Studies Organization* 30 (3): 379–95. https://doi.org/10.1111/j.1541-0072.2002.tb02153.x.

Snow, Dave. 2012. "The Judicialization of Assisted Reproductive Technology Policy in Canada: Decentralization, Medicalization, and Mandatory Regulation." *Canadian Journal of Law and Society* 27 (2): 169–88. https://doi.org/10.3138/cjls.27.2.169.

Snow, Dave. 2016. "Measuring Parentage Policy in the Canadian Provinces: A Comparative Framework." *Canadian Public Administration* 59 (1): 5–25.

Snow, Dave, Françoise Baylis, and Jocelyn Downie. 2015. "Why the Government of Canada Won't Regulate Assisted Human Reproduction: A Modern Mystery." *McGill Journal of Law and Health* 9 (1): 1–15.

Snow, Dave, and Rainer Knopff. 2012. "Assisted Reproduction Policy in Federal States: What Canada Should Learn from Australia." *School of Public Policy Research Papers* 5 (12): 1–28. https://doi.org/10.2139/ssrn.2056442.

Snyder, Steven H., and Mary Patricia Byrn. 2005. "The Use of Prebirth Parentage Orders in Court Proceedings." *Family Law Quarterly* 39 (3): 633–62.

Society of Obstetricians and Gynaecologists of Canada. 2016. "Clinical Practice Guidelines." https://sogc.org/clinical-practice-guidelines.html (Accessed 7 January 2017).

Stechyson, Natalie. 2013. "Part 2: Patchwork of Canadian Laws Creates Confusion in Determining Parental Rights for Gay and Lesbian Parents." *Calgary Herald*, 8 October. http://www.calgaryherald.com/health/Part+Patchwork+Canadian+laws+creates+confusion+determining+parental+rights+lesbian+parents/8947706/story.html (Accessed 7 January 2017).

Stern, Judy E., Marcelle I. Cedars, Tarun Jain, Nancy A. Klein, C. Martin Beaird, David A. Grainger, and William E. Gibbons. 2007. "Assisted Reproductive Technology Practice Patterns and the Impact of Embryo Transfer Guidelines in the United States." *Fertility and Sterility* 88: 275–82. https://doi.org/10.1016/j.fertnstert.2006.09.016.

Stevenson, Garth. 1993. *Ex uno plures: Federal-Provincial Relations in Canada, 1887–1896*. Montreal: McGill-Queen's University Press.

Subdhan, Abigale. 2014. "Vancouver Baby Becomes First Person to Have Three Parents Named on Birth Certificate in B.C." *National Post*, 10 February. http://news.nationalpost.com/2014/02/10/vancouver-baby-becomes-

first-person-to-have-three-parents-named-on-birth-certificate-in-b-c/
(Accessed 7 January 2017).

Supreme Court of Canada. 2015. "Statistics 2005 to 2015." http://www.scc-
csc.ca/case-dossier/stat/cat5-eng.aspx (Accessed 7 January 2017).

Tatalovich, Raymond, and Byron W. Daynes, eds. 2005. *Moral Controversies
in American Politics*. 3rd ed. London: M.E. Sharpe.

Toronto Star. 2010. "Supreme Court Ruling Muddies Issue." Unsigned
editorial, 23 December, A22.

TVO. 2016. "LGBTQ Parenting Rights in Ontario." *The Agenda with Steve
Paikin*. 29 June. https://www.youtube.com/watch?v=KHrr7qYD2g4
(Accessed 7 January 2017).

Vaughan, Frederick. 2010. *Viscount Haldane: 'The Wicked Step-Father' of the
Canadian Constitution*. Toronto: University of Toronto Press. https://doi
.org/10.3138/9781442693852.

Victoria Times-Colonist. 2011. "Law Needed for High-Tech Births." Unsigned
editorial, 9 January, C2.

von Tigerstrom, Barbara. 2011. "Federal Health Legislation and the Assisted
Human Reproduction Act Reference." *Saskatchewan Law Review* 74 (1):
33–43.

Vrielink, Mirjan Oude, Cor van Montfort, and Meike Bokhorst. 2011. "Codes
as Hybrid Regulation." In *Handbook on the Politics of Regulation*, edited by
David Levi-Faur, 486–98. Cheltenham, UK: Edward Elgar. https://doi.org/
10.4337/9780857936110.00052.

Weir, Lorna, and Jasmin Habib. 1997. "A Critical Feminist Analysis of the Final
Report of the Royal Commission on New Reproductive Technologies."
Studies in Political Economy 52: 137–54.

Whyte, John D. 2011. "Federalism and Moral Regulation: A Comment on
Reference Re Assisted Human Reproduction Act." *Saskatchewan Law Review*
74 (1): 45–58.

Williams, R. Stan. 2011. "Response by the Leadership of the Society of Assisted
Reproductive Technology (SART) to the Article 'Assisted Reproduction and
Choices in the Biotech Age.'" *Contraception* 84 (6): 652–4, author reply 654–5.
https://doi.org/10.1016/j.contraception.2011.03.021.

Index

Healy, Patrick, 50
historical institutionalism, 16–19,
   133, 154
H.L.W. and T.H.W. v. J.C.T. and J.T.
   (2005), 85
human cloning: in *Assisted Human
   Reproduction Act*, 44, 80, 136; non-
   reproductive, 38, 45; reproductive,
   9, 12, 14, 38, 65, 74; in Royal Commission, 21
hybrids and chimeras, 21, 38, 43–4,
   80, 136

ideas, 14, 18–19, 28, 154
Ignatieff, Michael, 54
Ingram, Helen, 26
intergovernmental collaboration, 40,
   42–3, 142, 145–7
intracytoplasmic sperm injection
   (ICSI), 112, 115, 119, 122, 129
intrauterine insemination (IUI), 115,
   119–20
in vitro fertilization (IVF), 8, 26,
   111–12, 115, 117–22, 125, 129–30,
   138–9, 141, 149
Italy, 137

Jackman, Martha, 49, 51
J.A.W. v. J.E.W. (2010), 100–1
J.C.M. v. A.N.A. (2012), 129
*J.C. v. The Queen (Dept. of Vital Statis-
   tics)* (2000), 98, 105
Judicial Committee of the Privy
   Council, 18, 58–9
judicial power and judicialization,
   14–15, 81–2, 103, 105–6, 129,
   147–8, 152

Kelly, Fiona, 102
Keyes, Stan, 45

Lam, Nancy, 97
Laskin, Bora, 59
LeBel, Louis, 67–9, 71–2
Lee, Ian B., 70–1
Legault, François, 56
legislative history, 71, 76, 78
Levine, Aaron D., 123
Levitan, Sherry, 84
LGBTQ rights and sexual orienta-
   tion, 87, 103–5, 137, 147
Liberal Party of Canada, 36–7, 45, 49,
   53–5, 77, 135
Lobo, Rogerio A., 124
Lunney, James, 47, 126

MacLachlan, Richard, 151
Manning, Preston, 48–50
Marleau, Diane, 36
Mathers McHenry, Jennifer, 103–4
McLachlin, Beverley, 66–7, 69–71, 78
McLellan, Anne, 47
McTeer, Maureen, 25
M.D. et al. v. L.L. et al. (2008), 101–3
medical organizations: academic
   scholarship on, 148–52; opposi-
   tion to regulations and prohibi-
   tions, 27, 39, 113, 153; provincial
   colleges, 13, 121, 123, 130, 143,
   148–51, 153; self-regulation, 13,
   22–4, 111–12, 117–18, 120–5, 130–1,
   136, 139, 149–51; support for as-
   sisted reproduction legislation,
   113, 153
Ménard, Réal, 49, 56, 62
Merrifield, Rob, 45
Millbank, Jenni, 85, 90
Minister of Health (federal), 36–7,
   39–42, 48, 50–1, 56, 62
Mitchell, Ian, 123
Montpetit, Éric, 54, 145, 153